JOSIAH CONDER

A Memoir

BY

EUSTACE R. CONDER, M.A.

ΙΔΙΑΙ ΓΕΝΕΑΙ ΥΠΗΡΕΤΗΣΑΣ ΤΗΙ ΤΟΥ ΘΕΟΥ ΒΟΥΛΗΙ
ΕΚΟΙΜΗΘΗ

LONDON

JOHN SNOW, 35 PATERNOSTER ROW

MDCCCLVII.

CONTENTS.

JOSIAH CONDER:

A MEMOIR.

------◆------

INTRODUCTORY CHAPTER.

FORMER GENERATIONS.

THE family records or traditions of the Conders do
not extend further back than to the sixth generation;
nor do they include any names illustrious for rank,
wealth, or genius. Happily, they are equally undistinguished by dishonour or crime; so that if JOSIAH
CONDER had not much to be proud of in his ancestry, he
had nothing to be ashamed of. Their arms are not to
be discovered at the Herald's College, and therefore it is
probable they never bore any; and their only estates were
their farms, which they cultivated themselves. But they
bequeathed to their descendants the inheritance of an
honest name and a religious example; and if worth and
piety can ennoble, and every true Christian is the child of
a king and the heir to a kingdom, there were not a few
of the stock who could show good claims to that sort of
nobility.

The family appears to have come originally from the
north of England. The name is found in Yorkshire and

without interruption, they might talk freely about the things of God; how they had heard on the Sabbath, and how they had gone on the week past, etc. I was admitted to sit in a corner of the room. One day, when I was there, the conversation turned upon this question—By what means God first visited their souls and began a work of grace on them? It was your great-grandfather's turn to speak, and his account struck me so I never forgot it. He told the company as follows :—

" ' When I was a young man, I was greatly addicted to football-playing, and as the custom was in our parish, and in many others, the young men, as soon as church was over, took the football and went to play. Our minister often remonstrated against our breaking the Sabbath, which, however, had little effect; only my conscience checked me at times, and I would sometimes steal away and hide myself from my companions; but being dexterous at the game, they would find me out and get me again among them. This would bring on me more guilt and horror of conscience. And thus I went on sinning and repenting a long time, but had not resolution to break off from the practice, till one Sabbath morning our good minister acquainted his hearers that he was very sorry to tell them, that by order of the King (James I.) and Council, he must read them the following paper, or turn out of his living. This was the *Book of Sports*, forbidding the minister or churchwardens or any others to molest or discourage the youth in their manly sports and recreations on the Lord's Day, etc.* While our minister was reading it, I was seized with a chill and horror not to be described. Now, thought I, iniquity is established by a law, and sinners are hardened in their

* A.D. 1617.

sinful ways. What sore judgments are to be expected upon so wicked and guilty a nation? What must I do? Whither shall I fly? How shall I escape the wrath to come? And God set in so with it, that I thought it was high time to be in earnest about salvation. And from that time I never had the least inclination to take a football in hand, or to join my vain companions any more. So that I date my conversion from that time, and adore the grace of God in making that to be an ordinance for my salvation, which the devil and wicked governors laid as a trap for my destruction.' 'This,' said the good man, 'I heard him tell with mine own ears, and I hope to my soul's good.' And, by this account, great reason is given to conclude that this our ancestor was godly, though not great in this world; and that is best of all.

"Richard his son, and my grandfather," continues Dr. Conder, "lived and died in the same farm, and partook of the same spirit with his father. Insomuch that upon the restoration of Charles the Second, and the ejection of such a number of nonconforming ministers, he joined himself to a congregational church, which was gathered by Mr. Fr. Holcroft and Joseph Addy, about Cambridgeshire. These two good men preached as they had opportunity, in private houses, and woods, and fields; in the night, when they could not by day. For which practice Mr. Holcroft was imprisoned for twelve years, and Mr. Addy six years, in Cambridge Castle. But the keeper of the jail favoured them, and often, let them out on Saturday evening after dark, and they returned on Monday morning before light; and in this practice they were never detected. N.B. The grandson of this jail-keeper, whose name was Prophet, was in the same office, and used to hear me, when I lived at Cambridge.

"Upon the Revolution, and liberty of conscience, Mr. Holcroft's church parted off into less communities, and chose their pastors from among themselves. Many of the members became preachers. Our grandfather, Richard Conder, was one who thus embodied with a little number of his neighbours, to whom he preached and administered in his own hall; and all *gratis*, to the day of his death, which was in 1718, æt. 69. Near his house was a fine spring, and a pleasant grove. Here, in the summer-time, his flock sat down in companies; ate their morsels which they brought in their pockets, drank of the fountain, and conversed of the things they had heard. The Lord seemed greatly with them; and the meeting continued some years under Dixey. After some years, about 1725, my father, Jabez Conder, second son of Richard, who was settled in a farm at Wimple, a member of the church, fitted up a meeting-house at Croydon, where he preached and became their pastor; and the interest seemed greatly to increase and thrive under him. But, alas! in a few months after his being ordained pastor, he was taken off by death. Two or three ministers were invited by the people; but being never used to contribute anything for the Gospel, they could not maintain their minister; till one Matthew Dutton, an anabaptist, came among them, made some converts to his opinion, so divided the church, and broke it up at Croydon, while he and his adherents removed to Great Gransden, and set up a Baptist interest there.

"The said Dutton was the first I have heard of who struck out into most parts of England, Ireland, and even Holland, preaching (where he was permitted), and begging money to build a meeting-house; and got money enough to do that, and to build two or three houses beside, which he left to his wife and heirs to this day, at Great Gransden aforesaid.

"Jabez Conder, at æt. 33, married (in 1713) Elizabeth, the eldest daughter of William and Frances Linkern (a farmer at Everton, Bedfordshire), at æt. about 20, by whom he had one son, born June 3, O.S., 1714, John Conder, baptized by his grandfather, who, with tears, kissed him, and said, 'Who knows what sad days these little eyes are likely to see!' it being then a very lowering aspect of things which then attended the Dissenters. But in two months after, the clouds broke with Queen Anne's death; and fair days succeeded ever after. So that these eyes have for more than sixty years seen nothing but goodness and mercy following them and the churches of Christ even to this day. . . . .

"My father's death took place October 18, 1727, by this awful providence: I boarded with grandmother Linkern, at Potton, and went to school there with Mr. Hicks the clergyman. Father and mother came over to see us from Wimple, early in the morning. Leaving mother with us, after breakfast he took his horse, and rode to Biggleswade, where he dined with his brother Linkern, and in the afternoon returning to Potton, his horse on the gallop, a cow, driven in a near path (which it seems had only one eye), hearing the noise of the horse, she started suddenly across his path. The horse ran against her, fell over her, and threw father off with such violence, as to give him a large contusion over his eye; and, withal, such a shock of his whole frame, as broke a blood-vessel within him. In which condition, a neighbour that was with him recovered his horse, set father upon him, and so he was conducted to grandmother's, sensible, but near gone, and expired in a quarter of an hour. I was gone to the barber, to put on a wig for the first time; and came back

with great pride, and pleasure of thought how father
would admire my new dress; but when I came to the
door, was met by Aunt Rebekah in tears, who abruptly
said, 'Your father is killed by a fall from his horse.' I
ran, speechless and benumbed with surprise, to the bed's
foot, where he lay asleep, and snoring as when in health,
but soon fetched his breath shorter and shorter. In a
few minutes it stopped, when the blood gushed out of
nose, mouth, and ears. So I stood like a statue, and
saw him breathe his last. Then I first knew that smaller
sorrows produce tears, greater ones stun and stupify. I
was but thirteen and about four months; but it made
very deep impressions for a time. A bright and cheerful morning, but shut up in a dismal night to us all. So
certain is it that we know not what a day may bring
forth.

"Father died intestate; poor mother was disconsolate, and left in a great deal of cumber, not merely by
her own farm, but father being an active, knowing man,
and taking delight in assisting the widow and fatherless,
he had engaged as executor to several of his neighbours,
and guardian for their children. And mother being of a
tender, delicate constitution, these things almost overset
her; but, after awhile, my cousin Joseph Porter came
and managed affairs for her, and helped her through her
difficulties.

"Mother being deemed a young and likely widow,
after a time had several suitors; and after about four
years she married to a young, tall, personable man, the
eldest son of Mr. Stephen Hawkes of Rockets. He was
thought too young for her by friends who dissuaded
her from the match; but her affections were fixed. And
as part of the stock was mine, and too much for him to
pay for, it turned upon my promise that I would let my

part continue, he paying me interest. My mother became petitioner to her son, that she should never know a
happy day more if I did not comply; and that surely I
ought to make her life comfortable who had given me
life and being. Her argument was too delicate and
moving to meet with a denial, though, as I judged, I ran
no small hazard, as it proved; for I lost upwards of a
hundred pounds, principal and interest, by him. George
Hawkes was a loving and well-behaved husband to
mother, and a very agreeable companion to me, being
but about five years older than his son; and in mother's
absence we went for brothers."

The manuscript from which the foregoing extracts
and some which follow are taken was penned by Dr.
Conder, a few years before his death, for the instruction
of his children. It does not appear that his childhood
and boyhood gave much promise of the unaffected,
humble, and laborious piety of his subsequent life. But
in this the prayers of his father were answered, though
he was not spared to see the answer; for from his birth,
he tells us, his father had conceived a strong desire, and
withal a strong impression on his mind, that he should
be a minister, and commenced his education, even as a
boy, with this end in view. John, however, did not
show any great love for study. Being sent, after his
father's death, to the grammar-school at Hitchin, his
"head ran much after going home and being a farmer,"
which his mother was much against, urging that it was
his father's purpose he should be a scholar, and she was
resolved to fulfil his will. However, Mr. Newman (his
instructor) persuaded her to take him home for the
harvest, and advised her to work him hard, and he would
then be glad to come to school again when it was over.

But he was loath to return, though after awhile he was brought to consent, upon her promising that, if he continued so averse to it, he should "come home and be the farmer." On his return, Mr. Newman behaved with much tenderness, and then he applied with cheerfulness, and never wanted to leave his studies more. "I continued," he says, "in this situation between three and four years, in which time I got near the top form in the school."

When he was about eighteen, it happened that a London minister, named Pain, was visiting his friends in Essex, and mentioned a society recently established, under the name of the King's Head Society, for educating pious young men for the ministry. The name of John Conder was mentioned as a promising and suitable candidate. "Upon which," says he, "I was sent for to Royston, to be conversed with by Mr. Pain; but he was in great haste, and directed me to write an account of my experience, and send it by post to him in town. I returned home that evening full of disappointment and concern, never having entertained the thoughts I ever had experienced the grace of God in truth. But as a letter must be written, I was put upon very close thought and examination what indeed I had to say with integrity of heart, and this was so little that I persuaded myself that, upon receiving my letter, the old gentleman would quite desist, as well judging I was not fit to be taken in by the Society.

"I had to write that I made conscience of secret prayer and hearing the word; and that, some time before, the Rev. Mr. Robert Wright had preached at Hitchin, text, ' *Nay, but I say unless ye repent,*' etc., which came with convincing power; and that when I came over to Royston, Mr. Pain's text was the same, which I judged a particular voice of God (as the message was thus repeated). Some texts of Scripture (as Isa. i. 18, John vi. 37, etc.) were added, as what gave some relief under these convictions. So the letter was sent, and by return of post an order came requiring me to come to be conversed with by a committee. I went with much fear and trembling; but was examined by the Rev. Mr. John Sladen, Mr. Jonathan Rowlet, treasurer, and Mr. Hartgrave. They reported favourably. I was admitted, and ordered to repair, as soon as convenient, to the Rev. Mr. Samuel Parson's care in Clerkenwell. Some time after, I was taken in member of Mr. Pain's church. But after two or three sacrament days, Mr. Pain unhandsomely left his church, and retired into the country and died. This event was matter of great discouragement to my mind, as if the Lord hereby rebuked me for joining so soon."

Soon after commencing his studies at Clerkenwell, the youthful nonconformist was subjected to a somewhat severe test of his stedfast attachment to principle. His mother having come up to London to be treated for cancer (of which, in the following year, she died), was attended by "the celebrated Mrs. Stevens," whose remedies attracted so much attention at that time as to obtain for her a parliamentary grant of six thousand pounds.

"The old lady," as he relates, who often saw him when he visited his mother, took a great fancy to the embryo divine, and "courted me much to go to St. Omer's for education, which she promised should be all gratis, and with a full supply of the pocket, etc.; by which I could see what religion she was of, and how diligent the Papists are to gain proselytes. I was helped to make Moses' choice; choosing rather to suffer affliction with the people of God, than enjoy the pleasures of sin for a season."

He was afterwards placed under the tuition of Mr. Eames, " a man of great knowledge, and a very able tutor." He commenced his ministry in 1738, at the age of twenty-four, and was ordained the following year at Cambridge, where he continued to labour during sixteen years. In 1734, he was invited to become Theological Tutor in the " Academy" established by the King's Head Society at Mile-end. His diary shows the surprise and unaffected humility with which he entertained this invitation, and the spirit of prayer and self-distrust in which he entered on the office, which he filled with honour until his death. The institution was removed in 1770 to Homerton, and is now merged in New College.

His diploma of Doctor of Divinity was conferred upon him, without his knowledge, by the University of Aberdeen, in 1762. He continued to discharge the duties both of his College tutorship and of the pastorship of the church in Moorfields (a co-pastorship part of the time) for one-and-twenty years. On May 30, 1781, he peacefully and happily departed for the better country.* An epitaph, found in his own handwriting, and

---

* On the morning before he died, he requested his son Thomas to sing a favourite hymn, which may be found in the *first edition* of the Congregational Hymn Book (No. 611), the first verse of which is as follows :—

> " Never weather-beaten sail
>   More willing bent to shore;
> Never tired pilgrim's limbs
>   Affected slumber more;
> Than my weary spirit longs
>   To fly out of my troubled breast
> Oh, come quickly, dearest Lord!
>   And take my soul to rest!"

engraven on his tombstone in Bunhill Fields, may not be out of place in these introductory memorials :—

PECCAVI

RESIPUI CONFIDI

AMAVI REQUIESCO

RESURGAM

ET EX GRATIA CHRISTI

UT UT INDIGNUS

REGNABO

An adventure which befel him when residing at Cambridge places his character in an interesting light, and is worth recording as a picture of the times. Returning on horseback from Peterborough, he was attacked by a mounted highwayman, whom he at once recognised as a former inhabitant of Cambridge, but had the presence of mind to conceal his knowledge. He at once surrendered his purse, but pleaded hard for his watch, which he valued as an heirloom; but the robber was inexorable. Throughout the affair, the man's inward uneasiness and agitation betrayed itself under all his assumed courage and violence. Mr. Conder civilly proposed, as the road was lonely, that they should ride in company; and the highwayman assenting, he began with great kindness and seriousness to inquire into the motives which could induce him to such a criminal course, which must issue so fatally, here and hereafter. The robber urged the plea of necessity; but as the conversation continued, his conscience was roused; he offered to return the watch, and, at length, the money also. The former Mr. Conder accepted, as he greatly valued it; but as to the latter—amounting to several guineas—he said that he would, on no account, take it back, but begged the man to regard it as a free gift, to assist him in escaping from this miserable mode of life. The man thanked him earnestly, and galloped off as they drew near Cambridge; but fell, almost instantly, into the hands of the officers, who were watching to apprehend him, on account of previous robberies. Great was Mr. Conder's surprise, on entering the streets of the city, to encounter his friend in custody. He visited him in prison, both before and after his trial, and had every reason to believe that the unhappy man died a real penitent.

Dr. John Conder left several sons, of whom the fourth, Thomas, was father to the subject of the ensuing memoir. He was a man of superior and cultivated abilities, amiable and kind heart, mild and quiet temper, and devout piety. He was brought up to the business of a map engraver. During his apprenticeship his mind was greatly impressed by a remarkable dream. He thought that he and a fellow-apprentice, with whom he was intimate, were in prison together, under sentence of death. The morning of execution arrived. They were brought out, ascended the scaffold, and the cap was already drawn over their faces, when there was a sudden agitation in the crowd, a distant shouting, and presently the word, "*Reprieve! Reprieve!*" rung from mouth to mouth. The messenger galloped up to the scaffold; the paper which he bore was snatched from his hand, and opened, and found to contain the name of Thomas Conder only. He was saved, and his companion executed. He awoke in great agitation, not a little rejoiced to find it but a dream. Not long after, this same fellow-apprentice and himself were seized with fever, and both lay ill at the same time, uncertain which would die first. His companion died; but, through the mercy of God, he recovered; and the correspondence of the event with his dream could not but deepen on his mind the impression of this deliverance. He had received a good classical education (having been accustomed to attend the College lectures -with the students); and many years afterwards he could repeat from memory long passages out of Homer. He was a man of excellent judgment, and well read, but shy, and making no ostentatious display of his abilities. One of his favourite amusements was painting butterflies or other insects from life, in which he displayed admirable skill. He ground his own colours, and painted before breakfast; and after eighty years, these insect-portraits, which are so minutely finished as to bear the magnifier, retain their freshness. He lived to the age of eighty-four, and then received the answer to his cherished wish and prayer, by a sudden and most easy departure. Though in the earlier part of his life his health had been often infirm and interrupted, his age was vigorous. At sixty, he left off his wig, and had a fine head of hair when he died. The day before he died he had walked into town; and within two or three hours of his death—being apparently but slightly unwell—he gave full directions to the friend who was to take his place at the committee meeting of Homerton College. He had held the treasurership to the College for many years, and had prepared the accounts and report for the annual meeting of the committee, which took place that very day. While it was being held, he was gently summoned to give in his account with joy in his Master's presence. He published, at the request of his friends, a little volume of essays, full of good sense and piety, under the title of " *Opinions of an Old Gentleman*," which reached a second edition.

Mrs. Thomas Conder, JOSIAH CONDER's mother, was a woman of excellent good sense and judgment, great energy and strength of character, and sincere piety. Her maiden name was also Conder, but there was no near relationship. She also lived to be upwards of eighty, retaining the full use of her faculties, and her characteristic love of independence and self-help, insomuch that her death was hastened by her stooping to tie her own shoestring.

An adventure which happened to *her* mother when a girl seems worth relating, as a pendant to that already related of Dr. Conder. Miss Esther Stonard, as she then was, accompanied by another young lady, was riding near Chelmsford rather late in the evening. A gentleman splendidly mounted rode up, and politely entering into conversation with them, asked if they were not afraid to be out so late alone, as Turpin was often on that road. Miss Stonard replied that they had brave hearts, and that, besides, she was sure Turpin was too much of a gentleman to attack ladies. Their companion, smiling, said that he believed she was right, but that some of Turpin's followers might be less scrupulous; and he would, if they pleased, accompany them until they were out of danger. On coming to a cross-lane not far from the town, he bowed courteously, and galloped off. As soon as they reached home, they recounted their adventure; and on describing their protector, they found that it was no other than "Dick Turpin" himself. When, some years after, Turpin was taken, and executed in the same town of Chelmsford, it is said that there was not a dry eye in the place. Compared with the forms, at once dastardly and ferocious, which crime has assumed in England of late years, these little incidents of the romance of highway robbery in the days of George the

Second are really quite refreshing. In these degenerate days, it is only here and there a banking baronet, or a director or secretary of some public company, who is found capable of executing his robberies in a thoroughly gentlemanly manner. In one respect, indeed, the Sir John Pauls and Leopold Redpaths of our day have made a decided advance on their predecessors. It is not related that Dick Turpin ever subscribed to benevolent institutions, or made any profession of religion.

The grass has long been green, and the leaves of many an autumn have fallen over the mouldering dust of those whose names have filled these introductory pages; but their prayers have not ceased to be answered, and the God whom they trusted and honoured has been the God of their children, and their children's children. This preliminary chapter will not, it is hoped, be deemed either tedious or out of place, though it must needs be more interesting to the writer than to most of his readers. Certainly, it is both an honour and a happiness to be permitted to think of the heavenly world as the home of former generations of those but for whose sojourn on earth we had not been; and they are to be congratulated who can say, as they turn the pages of their family history, how obscure or unattractive soever to the mere worldly eye, "THIS GOD IS OUR GOD FOR EVER AND EVER: HE WILL BE OUR GUIDE EVEN TO DEATH."

CHAPTER I.

EARLY LIFE.

Josiah Conder, fourth son and sixth child of Thomas Conder, citizen of London, and engraver, was born in Falcon Street, Aldersgate, on the 17th of September, 1789. He brought with him into the world a better inheritance than lands or gold, namely, a sound and healthful constitution, capable of enduring severe toil, and a cheerful, hopeful, elastic temperament, which stood him in good stead under the cares and disappointments and trials of a long and busy life. Unmistakable indications of more than ordinary mental ability and energy very early displayed themselves; and the circumstances in which his childhood was spent tended to cherish a quiet, sensitive, meditative turn of mind, and to form the man of letters, rather than the man of action. Above all, religion must be reckoned as the predominant influence in his education, and in the formation of his character. He counted it a great honour to be sprung from a family in which piety (as well as non-conformity) was hereditary. The prayers, example, and instructions of Christian parents presented religion to him, from his very infancy, under its happiest aspect; the Spirit of God seems early to have prepared the soil for the precious seed which loving and unwearied hands thus early dropped in; and the profound and stedfast convictions of religious truth, the devout habit of thought and feeling,

c

and the simple childlike faith which distinguished him through life, were but the ripened promise of his early years.

In an autobiographical fragment, commenced in his twentieth year, and designed for the inspection of himself alone,* he thus reviews the circumstances of his birth and childhood :—"It is, in these perilous and eventful times, a circumstance which calls loudly on my gratitude, that I am by birth planted in the happiest nation under heaven; the most enlightened, the most secure, the most distinguished, the most Christian; that I am born at an era in which, notwithstanding the pressure of various external and domestic evils, this happiest country may be said to have attained a higher degree of perfection than it has ever enjoyed with respect to the diffusion of general knowledge and of religious truth; a season of civil tranquillity and religious freedom. Add to this, that Providence has stationed me in that sphere of respectable mediocrity which is in every way the most favourable to happiness. I am not descended from the great and the opulent; but of what unspeakably greater honour is it to inherit the name, the prayers, and the instructions of the faithful servants of God! Has not God answered the prayers, and honoured the faith of his people in their third and fourth generations? And may I not, then, owe, in measure, what I enjoy to my pious ancestors? How gratefully should I reflect on the privileges of a pious education! Surely, memory will ever delight to recall the Sabbath evening's catechism and hymns, and

* "The plan I mean to pursue is, to reject all plan, and to set down my recollections and reflections as they occur. . . . It is designed for the inspection of myself alone, so I need not care about style; but let me be serious, faithful, and impartial, as exposed to the scrutiny of Omniscience."

conversations in my father's study. Perhaps nothing has tended more deeply to fix in my mind the belief of an overruling Providence, than the anecdotes which my infant mind heard with such interest of the remarkable deliverances and preservations of good men. These anecdotes I recollect frequently to have repeated at school to amuse the boys, and believe they had a good effect on my mind; for from my very childhood I have felt a firm conviction, accompanied with sweet consolation, of the truth of this doctrine."

Parental instructions are not seldom counteracted by the folly or wickedness of the servants to whom children are carelessly intrusted. It deserves notice therefore that, in this review of the writer's childhood, he specially records his great obligations to a faithful and intelligent nurse. This pious and worthy woman survives, at the age of eighty-six, and still loves to speak of the early piety of the little boy whom she nursed and instructed sixty years ago. At four years old he learned to read well, so that when at five years old he went to school, he was placed in the third class, and soon made his way to the head.

The circumstance which was the occasion of his being sent at that early age to a boarding-school, was a serious calamity which befel him, yet which in later years he "did not scruple to rejoice in, as the probable fountain of future blessings." This was nothing less than the loss of an eye. According to the practice at that period, he was inoculated with small pox, and, although he had it most favourably, the providence of God, often severest when kindest, ordained that the right eye should be one of the very few points at which the poison of the disease manifested itself; and the result was the irreparable destruction of that precious organ. "Perhaps," he writes, "no

other event has had such a merciful and decided influence
on my character and lot in life. The consequence was,
that I attracted a double share of care, sympathy, and
attention, and even from strangers met with the caresses
of pity. To try the effect of electricity in reducing the
eye, which then projected beyond the socket, I was sent
as a visitor to Mr. Palmer's; but here I by choice became a scholar, pursued the study of my Latin grammar
con amore, and thus got the start of my seniors in the
race of education."

In the same year, 1795, he had a dangerous attack of
scarlet fever, which nearly cut short his life. From that
time he never had any serious illness until he reached
manhood. The eye which was mercifully preserved, was
singularly brilliant and powerful; and the disfiguring
effect of the disease was almost entirely remedied, during
great part of his life, by means of a glass eye, until, in
later years, he was compelled to lay this aside and substitute a shade.

The school to which he was thus sent was at Hackney,
and was kept by the Rev. Mr. Palmer, the predecessor in the
pastoral office of the Rev. Henry Foster Burder. He made
rapid progress in the ordinary school studies, and became
a favourite both amongst his companions and with his
masters. One of his sisters, writing in reference to his
schoolboy days, records his unusual power of abstraction,
and of paying simultaneous attention to different and dis-
cordant objects; and the ease with which he acquired his
lessons under circumstances apparently most unfavourable.
" He never sat steadily at his desk like other boys, to prepare for the classes, but was sure to assume some grotesque
position, and, with pen or pencil in hand, would be scrib-
bling caricatures, or otherwise amusing himself, not heed-
ing the friendly warning of M. Paris, his excellent French

master. His mind was busy working while his fingers were playing truant, and never was he found unprepared for the master." He often spoke, in after years, of this worthy and kind-hearted Frenchman, with whom he was a favourite pupil, in terms of affectionate and respectful remembrance; and related how discouraged he used to be by the scanty meed of approval, and the harsh strictures awarded to his French exercises, until one day, having ventured to remonstrate, not without tears, that M. Paris seemed to deal much more severely with him than with the other boys, the good Frenchman burst forth with a tone and manner that quite made amends for the uncomplimentary epithet—" You *grate* fool, Josiah! you *grate* fool! Do you not see, zat it is just because you are ze only boy in ze school zat I care for, zat I am more severe wiz you zan wiz all de rest?" This was quite a new light on the matter, and the discovery communicated a new spur to the boy's mind, and fully reconciled him for the future to all M. Paris's fault-finding.

Recording, in the manuscript already quoted, his return to school after the Christmas of 1797, when in his ninth year, he continues:—" I recollect mixing but little in play with my schoolfellows, which I attribute partly to my eye. This also, as well as my youth and smallness, induced me to avoid all fighting. I remember but two boys with whom I came to blows. By this means I was led to choose more still and quiet pleasures and pursuits; and being under the protection of old Mrs. Palmer, it was thus, perhaps, that a foundation was laid for my domestic taste and literary propensity. Among my juvenile whims and projects—I believe first accidentally lighting on a sixpenny astrological book—I, with two others, set up as fortune-tellers. We amused ourselves, and succeeded in elevating ourselves by our eccen-

tricity above the undistinguished vulgar of our little
world. But I must confess that, whether my mind was
or was not predisposed to superstition, this fancy served
to strengthen ideas which were with difficulty shaken off
afterwards by reason. One of my astrological associates,
my fellow in age, class, and attainments, soon grew into
a rival, and exhibited in miniature all the jealousy, policy,
and ambition of a full-grown competitor on a nobler
field. I do not recollect to have myself felt, at least to
the degree I observed in him, that jealous spirit of emulation. Nevertheless, it operated as a stimulus to exertion, and taught me a little what to expect from the
world. I believe I began French at eight years old, and
well remember working at my French fables out of
school-hours; so that I had always translated three or
four beforehand, and transcribed them on long slips of
paper. On similar scraps I used, while the others were
in school-time getting their tasks, to compose my first
literary essays, in the shape of Eastern tales, etc.; many
of which, falling into the hands of my schoolmaster,
afforded him no small diversion. For this sort of stories,
perhaps from reading the 'Arabian Nights,' I had always
a strong partiality; but am convinced that, great as the
influence of books is over the tender mind, the nature
and the power of this influence must essentially depend
on the previous and attendant circumstances with which
the mind is enveloped. Thus, though I very early read,
was delighted with, and learned by heart extracts from
Pope's 'Iliad,' I do not recollect that I was at all
alive to its poetical beauties, so that they could contribute to form my taste; nor do I appear to have imbibed
any of those martial ideas and feelings, which in other
minds of the same age they have a great tendency to
produce. I was much interested in the characters and

narrative, and helped to form games from it, in which I chose voluntarily the quiet part of Ulysses, because of his wisdom, and of his being protected by Minerva, who, with Apollo, were my earliest favourites of the Pantheon, which I read with interest. The rival before alluded to gloried in assuming, when no one stronger claimed it, the congenial character of Achilles or Agamemnon. The friendship and history of Patroclus always delighted me, and Priam's visit to Achilles to beg the body of his son.

"The stage had its turn in my amusements, for which the public speeches naturally induced a taste. Dr. Young's 'Busiris' and 'The Brothers' I assisted in performing, taking myself the part of the heroine. Then there was a newspaper which I edited, and which reached a second or third number, so early was I seized with the *cacoethes scribendi.* My first poetical effort was the trying to bend some of Æsop's Fables—I recollect for one, Fortune and the Boy—into rhyme. These matchless poems I wrote out as well as I could, and prized like old gold, keeping them with religious care from the eye of every mortal.

"At ten years old I wrote my first essay for the 'Preceptor;'* and from that time till leaving school continued monthly to furnish for it an essay, criticism, or translation, by which my literary propensities and solitary habits were confirmed. I was thus obliged to read, and think, and digest. Two circumstances I remember attended these productions. I always wrote, or fancied I wrote, best at evening; and my principal difficulty in composition was keeping close to the question.

* The "Monthly Preceptor" was a collection of juvenile essays, to which several of Mr. Palmer's scholars contributed. Prizes were given to the best compositions, and two silver medals rewarded Josiah Conder's schoolboy skirmishes in the field of authorship.

"In summoning up the past feelings of my school-day mind, I behold the spirit of adventure appearing to influence my character, but its operations were too childish and trivial to appear of any importance on paper; such as stealing into the garden over the pales at night, and exploring the house, the only interest arising from a dread of discovery; the mysterious feeling inspired by darkness, and the daring to do what others dared not. This attached importance to midnight bolster battles, and reconciled me to sitting for half hours in the cold in my night-gown at the parlour-door, listening to the organ, long after we were sent to bed.

"It was at school that natural philosophy engaged more of my attention than it has ever done since. I used to steal out of school, and instead of writing and arithmetic, recollect many a delightful summer afternoon spent in the playground with Adams's Lectures (I think). Not confined to theory, I aspired to be a practical philosopher, and united with two other boys in the pursuit for a time with spirit. We got an old outhouse for a laboratory, and there I have passed many an hour. I must own I was not so active in the business, except with my book, as my companions; but I cannot help suspecting that this was a point in my life when I might have become a philosopher, had my mind been previously formed for such pursuits. From circumstances equally insignificant some have dated their career, which confirms me in the opinion of the original diversity of minds, and their adaptation to different pursuits. Books, circumstances, and associates may awaken a latent feeling, but cannot create a taste; they may colour, but cannot decide the form of the natural character.

"At a very early period I remember to have mused on the common error that school-days are our happiest.

I looked round, and examined our school, reputed one of the best, and noticed the lamentable oversight of the directors, the insufficiency of rules in the place of motive and principle, and many fundamental errors in the system; and I resolved then, if I lived, to take up the subject. I reasoned that the cares which then oppressed me were not insignificant, considering my youth; that I was deprived of the consolations of friendship; and that religion did not deign to prescribe for such petty nameless sorrows and complaints. I recollect, in particular, being struck with the impropriety of depriving the boys indiscriminately of the opportunity of retirement, by forbidding them to go up stairs into their rooms, locking up the school-room, and enclosing sixty boys in a little yard. I thought then, and I think now, school-days are not golden days.

"I cannot recollect that I was ever irreligious. I desire with gratitude to bear my testimony to the invaluable privilege of a pious education. Religion was with me—first compliance, then habit, till it grew into feeling and principle. I do not suppose a child has generally notions much above natural religion. The doctrine of Providence, the performance of religious duties, and heaven, were, as far as I remember, what principally engaged my thoughts and attention; and perhaps I was then more conscientious than ever I have been since. This was not unaccompanied with a reception of the doctrines of the Gospel, as far as my mind was able to receive them. I received them as part of Scripture, and of my education. I very early accustomed myself to variation of my prayers, generally founding them on some form, but often intermixing my extempore thoughts. This I consider as a very wholesome exercise, which may have had considerable effect on my religious progress.

I always loved the Sabbath. At ——* years old, I first began to write the text and heads of the sermon, a custom which I have continued with little intermission ever since, and must say, as far as I can judge from myself, that it is a most useful and impróving custom. It perpetually rouses the attention, and thus fixes what is heard upon the memory far more than what is merely listened to. It accustoms the mind to an attention to system and order, and habituates to a conciseness and facility of expression."

At this point these brief autobiographical memoranda abruptly break off. Their writer never resumed them; nor was he at any period of his life in the habit of making more than the very briefest entries, and those not continuously, in his diary. Almost the only remaining materials therefore at the command of his biographer, besides his works (published or unpublished), are a few packets of letters, and the reminiscences of surviving friends.

Mr. Thomas Conder had left the house in Aldersgate soon after the date with which this chapter commences; and after residing for two or three years in the neighbourhood of Blackfriars, he took a bookselling business at No. 30, Bucklersbury, which he continued to carry on for about sixteen years. This removal occurred about the same time that the little Josiah was making his entrance (as described by his own pen) into the miniature world of school, and laying the foundation of the opinion that "school-days are not golden days." Bucklersbury was the home in prospect of returning to which the schoolboy essayist, poet, and critic counted the weeks to the holidays; and the scene in which, when school-days were

* There is a blank left for this date in the MS., which was never filled up.

over, he made his acquaintance with the dull routine, burdensome cares, and irksome confinement of business life.

At the early age of thirteen he was removed from Mr. Palmer's school, and entered his father's shop. It was a life altogether unsuited both to his tastes and his talents. The natural element of his mind was knowledge, not action. However diligently and conscientiously he might, and no doubt did, fulfil the innumerable yet monotonous duties of his calling, and however cheerfully he inured himself to its endless petty cares and vexations, it was not in his nature to throw his heart and soul into what is technically called " business." If Pegasus be put in harness, his wings will infallibly get in his way. There is no help for it, but either to take off the harness, or to cut off the wings. Many a youthful Pegasus succeeds, after some little trouble, in getting rid of those ethereal appendages, and settles down into a good steady useful hack. Yet, though the beaten way be paved with gold, were it not better, somehow, after all, since he had wings, to have flown ?

Doubtless, moral discipline, not intellectual culture, is the essential aim of education; and therefore the principal point to which the providence of God tends, in arranging the earthly lot of his children. Were it not so, one could not but both wonder and lament that a mind of such capacity and facility, with so strong a native bent towards literature, and so athirst for knowledge, should have been denied the congenial and powerful aids of a university education, or some equivalent course of prolonged study. Circumstances, it is true, can neither create nor destroy intellectual power. But they may do very much to foster or to repress it. The strongest racer, in shackles, on a rough hill-side, will make poor progress compared to what he would easily achieve on a level course, and with free limbs. Yet, the shackles and the hill-side may be the training for future triumphs. Our earthly schooling will have done its true work, if the great ends of spiritual and moral culture be attained. Once the character formed, and the heart purified, ample scope and stimulus will be supplied to the intellect in the unbounded future.

From the time of his quitting school, Josiah Conder was self-educated. Denied the assistance of tutors, and of a prescribed course, as well as the enjoyment of quiet leisure for study, and the stimulus of competition, he was obliged to snatch what intervals he could find in the midst of business, or what fragments could be spared from the hours of relaxation and rest. His reading was necessarily desultory; but, though this was a hindrance to his attaining profound and complete scholarship, it helped to prepare him for his future literary labours. The bent of his mind was towards poetry, theology, metaphysics, and criticism, rather than towards science or classical erudition. Many of his early friends were literary; few of them were learned. At an early age, the recognised acuteness and soundness of his judgments secured for him, in the youthful literary circle of which he gradually became the centre, the dangerous post of acknowledged critic and *arbiter elegantiæ.* Poetry, however, formed his favourite study, and first kindled the ambition to be known as an author. A small volume, filled with extracts, from Young's poems, written in a close and very good and legible hand, at the age of ten years; and a similar volume, compiled at the age of thirteen, entitled "Cowperiana; or, Extracts from the Writings of William Cowper, Esq.," indicate at once the models on which his poetical taste was first formed, and the diligence with which, at that early age, he studied them. The poets who impressed, during the first twenty years of this century, a new character and impulse on English poetry had not yet emerged into fame. Byron and Shelley were schoolboys. Wordsworth was chiefly known by the unmitigated ridicule poured on his earlier poems; and Southey had rather promised than performed. When "Mr. Scott's new poem"—the *Lay of the Last Minstrel*—took the public admiration by storm, Josiah Conder was sixteen; and he speaks, in one of his letters, of reading it with delight. But his poetic tastes and susceptibilities instinctively inclined towards contemplative, tender, meditative communing with nature, and with the inward life of affection and emotion, rather than towards the region of stirring action and agitating passion, which is the native home of the poetry of romance. Hence, the writings of James Montgomery, then rising into popularity as a poet, attracted his warm admiration, and deeply interested him. Many of his youthful essays were submitted to the criticism of Mr. Montgomery, whose acute and unsparing, yet kind and judicious, strictures were of no little service, especially in leading him to a more severe and fastidious criticism of what he wrote. Their intercourse ripened into a friendship, valued on both sides, which lasted through half a century, until it was interrupted, not terminated, by the removal of the elder poet to that world in which Christian friendships will be reknit eternally.

The first appearance of the young author "in print" (excepting the childish prize essays before mentioned) seems to have been the publication of some lines, written at the age of sixteen, entitled "The Withered Oak." He says, in one of his letters, "Would it not be a proof of consummate vanity in me to send my ' Withered

Oak' to the *Athenæum?* I have been advised to do it." His scruples on the score. of modesty being removed, the piece was sent, and inserted in the 11th No. of the *Athenæum*, then edited by Dr. Aikin, who was so pleased with the young poet, that he called at his father's to see him, and asked him to dine at his house. The occasion of the verses is thus described in a letter to one of his sisters.

"The walks about Colchester are most enchanting. On Friday we walked to Barfield Common; set off about three, drank tea at the White Hart there, and returned about seven. The scenery and sky were most beautiful. On returning home, there was an old oak forcibly arrested our attention. All the surrounding trees and verdure were flourishing. This stood in the midst, leafless and blighted. The next day, the event of the preceding afternoon occasioned the annexed poem, which, as I have nothing better to offer, I send you."

THE WITHERED OAK.

'Twas Autumn. The sun, now descending the sky,
  In a robe of bright crimson and gold was array'd;
While the pale sickly moon (scarcely open'd her eye)
  Just peep'd thro' the forest, and silver'd the glade.

The voice of the evening was heard in the trees;
  Each chirper so merry was seeking his nest;
The anthems of insects were mix'd with the breeze,
  And Nature look'd pleas'd—all her children were blest.

E'en the trees appear'd dress'd in their holiday clothes,*
  And they wav'd their green arms, and they seem'd to rejoice;
While methought, as I listen'd, at times there arose
  From each oak's ivied branches a deity's voice.

* Old-fashioned pronouncing dictionaries give this word as to be sounded "*cloze*."

But ah! there was one that did not appear gay,
    Nor wave his long branches, now verdant no more;
The bird, as he views him, soars silent away;
    His genius is dead, and his honours are o'er.

Once green like the rest, strong and lovely he grew;
    The warbler once dwelt in each well-cover'd bough;
The breezes saluted his leaves as they flew:
    Yes, he has been;—but now—alas! what is he now!

The rays of the morning still shine on the tree,
    And evening still waters the trunk with her tears;
The wild flower and wheatsheaf around it we see;
    But a wintery ruin this ever appears.

Oh say, is it age that has alter'd thy form
    (For care and affliction thou never hast known);
Or hast thou been struck by the pitiless storm,
    That thou thus seem'st to pine and to wither alone?

Thou art silent. The silence, my fancy, improve!
    Come, pause here awhile. It is what thou may'st be.
Ah! oft in the heyday of pleasure and love,
    Old friend! I shall sigh as I think upon thee!

August 23rd, '06.

To the same date—the writer's seventeenth year—
belongs the following specimen of his correspondence.
It is the first of a numerous series of letters, kindly furnished by one of his earliest and most valued literary
friends.* It gives a glimpse at the scenes then rife with
the intense interest and vivid activity of the present—
now shadows on the mirror of the past, amidst which
his mind was being trained and ripened for future toil
and usefulness.

* Miss Ann Taylor, afterwards Mrs. Gilbert.

I. " Judge not, that ye be not judged," is the commandment of a greater than Solomon. Lord Nelson was a truly great man. His exertions, heroic and apparently disinterested, have freed us from the fear of invasion, and Britain will ever venerate his name. But with respect to his character before God, what he will be found when weighed in the balance of the sanctuary, we have no business to conjecture; but I would sooner be among those who waft him to Heaven, than of the number of those who presume to limit *His* mercy who promised heaven to a malefactor in the very arms of death. What passed in the mind of Nelson we cannot know. This is to his honour—he was, I believe, almost the first who publicly acknowledged the arm of the Almighty in his despatches. But it is a part of his character with which we have no concern. Therefore, though I, and and not I alone, greatly admire your beautiful verses, we regret that the last two should need an apology, and that the lyre of Poetry should recall to memory what we would consign to the silence in which he now reposes.

. . . . . As my letter has been delayed till this time, you may perhaps expect a line or two concerning Lord Nelson's funeral. With respect to the aquatic procession, many were disappointed; but as I had never witnessed anything of the kind before, I was very much gratified. The day was beautiful. Had the occasion been of a less solemn nature, and more music, it would have been delightful. On Thursday, carriages were in motion by five in the morning; streets crowded by six; and the houses in the streets through which the procession was to pass (which were fitted up for the occasion, and the seats in some sold for £1 1s. each) mostly filled by seven. The particulars you have, doubtless, seen in the paper. The sight of the colours of the "Victory," covered with blood and full of shot-holes; of the old Greenwich Pensioners, limping along in black cloaks; and of the crew of the "Victory," in black, who, though sailors, hung down their heads and appeared *real* mourners ; the muffled roll of the drums at intervals, and solemn sound of the trumpets, were really very impressive. There was too little music; but one of the bands played the Portuguese Hymn with fine effect as it passed. The shrieks of the bagpipes, belonging to the Highland regiment who were with Nelson in Egypt, and preceded the procession, were really lamentable. The hearse was elegant, without being showy. The long train of gentlemen's carriages, and the breaks and stoppages which unfortunately happened, lessened the effect which was evidently made. There were a few accidents, but they only took place among a numerous collection, from the adjacent parts, of rioters and pickpockets, whom they were obliged to quell by Horse Guards, and sometimes to charge with bayonets and drawn swords ; but, upon the whole, great order prevailed.

To the same correspondent he describes the impression made on his mind by Montgomery's poems ; and, subsequently, by those of Professor Smyth.

II. . . . You will, of course, look into Montgomery's Poems. Take special notice of " Hannah," the last verse of which is masterly. " Ocean," generally reckoned his *chef d'œuvre*. " The Daisy" *I* like ; whether it will attract you, I can't say. I think it is characteristic of its subject. The " Battle of Alexandria " is sublime. What says Martin to it ? The " Joy of Grief," when it appeared in the *Poetical Register*, was

D

the first poem signed Alixus that arrested my notice. I have never yet felt the agony of grief. I have never yet experienced the loss of a friend, a brother, a parent, or felt the charms of any Anna, but as a poet; but there was a power in the lyre of Alixus that "exquisitely thrilled my soul!" . . . But I am again running upon *self*—that dear intrusive being. If we knew him better, we should, perhaps, be less fond of him. (I beg pardon for saying "we.")

. .. . . There is another subject which I cannot pass over, that of Smyth's Lyrics; and yet, why should I, for the sake of an unknown individual, hazard my reputation for correctness of taste and accuracy of discernment? Why should I unblushingly confess to those who are far better judges of their respective merits, that the spirit that breathes through the "English Lyrics" is more congenial with mine than that which animates the bosom of Alixus—that the music of the lyre of the Cambridge Professor of History has more power over my heart, and accords more with my feelings, than that of the still much admired author of "The Common Lot," "Hannah," and "The Joy of Grief"? I'll tell you why I hazard this confession. Not in deference to J. S., or the Edinburgh reviewers—not from a lessened partiality to Montgomery, but out of gratitude for the pleasure received from Smyth. And here, as a sort of defence, I would observe that—1st, I do not wonder that those who merely "skimmed" him over should overlook the peculiar beauties of his muse, whose characteristics are tenderness and delicacy; 2ndly, that a certain degree of prejudice naturally attends the opening of a book of poems on subjects not in general striking, to which the name of an unheard-of simple somebody is affixed, without title, prefatory or annexed; 3rdly, that poems like Cowper's and Smyth's, which address the heart, are not calculated to be read aloud in full critical tribunal. Perhaps these remarks may not, in this case, be applicable. I am otherwise at a loss how to account for this mortifying diversity of taste between Miss Taylor and Josiah Conder. I shall therefore dismiss the subject.

There was a certain annual publication, entitled the *Minor's Pocket-book*, which formed the centre of a little world of poetical activity and interest, and in whose pages the initials J. C. B. (Josiah Conder, Bucklersbury) are of frequent occurrence. In reference to some verses which he had contributed, he writes :—

III. I don't recollect anything that needs alteration, unless it be some slovenly lines, which I should thank you very much to correct. I am much obliged, I assure you, for your remarks, and should be more so if you would take the trouble of pointing out those pieces which are most objectionable on this ground. I am in part conscious of this, but often remain ignorant of the defect till I hear them read by some one that misplaces the accents, murders the cadences, and puts my poetical feelings to exquisite torture. I enclose my " Sun ;" the " Moon" is at Camberwell; it shall follow. Be so good as to look over them, as I think of sending them to Dr. A. His attention to me and to my muse has given birth to a feeling new to me—the anxiety of an author that he does not disgrace himself, nor forfeit commendation which he is half conscious of not wholly deserving. .... I have some thoughts of sending, in the first place, the song last written, " How bright the sun's declining rays," etc. My father thinks it to be one of the best of my productions. Also that founded on Montgomery's story of "Hannah," or rather suggested by it. On these your opinion and remarks will be very acceptable.

Literarium, June 9, 1808.

IV. DEAR LADIES,—A leisure quarter of an hour has sent me up into my workshop, and the sight of my inkstand reminds me of Colchester; and though I have been rather loquacious of late, having some business to transact, I shall, without further apology, proceed thereunto.

A packet of communications for the *Minor's Pocket-book* will accompany this; among which are three enigmas by your humble servant, which are to serve for my quota. The pigeon verses may, if you like, go into the original poetry. Mr. Suttaby desires me to mention, that anything you may have to spare he will be very glad of for other pocket-books, which have not such a reputation to support.

. . . Herewith I send you the Green Book. When you come to any unworthy piece, be so good as recollect that I have therein inserted *everything*. The necessity of selection, both in justice to myself and in kindness to my readers, would have prevented my lending the volume in a general way. I request you, in return, will exercise all your criticismatical faculties upon its contents. Do not be afraid of making too many pencil-marks. I need not say how much obliged I shall be by any remarks from Dr. Mackintosh. . . . . .

Miss Jane mentions the Exhibition. I have been twice; not because I could afford it, but because the first time I came away without seeing or knowing anything about Mrs. Grant!!! She is indeed placed about even with your knee, so that I do not wonder at my overlooking it. She is handsomer than I was led to expect, and there is all the characteristic sweetness and refinement in her old features which breathe through her letters. It is only a small drawing. "Who is that?" said a young lady by-standing. "Only *a* Mrs. Grant of Laggan," was the reply. I should like you much to see Southey's miniature. H. discovered it by its likeness to Neville White. In the catalogue of the Exhibition, herewith sent, I have marked those which struck me most. Daniel's Eastern landscapes are always admirable. Woodforde is with me a favourite; he has what I think the best of all, viz., Scott's Minstrel. West's picture I like very much. Westall's is spoken variously of. But my paper and your patience failing, I hasten to subscribe myself, yours dutifully,

JOSIAH CONDER.

V. ... I am hardly yet awake from a most delectable dream. July 20, I began "Thaddeus of Warsaw," vol. i.; and July 23, I finished "Thaddeus of Warsaw," vol. iv. It was indeed a treat; and the impression left on my mind was not that of a novel, but that of having known and been in company with Sobieski, the Palatine, etc. I am actually in love (don't say anything) with Mary Beaufort. When you see her next, you may tell her so; and poor Lady Tinemouth, and Mrs. Robson too! Bless them all. The delineation of character is so masterly, the fable is so natural and interesting, the descriptions so well drawn, and the sentiments so just and therefore beautiful, that I quite long to see the authoress.

I am now about to enter upon Miss Hamilton's "Cottagers of Glenburnie," out loud after supper; but I don't intend to read another novel for I can't tell how long. Only, in French, I am reading "Gil Blas." I continue, on the whole, to persevere in getting up earlier in

the morning. I this morning read half through "Castle
Rackrent" before breakfast; but—hush! that was in bed.
This is not a specimen. By seven and half-after seven
I have usually been (of late) in my study; but what
with the weather and a bilious attack, I have not felt
quite the thing for a few days past.

VI. If the receiver is as bad as the thief, you are
actionable if you make use of the enclosed riddlemerees,
since they have been stolen from sleep, from Greek, and
from a third gentleman I met on the king's highway, of
the name of Business. On the latter, indeed, I did not
levy much, and the guilt of it all rests on you. To hear
that the poor dear Pocket-book (my first love!) was
starving was too much, and thus I am not the first poor
man driven by the distress of his family to acts of dishonesty.

Well, to proceed. Your note arrived on Thursday.
Now, Monday being the last of the month, here was
abundance of time for a man of my engagements to
manufacture two or three score of rhymes. An enig-
matical solution, indeed, was quite out of the question,
not only because it takes twice as much stuff and thrice
as much labour, but because I did not know the solution.
Thursday night produced, after eleven o'clock, eight lines,
squeezed like drops out of a wrung lemon, and four of
which were blotted out in the morning. Saturday being
completely occupied, Sunday not being in general devoted to such studies, and Monday the last of the month,
all the work devolved upon poor Friday and me Robinson Crusoe. However, I send you two enigmas and
three charades. . . . . And pray, Mr. Isaac, what is the
reason that your pride cannot come down to the poor
roof of a pocket-book; but that, on pretence of taking a

sketch of the place, you leave us to go and help the poor women on with their spinning? O the pride of you artists!

The following lively and amusing picture of a visit to an editor's den, on behalf of his fair and aggrieved correspondent, is suggestive of the scenes amidst which the writer was preparing to occupy the editorial chair himself. It will touch a sympathetic chord in the heart of any aspiring and indignant author not yet emerged from his teens and his pseudonyms :—

Bucklersbury, September 9.

VII. My poor dear Sister in sorrow and rhyme,— I yesterday afternoon went up to Hatton Garden on the melancholy embassy which your letter enjoined. C. T., junior, was in the shop, and on my entrance, after the customary salutations, began with, "I fear certain odes are printed not quite in the state that—" Here I, with broken voice, stopped him short. "That is done," said I; "and what can't be cured, etc., as the old proverb says. I am only come now to prevent another murder." I then detailed my commission, informing him that I (of course) had written down to Colchester a narrative of these bloody proceedings, and repeated to him, as near as I could, your answer thereunto. "No corrections!" exclaimed the young editor of the *Records*, "that, I am sure, will never do." I then begged a sight of the piece. Here his sage father entered, to whom Charles, seeing perhaps the conflict of my feelings, briefly mentioned my business. Upon this the old gentleman threw his head on one shoulder, and bursting out into a peculiar species of critical and literary laugh, began an oratorical flourish. "He had no notion"—"And these young authors"—"And this polite age," etc. I said little, but renewed my request for a sight of your verses. I was ushered up stairs, where a paper was put into my hands, which I could hardly read for *corrections*. Two or three only I can at present call to mind. " Autumn rustles by in all his golden panoply." There Mr. T. remarked that autumn does not rustle more than summer; that if it was rustling by it could not be approaching; and, lastly, that you did not mean panoply, for that panoply signified *complete* armour. " It signifies armour," said I. " Nay," quoth he, "it is complete armour. *Pan*, you know, all, universal; *oply*, is——;" and so he went on displaying his Greek. Another offending line was, " Probing the lacerated vein." " Now," quoth he, " you do not probe a vein, you probe a wound; but you only probe to heal." Here, perhaps, he was right; but what did he substitute? As near as I can recollect, it was—" Will every pang recall again;" that is, " a spear recalling;" beautiful prosopopœia! And " recalling again," too; that is, calling again, again. Admirable critic! " Fragile flower," likewise, was strongly objected to, and was supplanted by a word very descriptive of the criticism, "*feeble* flower." I stood up for "fragile.' " Well," said the Dr., "I'll turn to a Latin dictionary. It is, you know, a Latin word. *China* is *fragile*, easily broken; but a flower——" I saw it was useless to say anything more, so I proceeded to petition that a proof might be sent to Colchester. " That was impossible; it was designed for the October number, and there would not be time." " Better delay its insertion till November, then." Well, at last I got a sort of promise that, if a proof could not be had, the *corrected* copy should be sent down for your inspection; and having accomplished this, I made my bow and departed, inwardly soliloquising. I just threw a few words at Charles, as I passed through the shop, who told me, when I asked him whether his creed was with mine or his father's, that he had two, a Latin and an English, a political and a literary one: and so we parted. And now I can do nothing but exhort you to the exercise of the Christian virtues, and to beware of editors. Before I conclude, from what I could *see* of your verses, I like them exceedingly. Grandmamma sends her love, and has been much concerned to hear of Isaac's illness. I remain, yours, in tender sympathy,

"JOSIAH CONDER."*

The foregoing extracts, with some others which will be given from his correspondence at this period, sufficiently show that whatever disadvantage the writer suffered from the early termination of his school studies, and his confinement to the ungenial drudgery of business, his position was not altogether unfavourable for literary culture. He lacked the inestimable advantages which a university course would have supplied, with its masculine discipline, wholesome emulation, and quiet thoughtful solitude. But his business itself brought him into constant contact with

---

* Here followeth, in the original, a quaint and amusing *jeu d'esprit*, in the shape of a fragment of a ballad: "*A new song, and a true song, entitled The Poet's Tragedy.*" The giant of criticism is depicted, seated in his castle, "high on a throne of self-conceit."

> "Stood by a wight in solemn guise,
>   With spectacles and band,
> Hight Pedantry; and near him sat,
>   With hatchet in his hand,
> Old Dullness . . . . "

The cruel treatment to which the tender offspring of the poets were subjected is then described; from which, when they escaped with bare life, their unhappy parents could no longer recognise them, "but said their sons were dead."

literaturé and literary men. He was happy, too, in having a circle of friends all fond of literature, and especially of poetry, and with some of whom authorship was a profession. Friendly admiration and animated mutual criticism stimulated him to the laborious improvement of the powers which he was conscious of possessing. The ambition of authorship was roused, and skill and facility in composition and criticism gradually acquired. And thus it happened that he escaped the fate, or the good fortune (whichever the reader is pleased to consider it), of many a youth, who at the age of eighteen has felt perhaps quite as strong a passion and vocation for literature, but, yielding to the influence of unsympathising friends and the claims of business, has consoled himself with the acquisition of actual cash, for the loss of possible and prospective fame. " Poetry," some of his friends said, " was his bane." And so, no doubt, it was, if the great end of life be to " get on in the world," and a balance at a banker's be better gain than the immaterial wealth, and triumphs neither to be reckoned, weighed, nor measured, won in the world of thought. Still, he does not appear to have devoted any large amount of time to literary pursuits. His Sabbaths were always kept sacred. Fragments of busy days and corners of careful weeks were all that he could secure for his beloved studies. Yet these moments of study and composition, and not the hours of business, were shaping his character and future life. So true is it, that not what we are employed in, but what we love, both shows and makes us what we are. The following extract shows that the writer was conscious of the growth of these irrepressible tendencies in his own mind ; and also, that among other studies the study of his own heart was not overlooked :—

November 9, 1808.

VIII. This afternoon brought me your welcome packet, and as I have only run over your letter twice, I intend merely to notice, in a cursory manner, a few of its contents, while the impression is yet warm on my mind. In the first place, my green book; I am disappointed at finding its margin quite free from pencilmarks, upon which valuable accession I had also lately counted. No, not one critical query or asterisk! Not one friendly *dele;* and worse, not one remark on one of the poems to inform me which pleased and which did not, or to enable me to judge of their comparative merit, or to make any corrections; and this after having passed through the hands of two poets, an artist, and a doctor! . . . .

2ndly, As to your ode. You are one of a thousand to take our remarks so good-naturedly. It was only my conscience, I dare say, that made me feel apprehensive you would not. But, yes, I will tell you another reason; and here I am going to be serious. There is a certain failing known by the name of Vanity, which, I understand, is the too general attendant of youth when, emancipated from scholastic shackles, he is looking forward to the period when he shall be a man; and it is said that this weed is particularly luxuriant by the side of the waters of Helicon. And there is another passion which is too often the bosom friend of the poet, yclept Jealousy. Now, however conscious I may be (for I am both young and a poet by name) that I am not exempt from either of these vices, I am yet solicitous, as far as I can, both to check and to conceal them. I am diffident of myself, lest I should appear to be actuated by motives which I abhor and disown. To come to the point, I was only fearful lest the way in which I criticised your poem should seem to savour of puerile vanity, or a rival's jealousy; that, exalted in my own estimation, by an overrated opinion of my powers, or the soul-seducing praises which friendship or politeness is often lavishing upon me, you might think I looked down upon your production, and was pleased to show my critical sagacity. I am happy to found a hope on your letters that my apprehensions were groundless; and I have therefore only to entreat, that if ever you should discover in me any approaches to this character, you will assert the prerogative of friendship, and fulfil the duty of (may I say) a fellow-Christian, in pointing it out to me. I will not assert a modesty which I do not possess, or an indifference to fame which I cannot feel. When first I courted the Muse, it was in idle amusement; but the passion has strengthened—I have gone too far to recede. I have published proofs of my attachment, and am her lover professed. And now I find I have some character to support. Fame invites me on. But as I ascend the hill, the path grows steeper, though the bursting prospects well repay the toil. At first I heedless wandered on; now I must climb. I own, then, I aspire to the character of a poet; but, believe me, I am still more anxious to sustain and deserve that of a friend, and your friend too. But there is a step higher—the friend of God. O may my ambition be more directed to this great end! These reflections are irrelevant, but I think you will excuse them. But to return. You "would rather thank my fidelity than my politeness." Well, I can assure you, it was not politeness which dictated our few remarks of a complimentary nature. The opinion I have always demonstrated of your poems was never feigned, and is not altered. Could my Muse but ensure an existence coëval with the "Original Poems," she would not complain. . . .

I boasted that no piece of mine had undergone so few alterations as "Fancy." Alas! Montgomery taught me that excellence was only to be attained by laborious correction and study. He almost discouraged me by some of his minute and keen criticisms. How much bad poetry would have been saved, if persons could have thought their verses capable of improvement, or had had some judicious friend at their elbow to point out their deficiencies. Montgomery showed me several incorrect lines in " Silence," and has improved my " Fragment." I beg you to believe that I can fully sympathise with you in the pain and drudgery of revision; and while you may expect me to be less disposed to tolerate in you anything short of the excellence you possess, I shall with increasing tenderness respect the feelings and love the offspring of the poet.

An earlier letter, to another correspondent, thus playfully confesses the drawbacks in the way of a too serious devotion to poetry :—

IX. So you really think it was only by my "*good fortune*," more by luck than by wit, that my ode got admission into the *Athenæum ?* Very pretty! If you were not my cousin, I don't know whether I should readily pardon such an affront to my Muse. Disrespect to her ladyship I cannot but consider as disrespect to myself. "I've courted her mickle and lang;" and entertain the same affection for her as if we were real man and wife, and she bone of my bone and flesh of my flesh. Whether we shall ever marry at last, I cannot tell. She has many virtues and accomplishments, sings sweetly, is a delightful companion, and, I dare say, she would be a good nurse. But, then, she has no fortune. Her parents are poor. She is no housewife. She hates a kitchen.

She can't cook, nor bake, nor brew, nor work with her needle; though she can amuse children, and is quite a favourite in the nursery. But, again, I am sadly afraid she would never get through the marriage service. "Wilt thou *obey* him, and serve him—love, honour, and keep him in sickness and in health—and, forsaking all others, keep only to him so long as he lives?" "No," quoth she.

After one of those country visits, which afforded a rare and precious relief to the monotony of his citizen life, he says, "I found my lyre again at C——. Some kind spirit dropped it in Isaac's loft, and sent me down laughing with an ode to cheerfulness. With this, I have concluded my brown book. Yea, verily, it is full. And now I have sent Pegasus to graze, and laid my lyre under the ledger."

Interesting light is thrown on the direction and extent of his studies during these years, by some brief entries in his pocket-books. In his fourteenth year, after he left school, we find him beginning the Æneid, and reading with some perseverance. These self-appointed studies, however, were subject to serious interruptions, as may be gathered from an entry in the following February:—"Fifty-three lines of Virgil; 1st time for 2 mo's." In the year in which he ventured to send his "Withered Oak" to Dr. Aikin, his pocket-book exhibits the following "Journal of Books":—

"1807. *Jan.*—Finished vol. iv. 'Boswell's Johnson.' *Feb.* 16-19.—'Scott's Lay of Last Minstrel.' About *Feb.* 9th.—Began reading in the morning vol. i. 'Horne on the Psalms.' 23.—Begun 'Gellert's Life.' *April* 22-9. —'Wilberforce's Address.' 20.—Begun 'Adolphus's France,' vol. i. 26.—Finished 'Buck on Experience.' *May* 3.—Finished 'Foster's Last Essay.' 8.—Begun

'Marmontel's Life,' vol. i. 24.—Finished 'Pleasures of Religion.' *June* 7.—Begun 'Temple of Truth.' 10.— Finished 'Marmontel' vol. iv. 24.—Read 'Grahame's Sabbath.' 18.—Begun 'Mickle's Lusiad' vol. i. *July* 6. —Finished ditto, vol. iii. 16-19.—Read 'Letters of Scævola.' 15-19.—Read 'Obsolete Ideas.' *August* 2. —Begun Hall's Works. 11.—Finished 'Horne,' vol. i. 12.—Begun 'Letters from the Mountains' (aloud). 'De Salvo's Travels.' 15.—Finished 'Adolphus's France,' vol. ii. 16.—Begun 'Life of Rochester.' 23. —Finished ditto. 24.—Finished 'Epics of Ton.' 22. —Begun 'Froissart,' vol. i. 16.—Begun 'Calmet's Dictionary,' vol. i. *Sept.* 20.—Begun 'Price's Dissertations.' *Oct.* 25.—Read 'Britain Independent of Commerce.' 18.—Begun 'Henry's Christian Communicant.' *Nov.* 21-30.—Read 'Sir R. C. Hoare's Tour.' *Dec.* 6. —Finished 'Price's Dissertations.' 20.—Begun 'Edwards on Religious Affections.' 24.—Finished 'Froissart's Chronicles,' vol. xii. 27.—Begun 'Scott's Force of Truth.' 26.—Begun 'Memoirs of Condé.' 31. —Finished 'Letters from the Mountains,' 3rd vol. (aloud)."

In the following year (his nineteenth), the list of books "finished" includes "Scott's Force of Truth," "Walter Scott's Marmion," "Horne on the Psalms," "Introduction to Literary History of 14th and 15th Centuries," "Fox's History," "Newton's Life," "Gil Blas," "Thaddeus of Warsaw," "Castle Rackrent," "Cottagers of Glenburnie," "Milton's Poetical Works," "Denham's Poems," "Pack's Poems," "View of Antiquity," "Crabbe's Poems," "Bennet on Man," "Waller's Poems," "Winter's Life," "Hutchinson's Life," "Joan of Arc," "Edwards on Religious Affections," "Doddridge's Harmony," "Zouch's Sir P. Sidney," "Elizabeth," "Orton's Life of Doddridge," and two books of "Ovid's Metamorphoses;" besides a number of others begun, among which are "Butler's Analogy," "Spenser's Faerie Queen," "Prideaux's Connection."

That his pen was not idle is attested by the following list of compositions, mostly in verse, during the same year, which is headed, "*Journal of Scribble-ations.*" A note at the end states that those marked with an asterisk had "appeared in print in the *Athenæum, Literary Panorama, Evangelical Magazine, Minor's Pocket-book*, and 'Remains of Henry Kirke White.'"

> *January* ....For January 6th, Rhymes.
> Verses to Uncle and Aunt.
> *February* ......Answer to a Valentine.
> *Ode to Forgetfulness.
> *"But art thou thus indeed alone?"
> *March* ....For March 19th.
> Gumption, part 2.
> " Yet if the soft complaining string."
> *April* ....To Susette.
> On the Misapplication of Scripture.
> *May* ....*Fragment: Morning and Evening.
> The Snowdrop.
> Fancy.
> *Enigma, "*Arms.*"
> *Enigma, "*Temple.*"
> The Snowdrop transformed into a Myrtle.
> *June* ....*Enigma, "*Paper.*"
> Hymn.
> Enigma, "*Bull.*"
> To J. B. C. in his Glen.
> *July* ....*To Duty.
> *August* ....Translation of Musculus's Soliloquy.
> " Give me a harp."
> " A feeble hand."
> " Ah! say, was the lyre."

September, October. .Silence.
September ...." And when within his castle gate."
August ....The Frenzied Sybil.*
September, October. .Thoughts on Life.
August, September . ." Welcome, sweet eve of peace."
October ....Letter to Editor of " Evangelical."
November ....*Review of Gilpin.
December ....Praise.
                     H——'s Commission (verses to his sister).
                     " Veil your bright heads."

A few years later he wrote, in reference to his early studies and projects, " There was a period when, with all the ambition of eighteen, I aspired to the fame of a poet, and I once entertained the hope of producing a work, that might, more worthily repay the public for the favour shown to an anonymous volume, the joint production of a knot of youthful associates, which contains my earliest effusions. But my pursuits have been determined in other directions, and poetry has long ceased to be with me more than a record of feeling, and a source of quiet enjoyment."†

The " anonymous volume " thus referred to, was entitled " The Associate Minstrels." First published in 1810, it reached a second edition within three years. The second edition contained " *The Reverie* "—probably, of all the author's productions, the one which has attained the greatest popularity, and by which his name has been most widely known out of the circle of his own religious communion. It was suggested by a work on the state of separate spirits, entitled, " *Olam Haneshamoth*," which appears deeply to have interested him. It was composed

---

* An error in orthography, which may be pardoned in a self-educated author of eighteen, since Mr. D'Israeli is not ashamed of it on one of his title-pages.

† Preface to the " Star in the East," 1824.

E

in his twenty-second year, with an interval of several months (as appears from the memoranda in his pocket-book) between the commencement and completion. As it is probable that many readers are familiar with the second part (commencing " Oh, the hour when this material shall have vanish'd as a cloud!") who have never seen the first part, it is here inserted. It may fitly be regarded as a page of the author's private journal; for his poetical compositions seem to have been the only record, saving his letters, of the deepest feelings of his heart.

> " Animula vagula, blandula,
> Hospes comesque corporis,
> Quæ nunc abibis in loca,
> Pallidula, rigida, nudula?
> Nec, ut soles, dabis jocos."
>
> *Emperor Adrian to his Soul.*

Oh, that in unfetter'd union,
   Spirit could with spirit blend!
Oh, that in unseen communion,
   Thought could hold the distant friend!
Who the secrets can unravel
   Of the body's mystic guest?
Who knows how the soul may travel,
   While unconsciously we rest?

While in pleasing thraldom lying,
   Seal'd in slumber deep it seems,
Far abroad it may be flying :—
   What is Sleep? and what are Dreams?
Earth, how narrow thy dominions,
   And how slow the body's pace!
Oh, to range on eagle pinions,
   Through illimitable space!

What is Thought? In wild succession
   Whence proceeds the motley train?
What first stamps the vague impression
   On the ever-active brain?

What is Thought? And whither tending
  Does the subtle phantom flee?
Does it like a moonbeam ending
  Shine, then melt to vacancy?

Has a strange mysterious feeling,
  Something shapeless, undefined,
O'er thy lonely musings stealing,
  Ne'er impress'd thy pensive mind,—
As if he, whose strong resemblance
  Fancy at that moment drew,
By coincident remembrance,
  Knew your thoughts, and thought of you?

When, at Mercy's footstool bending,
  Thou hast felt a sacred glow—
Faith and Hope to heaven ascending,
  Love still lingering below—
Say, has ne'er the thought impress'd thee,
  That thy friend might feel thy prayer?
Or the wish at least possess'd thee,
  He could then thy feelings share?

Who can tell?—that fervent blessing—
  Angels, did ye hear it rise?
Do ye, thus your love expressing,
  Watch o'er human sympathies?
Do ye some mysterious token
  To the kindred bosom bear,
And, to what the heart has spoken,
  Wake a chord responsive there?

Laws, perhaps, unknown but certain,
  Kindred spirits may control:
But what hand can lift the curtain,
  And reveal the awful soul?
Dimly through life's vapours seeing,
  Who but longs for light to break?
Oh, this feverish dream of being!
  When, my friend, shall we awake?

"Yes, the hour, the hour is hasting,
    Spirit *shall* with spirit blend.
Fast mortality is wasting:
    Then the secret all shall end.
Let, then, thought hold sweet communion,
    Let us breathe the mutual prayer,
Till in heaven's eternal union—
    Oh, my friend, to meet thee there!"

The plan of "The Associate Minstrels" was projected in a long country ramble among the same scenes which had suggested "The Withered Oak." The correspondence of these years shows how much interest, hope, and labour centred in this little volume; and how long, to use the words of one of the surviving contributors to its pages, "it filled and brightened their horizon." The minstrels, and other members of that larger circle of closely attached friends of which they formed a segment, were known among themselves by the names of certain favourite flowers. Josiah Conder's favourite emblem was the myrtle, and many of his letters to his youthful friends are signed "Myrtus." It was therefore proposed to call their joint production "The Wreath;" but Montgomery (to whom the young poets dedicated their volume) inexorably condemned this title as hackneyed; and the editor's ingenuity was taxed to suggest a list of new ones, of which "The Associate Minstrels" was deemed best and most appropriate. Not without fear and trembling did the little barque at last get launched, and the minstrel company put out to sea.*

X. O for the reviews! When do you send to Miss

---

* The contributors (whose pieces are distinguished by initials) were Misses Anne and Jane Taylor, Miss Eliza Thomas, Mr. Conder *senior*, the Rev. I. Taylor, J. G. Strutt, and Josiah Conder.

Edgeworth? 1 meet with nothing as yet but encouragement. Mr. Savill is really a man of sound judgment and fine taste, is he not? Mr. Rogers's tacit testimony I told you of. Besides which, I could only tell you of the kind expressions of my friends. I long to hear from Southey, and Montgomery, and Aikin, and Dr. Mackintosh. Oh! I am as ravenous for praise as ever, because I do not stand alone. I look round on my famishing sister minstrels, whom I have tempted to embark with me; and if but a squall arise, or the provisions threaten to fail, or there be danger of being becalmed, I feel all the brother and the editor in my heart. Poor E. gets sadly pitied and teased by her sister and Plato. "We think the pieces signed E. rather poor:" this is the review they threaten her with. "Well, I shall not mind, any further than my pieces may injure the work." Ah! my magnanimous friend, I am glad I have no apprehension you will be put to the trial. Yet—oh dear!

I am growing a Methodist. I actually went to hear Dr. Collyer at Surrey Chapel, and very much pleased I was. He was simple and striking. And then the next morning, what a treat at the Tract Society! I cannot detail to you the intelligence, the letters, the anecdotes, the addresses, which conspired to render the meeting most solemnly delightful and impressive. I should think above 800 at least were present. I really felt it. The present times, said Dr. Smith—but I cannot give his impressive language—are such as can be paralleled by no age, by no era in the history of the world, unless by that time when the apostles were assembled in an upper room of the temple,* and the Spirit of God was poured out upon them. And it is so. The signs of the times are awful, but

* Whether this inaccuracy is the speaker's or the writer's, does not appear.

encouraging. Great things we may live to see; and from contemplating the factious tumults of demagogues, the infatuation and imbecility of ministers, the profligacy, the venality, and the seditious violence of the opponent parties, which threaten to revive the times of anarchy in our oppressed country, how consoling to soar above the petty squabbles of the day, and contemplate the great designs of Providence gradually unfolding, and behold the first dawning promise of that universal day, when the Light of the Gentiles and the Star of Jacob shall illumine the whole world; and, to use the words of Dr. Collyer, "the Hindoo shall bring a broken heart instead of a bleeding body to the altar of Jesus; and the Persian bow to a more glorious Sun than ever irradiated the visible firmament." But this is not a subject which I feel competent to touch on. It is almost too vast for comprehension. Farewell.

The following extract from an earlier letter (Sept., 1808), affords an interesting glimpse of the state of religious parties. It refers to the *Remains*, then recently published, of Henry Kirke White, in whose character and writings it was natural that one who had so many points of sympathy with him should feel deeply interested.

XI. Your ideas and mine quite harmonize on this subject; but while I approve of your selection, I must be permitted, as in a former case, to add to it, by naming as of merit not inferior—"To Disappointment," "The Early Primrose," Sonnet 8 and 9 of First Series, "The Lullaby," "To a Friend in Affliction," and "Written in the Prospect of Death," and almost all the later Sonnets. But where shall I stop? And why do you say "a few

lines" only, in "Yes, my stray steps have wandered"?
But, after all, it is not as the poet that he is *alone,* or
even *most* interesting. I do believe I felt for once
humble in perusing his life. His memoirs *have* been
made useful. A gentleman told me, the other day, that
he knew an instance in a young man, since entered at
college with a view to the ministry. By the way, the
increase of evangelical clergymen within these five years
past has been astonishing as well as pleasing. Rev.
Samuel Burder, you may perhaps have heard, has con-
formed. He told me, on the authority of (I believe) a
dignitary of the Establishment, that about five years ago
they could not reckon above 200 who were decidedly
evangelical, and now they are upwards of 1200. The
Bishop of Gloucester has lately ordained seven young
men who were well known to be decided *Methodists ;*
and he had previously provided them curacies in his own
diocese. Bishop Durham, by whom S. B. is, or is to be,
ordained, was very particular in inquiring, at their different interviews, his sentiments, and expressed his
cordial approbation on discovering them to be Calvinistic.
I heard last Sunday an excellent sermon from the Tutor
of Lincoln College, Oxford, which is, as well as Edmund
Hall, Methodistic. Are not these good tidings ?

Affairs of a different nature now engross the attention of the public, namely, the surrender of Junot, Lisbon, and the Russian and French fleets; but on terms
very disgraceful to our commander, Sir Hew Dalrymple.
The town is quite in a ferment. What will be the issue
of these wonderful events ?

In the same year in which "The Associate Minstrels"
was published, Josiah Conder came of age. In the career
opening before him there was little to dazzle or intoxi-

cate with dreams of worldly wealth and success. Already
he had learned that life is worse than vain, unless both
its aim and its treasure—its chief ambition, and its chief
joy—be above this world, and beyond the reach of its
uncertainties and changes. His view of life seems rather
to have erred in being too sombre, than in being over-
coloured. An error on the safe side! For is it not
better that our joys should take us by surprise, than our
sorrows?

What progress his inward spiritual life had made,
during these years; how truly he had learned to subordinate both business and taste to higher aims; and
how far he had been preparing, by a living faith, and by
the study of his own heart, for the heavier burdens and
severer toils which now awaited him, will be best seen
from a few extracts from his correspondence. These
claim a fresh chapter for themselves.

Meantime, this chapter may perhaps not unfitly be
closed with a charming and lively birthday epistle,
written to a little girl, in which the young man of one-
and-twenty, tries to set his views of life before the child,
whose own early years were not unshadowed by some
clouds of sorrow. The letter accompanied the present of
a small terrestrial globe :—

XII. For Jemima's Birthday.

Dec. 10, 1810.

My dear Jemima,—Or rather *our* Jemima, I should
say, for I now take pen in hand in an official capacity,
as secretary to the illustrious house of Conder. We,
whose names are undersigned, as a token of our unanimous regard, unite in requesting Jemima Taylor's acceptance of—*the world*.

And now, what can you wish for more? The whole

world is your own. Alas! you see what it is—light, empty, and all *outside!* What more can you wish for, did I say? I forget that he who conquered the world sighed for further conquests. There is a sweet verse I sometimes repeat—

> " While glory sighs for other spheres,
>   I feel that one's too wide,
> And think the home that love endears
>   Worth all the world beside."

And is not my Jemima of the same opinion? Is there not a little spot, which she will hardly be able to descry on this little miniature globe, but which is more to her than half the cities in the world? And the longer she lives, the more she will have the conviction forced upon her that the happiest, sweetest, safest spot is—Home. Oh, how good Providence has been to her in fixing her lot in such a home. I am sure Jemima would not wish to change situations with the richest child in England. I say England, for out of England, on what spot can envy fix? All is now darkness and distress. I do not know that *in* England I could find a child with greater advantages. Such parents, such brothers and sisters, and, I will add, so many friends too, who love you and are anxious for your welfare. And, my dear Jemima, as to the very sorrows which extend their shadows over your childhood, you will one day count these amongst your *greatest* advantages. God is gently teaching you by degrees, that the good things of this world are not the good things which He designs for those He loves; that affliction is only a name for one of his angels; that what men are most earnestly pursuing, He considers as too insignificant to bestow, or what it is mercy to refuse. Did you ever read of a person who lost a race by stopping for a golden apple? What better than this is the world? Life is the race, and the prize—Heaven.

The world is my text; and it is a text that has as many heads as a Hydra. Shall I go on? I will just observe, that on this little globe there was not room to delineate any but the great outlines by which the world is subdivided. You must refer to maps and charts for more minute information and more recent discoveries. When I publish my new system of geography, I shall adopt quite a different plan. In the centre, I shall place my native country, and make the metropolis Home. By the side of its walls flows the river Care, which, rising many miles distant, receives the influx of several petty streams, and loses itself in the Black Sea. Nearly in a parallel course, on the opposite side of the city, a clear and salubrious stream, whose waters make glad its inhabitants, rolls its refreshing waters. Its source is unknown, and its current eternal. There is a beautiful lake a little way out of town, on which it is delightful on a summer's day to make an excursion of pleasure. It is the Lake of Friendship, but I am told it is sometimes a little stormy, and that there are rocks and shallows, on which those have struck who have had no pilot. But then, beyond this, and indeed almost all round the city I am speaking of, you meet with a cheerless desert, which it is dangerous to travel; but through which the high road lies to a better kingdom. I cannot give you a very particular account of the country, for it is a singular fact, as to the country I am describing, that perpetual mists hang over the valleys, so that you can see little before you. And all beyond a certain point is undiscovered land. Dear me! What is become of my scheme of geography, that was to embrace the world? And yet I have described all *my* world; and what use would it be to lead you to those chilly regions, or fiery deserts, where others dwell ? To show you the world in the shape of a moral Ætna (gardens covering destruction), or of an Iceland ? There was an old geographer of great wisdom, who divided the world into two great continents; the one he named Vanity, and the other Vexation; and I know of no modern work that supersedes his. O, my dear Jemima, to drop all metaphor at once, it is a *poor* world. It is strange we should all love it so : that we should loiter so in our pilgrimage through this wilderness, that God is obliged to send storms and tempests to quicken us in the road to heaven. Do you know what I mean by loving the world ? Yes, I think you do. You feel there is something in your heart that dares to rival God. And is it not, too, an *evil* world ?

But perhaps this is rather in too gloomy a style for a birthday. No, but my dear Jemima, we do not want the world to make us happy. Come, let us shut it out. We have friends enough to make us cheerful within. What shall the song be ? Shall it be of the past year, about its mercies and comforts; or shall Hope take her harp, and sing of the Future ? Suppose, rather, that we talk over the Present—present comforts and privileges. And when I say the present, I do not mean to exclude that world which, though now unseen, is always *present*. We are never separated from an eternal state by any more than a moment; and perhaps some of the inhabitants of what is called, in accommodation to us, the world to come are ever present with us. Certain we are, that that Merciful and Omniscient Being is, in whom we live and move and have our being. O, my dear little friend, may He guide you through this new year by his counsels ! May the Good Shepherd, who died for you, carry you in his arms ! May you be preserved from those sins and evils, at which now your little heart would shudder, but from which nothing but divine grace can preserve you. And may you be spared many years to reward the love, to realize the hopes, and to fulfil the prayers of your tender parents, and all those in your family, and out of its beloved circle, who feel an interest in your welfare. Farewell.

CHAPTER II.

COMING OF AGE.

It is not designed, in the present memoir, to enter deeply into the minute details and sacred recesses of private life and personal history. It is designed, as far as the editor's materials and skill may avail, to portray Josiah Conder (principally by extracts from what he has himself written) in those aspects in which the public is chiefly interested in hearing of him—as a Writer and as a Christian; it may be added, as a Protestant Nonconformist, whose Nonconformity was always subordinate to his Protestantism, as his Protestantism was to his Christianity.

A biography should be a picture, not an anatomical preparation. There are cases, no doubt, in which a man's life and character are so completely public property, and the importance is so great of rightly understanding and estimating his conduct and motives, that public welfare may demand a *post mortem* examination of the severest and minutest. But this is not commonly either wise or needful. It is not thus that you would have your own friends treated. You would wish them to be seen on the printed page as their friends saw them in life; not with a critical magnifying glass applied to every speck and blemish, nor with all the most secret recesses of their heart and history wide open to common gaze; but robed with that comely reserve which it is the special privilege of intimate friendship to draw aside, and which, indeed, few can bear wholly to throw off before any eye but God's.

The inward religious life, however, of any one eminent for piety and usefulness, comes under a principle of exception to this proper reserve. Natural as it may seem, at first sight, to

> " Reckon faith and prayers
> As the most private of a man's affairs,"

yet, in fact, they are exactly what the largest number can sympathise with, and are interested to hear of. In all other regions our tastes, pursuits, joys, loves, sorrows, defeats, triumphs, may be so specially our own, through character or circumstance, that they command a very narrow range of sympathy. But all real Christians have a fellow-feeling, and belong to one family, and share a common life. They have a deep interest in one another's character, experience, and progress. The strife, the perils, the infirmities, the successes of their brethren are their own. The crown is the same which they hope to wear ; the goal the same which they strain, with eye, and foot, and panting breath, to win. They weep with those who weep, and rejoice with those who rejoice. So far as any life is a Christian life—be it that of king or peasant, soldier or slave, the grey-haired prophet, or the little child who early falls asleep in his Saviour— so far it has a hold on what is deepest, and purest, and most enduring in the heart of every other pilgrim to the better country. It is a page of the great family history, to which every true child of the family carries the key in his own heart.

JOSIAH CONDER's early religious history has already been briefly sketched in his own words. His piety was, under the blessing of God, the early set and timely fruit of those happy influences of instruction and example, amidst which he grew up to manhood. It furnishes a commentary upon the wise and weighty words : of Richard Baxter, who, after referring to his own doubts, lest his religion was nothing but the result of education, adds : " But afterwards I perceived that education is God's ordinary way for the conveyance of his grace, and ought no more to be set in opposition to the Spirit than the preaching of the word ; and that it was the great mercy of God to begin with me so soon, and to prevent such sins as else might have been my shame and sorrow while I lived ; and that Repentance is good, but Prevention and Innocence is better ; which though we cannot attain in perfection, yet the more the better."

The following letters and extracts, although not all confined to religious topics, will indicate the progress of their writer's religious history as youth matured into manhood. The first, written in his twentieth year, and addressed to one of his cousins, refers to his joining the church at Moorfields, then and for many years under the care of the Rev. Mr. Wall. It is only upon the grounds already indicated that the present editor feels justified in laying before the public eye such confidential and sacred records of personal feeling. These pages are designed for those who can understand them, not for those who cannot.

June 24, 1809.

XIII. DEAR ——,—As we have always more words than time when we meet on Sabbath Day, I am beginning on Saturday. . . . I drank tea last night at Wine Office Court with Messrs. M. and H. It was by no means an unpleasant meeting. They were very friendly, and, I was going to say, rational; but you will understand me. The only question that at all went close was, whether I knew of any particular time or period from which I could date a change (or something of that kind). But when I answered, that I hoped, from my infancy, I had been sensible of the privileges of a pious education, and experienced its advantages, they were pleased and satisfied. I was, indeed, much pleased with many things Mr. H. said; among the rest, that the best test was not to be founded on feelings, but on a, growing desire after conformity to God—that he had for a long time been fettered by the tempter with the fear that he had not experienced (as he said I expressed it) the whirlwind or the storm; and, therefore, was not the subject of a real change. And he mentioned several anecdotes; observed also the faithfulness of a covenant God, as it appeared in our family to the third and fourth generations; and in his prayer, which was truly excellent and affectionate, you were particularly mentioned.

I sometimes should feel disposed to introduce various topics, but unless we had a greater security for either meeting with an opportunity for a little chat together, or else for a regular interchange of letters, it appears useless, as the feeling cools, and the thought vanishes, before the subject has obtained a hearing. I was thinking the other day, how far it is lawful or desirable to expect and to endeavour after what we fancy would ensure our temporal happiness; and how far we might be permitted to apply to our present welfare and lawful endeavours that promise—'*Delight thyself in the Lord, and He shall give thee the desires of thine heart.*' You may not understand me, nor may I be able to convey to you the feeling. Certain I am that true happiness cannot be found in anything out of the mind; nor unmixed and permanent happiness anywhere out of Heaven. But, somehow, it is difficult to make up one's mind to unhappiness, even on earth; and our comfort must, in great measure, depend on circumstances and events. My expectations are not, at present, sanguine, nor my hopes ambitious; but in looking forward on the probabilities of my future life, which the wisest at times cannot forbear to do, especially when clouds and dark- ness overcast the sky, and I fancy I see a gleam of sunshine on the distant horizon—I say, at such times, hope raises the phantom of a modest, peaceable happi- ness, for which, could I secure its attainment at length, I would contentedly toil and sorrow for a painful ap- prenticeship to Time. But then, again, I say to myself, this can never be yours, because it would make you happy; and happy you must not look to be in the present world. For instance, I sometimes think, that if by my endeavours and the blessing of Providence, I could annihilate the grievous burden of care which is weighing down perpetually my father's health and spirits; could I procure, I won't say wealth, but that comfortable com- petency which should set me above anxious fears and ceaseless drudgery; why, from such a state I cannot withhold the name of comparative happiness. How far, then, may I dare to hope for it? But Fancy, a wild, daring, romantic creature as she is, sometimes makes what I can only call possibilities dance before me, and leads me to a mountain as high as Pisgah, or, at least, as Parnassus, and shows me a promised land which, I am afraid, can only be reached by crossing Jordan's flood. Surely, I think, if I could arrive at that point I should be too happy. And yet, others have attained as high. And then I endeavour to entertain right views of the transitory and trivial nature of earthly afflictions and

F

earthly joys; and sometimes, in the fulness of the feeling (and especially sometimes at the throne of grace), I forget the world, and can almost exclaim, "There is none on earth that I desire in comparison with Thee, my Father, who art in heaven." But I am soon called down from the mount, and a crowd of fancies, hopes, and fears rush upon me as I enter again into the world, and cling to my pride, my passions, and my affections, and almost usurp my heart. At such times, what a luxury would it be to have a friend at hand to compare notes with! I did not think of writing so much. If you do not understand or enter into these ideas, I pray you not to condemn them or laugh at them altogether.

July 23rd, 1809.
Sunday Evening. After Supper.

XIV. DEAR COUSIN,—It is not often that I take up my pen on this night, but some of the thoughts that have passed through my mind this evening, I am unwilling should leave no vestige behind them; nor do I know how I can better employ the closing half-hour of the Sabbath.

I lament, and in part reproach myself, that our conversation (particularly on these days) does not respect more things of the first importance, and which should be of the dearest moment. And I am grieved, too, to find how miserably dependent I am on the ever-changing frame of my mind; and that even now, while I am writing, the feeling which excited me to write is cooled, and the ideas with which my mind was impressed are no longer at my command.

I do not know whether I am going to be interesting —I am going to be confidential. The sermon of this afternoon was very impressive. One passage, in particular, set my mind at work, where Mr. W., addressing himself to those who now were led to mind the things of the Spirit, appealed to them whether it had been always so. The answer which arose in my thoughts was, *Yes.* I have been always impressed, in degree, ever since I can remember the actings of my mind, with religious things. But then, I afterwards thought, how very much exposed am I, from this very circumstance, to overrate my own attainments; to mistake the work of education for that of grace, spiritual notions for feelings, and feelings for principles. And then I could not help confessing how much I still mind earthly things, and how earthly I am in spiritual pursuits. But the thought which my mind most dwelt upon this evening in my study was, the very inadequate ideas of the evil of sin which I feel to possess. I do not know what good I do in going on to disclose my feelings on this subject; because, if your friendship excite you to endeavour to satisfy my mind on the subject, you may be doing me an injury.

I find it difficult to pursue in thought a train of close self-examination, or to excite in myself, by mere meditation, any warmth of feeling. But sometimes when on my knees—I hope I am not wrong—I can indulge my feelings. I can, while I am addressing God, reason with my soul. It was with a train of thought, I can scarcely say feeling, excited by the two sermons of the day, that I addressed myself this evening to the Almighty. I felt at first at a loss how to begin, till at length I roused my mind with invoking Him as the heart-searching God, who knew all the secret operations of my heart, and knew, before I uttered them, the words of my tongue. Among my reflections it occurred, that though I at times had felt displeased with myself for sin, and out of temper, how little I had known of David's righteous sorrow—how imperfect were my ideas as to *God's* displeasure against sin, one drop of whose wrath was sufficient to sink me into endless misery; that sorrow for sin had never cost me a sleepless night or an anxious day; that my sorrow, if real, was soon forgotten with the occasion; and that, perhaps, if I were stretched on the bed of languishing, a long array of forgotten and unrepented sins would start from oblivion, and overwhelm me. And for a moment I had some faint view of the deficiencies of my past life, and felt that to have been preserved from acts of outward enormity was matter indeed of thankfulness, but not of boasting, nor even of consolation, since I had never been placed in circumstances of temptation. Alas! in the sight of God—how dreadful to reflect!—all the sins of childhood and youth, of thought and action, sins confessed and unrepented, however distant, however deplored, however forgotten, all stand in unfading and distinct enormity. His justice can never excuse, can never forget, can never palliate. But there is a fountain filled with blood, drawn from Immanuel's veins, all-sufficient to wash away all our sins. How infinite the value of his sacrifice! How immeasurable his love! Here then, again, how disproportionate our feelings! My dear cousin, I say it not from humility, real or feigned, but I have cause to tremble as well as to sorrow, that I do feel so little—that even the tearful feeling with which I besought Divine mercy, that I might not, after all, be deceived, and that I might sooner die this evening than grow old in forgetfulness of God, that this feeling should have left so little trace on my mind; and to-morrow I shall return to my merchandize, and my mind be again engrossed with "earthly things." I fear I have overrated my attainments, but I repent not of any step I have taken; and I was enabled, with something like devotional feeling, to commit my soul and all my concerns to Him whom we, though sinners, may still call Our Father—to commit to Him my cares, my temporal affairs. But I dared not ask for happiness. Oh, my dear cousin, whom have we in heaven but God ? Who else constitutes heaven ? I feel sometimes sweet pleasure in the idea of meeting you and S——, and our parents and family, and A—— and J——, and E—— and L——, in the world of spirits. I cannot separate this idea from that of heaven; but even in this idea I feel I am earthly. It is the holiness of heaven, it is the presence of God, that I should be aspiring after; for whom have we in heaven but God ? and whom, if we look round on our dearest friends, on our nearest affections, whom have we on earth that we should desire in comparison with Him ? Alas ! whom do I habitually, though I trust not really, delight in and desire so little ? Let me draw the gloomiest picture—bid Death draw his curtain round some of the scenes of my enjoyment, and Poverty wither all my hopes ; suppose myself deprived of friendship and peace, the Eglantine dead, the Rose plucked, and Myrtle faded —yet, what would all these afflictions be in comparison with eternity ? What Providence designs me for, or prepares for me, I must leave to Him. Oh, that I could be more dead to the world—that I could live above it— that I could count all things but loss, so that I may win Christ, and be found in Him !

Your letter, I repeat the assurance, has done my heart good . . . . I do not know whether my prayers do any good to those for whom I pray. They have, however, the effect of exciting in my own mind a more tender interest in them . . . . I have no doubt I share, as I value, your prayers. For the present, farewell.—I enclose a version of the 23rd Psalm, written principally

for the sake of the metre, that I may sing it to Bethesda
tune. But it borrows some of its ideas from Laving-
ton's sermons. Farewell.—Yours affectionately,

JOSIAH CONDER.

Monday morning. On reviewing what I have
written, I am far from being satisfied with it. I have
not conveyed all that I exactly intended; but I am determined to send it, because it is to you I am writing.

Bucklersbury, July 4, 1810.

XV. MY DEAR FRIEND,—What a beautiful evening,
after a day so wet without doors, and busy within!
I have not yet crossed the threshold, and feel quite
muzzed. Suppose I take a walk. Shall it be to Clapham, to call on the mother and sister of Kirke White,
at Mr. Beddome's, or shall I go and see J—— at the
Forbes's? If I thought Plato was at Battersea, and it
was not so late, I would walk over there. But no; I
have altered my mind. I will sit down and write to Colchester, and it shall not be a letter of business . . . .
Southey's letter is, on many accounts, the most gratifying
(to the individual, at least, to whom it is addressed) of
any yet received. It is the friendly tribute of as fine a
genius, and as warm a heart, as any who have honoured
the minstrels with their praise. Shall I say the finest
genius? I know you are unacquainted with him but as
the author of some of his juvenile puerilities. Besides,
it will not do for *me* to praise him now; but pray read,
in the last "Christian Observer," a very fine, and what
is more, a just, and in every way excellent review of the
"Lady of the Lake," and see what is said of Southey there.
And then if, by way of contrast, you want to see how
much a man of great mind and strong judgment can
write in the flippant, snappish, would-be witty style of

some young sprig of law, just manufactured into a critic, with as little taste as good nature and sensibility, read a review of the same work in the last " Eclectic," by —— ——!! Yes, the essayist. Why will he waste his time, and debase his powers in reviewing ? Oh! I am out of patience with all the reviews; but I must get clear of the ranks before I speak out.... I do not know whether Southey and Haley will travel together without quarrelling; but the letter of the latter, if not from a man of the first order of genius, is that of a scholar and a gentleman. I assure you I prize it. Such tributes are very gratifying and very refreshing to one toiling through the arid deserts of Plutus. How far they tend to promote vanity, I cannot judge; for so many circumstances conspire to keep down the tone of my spirits, to engross, to harass, and to mortify my mind, that the antidote which they administer will, I hope, sufficiently counteract any such influence. But it is not such things which pre-eminently induce vanity. They may create ambition and self-confidence, but they are also calculated to humble, and surely they ought to inspire with gratitude. I do feel I have much to be grateful for, and I cannot help sometimes hoping I may one day or other be, and do something. At present, my genius is but a minor, serving a hard apprenticeship, during which it has to sacrifice its inclinations, and conform its will to the stern command and dull employ of its master. Nevertheless, I have actually written a sonnet to-day. Ay, a sonnet—correct enough for Capel Lofft; and there's truth in it, if little poetry. And so here it is :—

.Two voices are there. From the inmost breast,
    Its seat oracular, the one proceeds,
    Prompting the noble soul to worthy deeds,
And rousing Fancy from inglorious rest.

The öther, from above, Heaven's high behest
 In still small accents speaks, which he who heeds
 Is wise ; for sure, the path where duty leads,
Though dark, is safe ; though rugged, yet the best.
Nor would I, at the call of pleasure, dare
 Resist that voice ; but rather wait resign'd,
Perform my daily task with duteous care,
 And quench the proud aspirings of the mind,
Till happier days arrive, and blithe and free
My soul shall warble songs to peace and liberty.

I had better mention that Wordsworth has a sonnet beginning 'Two voices are there,' but there is no
further similarity of idea or expression.

But I intended this letter for other themes. I am
much concerned to hear how much your health and
spirits appear to suffer from the repeated demands recently made upon both. I wish circumstances would
permit a short interval of relaxation. The life you lead
is very unfavourable to that vigorous health of mind
which is produced by its regular moderate exercise, and
which can alone inspire with cheerfulness ; and you have
thus not only to cope with the trials of every day, and
the anxious cares which are now assaulting you, but this
with a mind so unstrung, that the sweet voice of hope
awakens no vibration of joy. I wish anything that I
could suggest had power to impart consolation. But
this is the prerogative of " the God of comfort." Were
I to prescribe a cordial for a fainting pilgrim, I know of
no better than the 8th of Romans. What a comprehensive, eloquent, sublime chapter is that ! I am sorry that
feelings which gave birth to the beautiful lines your note
contained should ever recur, and yet I know—I mean, I
have heard and read—how subject the most eminent
saints have been to seasons of similar doubt and despon-

dency. And doubtless, when they are only seasons, they are subservient, under the Divine blessing, to the quickening and eventually establishing the soul in hope. You have, however, no right, nay, I question if it be not wholly wrong, to indulge such feelings; for, my dear friend, as you cannot in judgment doubt the reality of the grace of which you have been made the partaker, as you must feel how dear to you the Gospel is, as you believe in the truth, the mercy, and the omnipotence of your heavenly Father, whatever cause you have, in common with other Christians, for humility and contrition, still you should not suffer the tempter to abridge God of that glory which accrues from a cheerful confidence in Him, a grateful sense of what He has done, and a joyful though trembling assurance of faith, that nothing shall separate you from the love of God; that all things are yours; that the issue of all present troubles shall be good, and that He who has imparted grace will perfect the work of his own hands in everlasting glory. I had rather not speak of myself, for then I shall be reminded of my incompetence, of the almost impropriety of my addressing you on such a subject; but I cannot help noticing how painfully, in my own experience, I feel the truth of what you say respecting the difference of feeling on Sabbath eve and Monday morning. How well Cowper knew the heart, when he closed one of his beautiful poems thus :—

"But ah! my inmost spirit cries,
    Still bind me to thy sway;
Else the next cloud that veils my skies,
    Drives all these thoughts away."

O this chilling, distracting, harassing world! When in league with such traitorous hearts, no efforts of ours, unassisted by Divine influences, can withstand its power.

But let our prayer be in unison with His who said, " I
pray not that Thou shouldest take them out of the world,
but that Thou shouldest keep them from the evil." O
what a prayer was that which our Saviour offered! How
full of consolation! All the boundless mercy, the Divine
majesty, the condescending and mysterious love of the
Mediator, shine through it in full glory.

My dear friend, we *ought* to talk of such subjects.
As to any natural difficulty, it is soon to be conquered.
It is only a few exertions, and the habit will be formed.
It is thus the blessing of a spiritual mind is to be obtained. Ought I to speak thus, whose heart and mind
are carnal? Yes, I will. There is no hypocrisy in instructing yourself through the medium of others, nor in
adopting language which applies to your desires rather
than to your attainments. For my own part, I find
that I must be content that my friends be deceived in
their estimate of my character; and by using that humble
language which would well comport with it, I should but
strengthen the deception. They would then give me
credit for what I at least possess—humility. This I
remember: God knows my character. Before Him let
me humble myself in the dust; but before men, let not
our faces wear sadness, nor our lips be sealed; and
among each other, let us exercise our stammering tongues
in the language of that country to which we are all
journeying. The Bible shall be our grammar; and however deficient our knowledge and imperfect our pronun-
ciation, still we can understand one another. It may
promote our mutual improvement, and will be a source
of pure delight. Why should you be afraid to use the
language of Canaan? We are none of us natives of that
better country; but still, is it not the home of our
desires? Ah! we wish it were, in one sense; but I

mean, is not the deliberate determination of our souls for heaven, whatever be our wanderings? I hope I may rejoice in this, while with fear and trembling I would work out my salvation, that God has begun to work in me to *will*, and in Him I trust that he will also work in me to *do*, of his good pleasure. But my letter is exceeding all bounds. One word more, about E——. Circumstances *will* put it in your power to benefit her. Who is there, how poor soever his ability and small his attainments—and yours it would be ingratitude in you to consider in this light—who is there but is capable of benefiting in some measure a fellow-creature, much more a fellow-Christian? And when a child, all impressibility, that looks up to you with love and deference, is thus lent you as a companion, can you say that nothing is in your power? You may do good both to her and yourself.

. . . Oh! it is hard thus quietly to wait; but be of good courage. Do not, I beseech you, yield to melancholy. I can counsel others, for here I am experienced. Do not say, I do well to be sad. "Seize present joys while rushing by"—the pleasures which Fame and Fancy scatter, the cordials which Friendship and Hope administer, the daily comforts designed for your refreshment. "Only be strong and of a good courage," for God shall bring you into a land of peace. Rejoice in your talents, your reputation, your family, your friends, your privileges, your promises, and your hopes. Rejoice in God. He is your God for ever and ever. My dear friend, farewell.

JOSIAH CONDER.

In prospect of the annual family gathering at Christmas tide, he writes:—

XVI. Our families have been wonderfully preserved. Year after year the same faces are seen round the same table, and not a vacant chair to repress the festivities of Christmas! Another year is drawing to a close. I look forward with new sensations to the period when Hope pictures us again assembled. . . . . . But we have got two months to travel through first; and what dangers and perils may await us in the interim it is in infinite wisdom ordained we should not know. Yes, L——, such is life! Let us hold fast by each other as long as we can. When the winds and the tempest are raging without, we should draw the closer to each other. Let us stir up the fire of friendship, and talk over old times; or rather let our conversation be of that world where all the children of God shall meet from all the families of the world, where sorrow and sickness shall be known no more, and an anthem of praise ascend from myriads of ransomed souls for ever and ever. The Conders, we have jokingly said, *are not born to riches.* D.D. is the highest honour yet attached to the name. We have been styled a family of quizzes, and Providence has doomed us to plod on in unassuming mediocrity; while Gout, and Bile, and Care, and sometimes Affliction, have knocked at our doors, and pruned luxuriant joy; but yet how highly are we privileged, that we can look up to parents whose death will (we doubt not) be their gain—parents who in the world and church fill up respectable places, and shine with steady if not dazzling light, whose prayers and examples we may well deem a blessing. The name of Conder, unstained with crime, will be long remembered with honour in many a religious society. Do not think I assume a style too patriarchal or affected, in saying what satisfaction it affords me to look round on friends and cousins, whose example I may follow also, whose value is not extrinsic. I expect much from you, and count upon your friendship.

This chapter may appropriately close with some lines written on coming of age, a copy of which was accompanied with the following note to two of his cousins :—

XVII. DEAR COUSINS,—I have been acting on the plan of "every man his own laureate." The annexed verses, whatever merit they want, tell the plain, unvarnished tale of my own feelings ; and there is one passage in which I hope you will feel an interest congenial with the sentiments that inspired it. I hope to find you at our table on Monday evening, but preferred sending to giving you the verses. They are not meant for every eye, but you are welcome, if you think proper, to show them to "The Roses." I have not read them to Bucklersbury, and do not know whether I shall. . . . . I quite enjoy feeling well and cheerful this evening, and look forward to a Sabbath with feelings of hope and thankfulness ; and father, too, seems pretty well. I think a little would make me happy yet. God bless you both.

SEPTEMBER 17, 1810.

Once more the months their round have run,
And the hand points to twenty-one.
Thy blessing, Father Time, I pray—
They tell me I'm of age to-day.

Of age! What then? No rich domain,
No noble heritage, my gain :
Say, will the year unchain my will?
Alas! I am a minor still.
Hope's prisoner I still must wait,
And serve the apprenticeship of Fate.

Of age! Ah, yes: I long have been
An actor in the busy scene.
My skiff has left the quiet shore,
And my hand grasps the heavy oar.
I hear the elemental roar,
And shudder at the rising strife
That heaves the troublous sea of life.
Long have I been of age to fear,
To hope, to shed the anxious tear,
To wish, to strive, to do, to dare,
Of age to suffer and to bear.
Of age to love? Yes, if that name
Be given to Friendship's holy flame;
For that is Virtue's tender claim.
But me should other passions move.
Oh, no! I'm not of age to love.
For once, as I with Fancy strayed,
Love met me, and half smiling said,
A Poet's heart was his by right:
I had assented if I might;
But I a nobler name have known,
And, as a Christian, claim'd my own.
Thine empire, Love! thy peaceful clime,
Lies not beneath the reign of Time,
Where all is change, and wintry storms
For ever rear their threatening forms.
No: through a wilderness we roam,
Poor pilgrims to a better home.
But oft the road is steep and bare:
My scrip—— Ah! nought but Hope is there.
And this my harp is all my store,
For Fortune gave me nothing more.
And will my harp's unskilful lay
Keep the fell spectre Care away?

But if in sweet reserve there be
No sunshine days of love for me,
Why should I waste a fruitless sigh,
As the light-treading years go by?

If bliss to me the world denies,
I'll snatch enjoyment from the skies.
Come, Friendship, for thy joys are mine,
And round my brow thy chaplet twine;
Thy Jasmine dear, sweet Eglantine,
Geranium, too, of brilliant hue,
And Violet clad in tender blue;
While thy own Roses o'er my head
Shall never-dying fragrance shed.
Oh, mystic wreath! far be the hour
That spoils thee of one breathing flower.

*   *   *   *   *

But my heart sinks, my spirits fail.
Oh! what can strength like mine avail?
God of my childhood and my youth!
I trust Thy mercy, and Thy truth.
My times are in thy hand. To Thee,
Who hast my helper been, I flee.
Oh! save me, guide me to the last,
Till Life with all its storms be past;
And till my soul shall be of age
For her eternal heritage.

CHAPTER III.

In the autumn of 1811, Mr. Conder senior, whose health was at that time very feeble and precarious, and whose business was not in a prosperous condition, by the advice of his friends, relinquished business entirely, and was succeeded by his son JOSIAH, whose pocket-book contains the following brief entry:—" Dec. 11. Began business on my account." In prospect of the opening of this new and important chapter of his life, he had written a few weeks previously:—" I have had, for some weeks past, peculiar anxieties to sustain. My father's state of health was such as to render his going from home indispensable, and he has, accordingly, been spending a fortnight at Melbourn, from which he returned much the better in his *looks*, and *really* the better, if not *essentially;* he could not have lasted as he was. The clouds, however, have returned. . . . . He cannot continue the work; but I must, and it must be by turning over the leaf. . . . . Everybody that has yet been spoken to seems to agree as to the propriety of this step, which I look forward to with trembling hope as that turn in the road of life which will introduce my dear father to a peaceful and shaded bye-path, more soft to his weary feet, and which shall gently conduct him to the close of the pilgrimage. For myself I have neither hopes, nor fears, nor anxieties; but I am convinced it is the best, the only step to be taken for my own advantage; and if I can once get the load that has been pressing on my heart and health into my hands and my head, I shall run on as lightsome as can be. In such a crisis, I trust I feel where wisdom must come from, and where strength is treasured. This very crisis is, I trust, the answer to my prayers, and I will pray and hope continually; and I shall have the prayers of my friends too. At present I feel relieved rather than depressed. . . . I heard a very plain and interesting sermon yesterday evening from Rev. Mr. Montgomery, brother of my friend James, at the Moravian Chapel, Fetter Lane, where he is come up with the prospect of settling. I called on him afterwards.

The following letters bear date a little earlier, in the same year :—

Bucklersbury, August 17 (St. Isaac), 1811.

XVIII. If you will accept the world's leavings, which is all I have to set before you, I will spread the cloth, and we will sit down together. You remember the old proverb, " Better is a dry morsel with love," and this I can offer you; but so many harpy cares have been quartered upon me that I have little mind, and not all my heart left for you. . . . As far as I can ascertain, I am nearly what and where you left me, perhaps a little wiser for the cares and trials of the intervening months, and a little more advanced into the unexplored regions of the future. Were I to give reins to my pen it would, very likely, take little notice of the mercies, the comforts, and enjoyments which have been crowded into this little space; and only dilate on the burdens and sorrows which oppress me. In this, however, I ought not to indulge myself, and especially now,

G

you are enjoying yourself (as I hope) in Devonshire. All I want you to remember is me, and not my circumstances; for if I were half that distance from town, it is probable I should half forget them too. Two days of this delightful forgetfulness I lately snatched in the beautiful and romantic vicinity of Dorking. . . . . I do not know whether you have heard of the melancholy death of Spencer, who was going to be married to Martha Hamilton. He was drowned in bathing; and the news seemed to open afresh Mrs. W——'s wounded heart. Ah! see, I have imperceptibly summoned up afflictions keener than mine. How much does it become me to be silent! And yet there are dark moments when all the stars go in, all the hues of fancy vanish, and friendship's voice is mute—earth is all desolate and gloomy—there is nothing around me but God; and from this infinite presence, this almighty support, the soul, half unbelieving, half distrustful, as well as painfully conscious of her unworthiness, shrinks back, and clings to the receding hopes of earth.

" Oh, for an overcoming faith to cheer these lonely hours!"

How different is it to exercise faith and resignation, as it were in the abstract, from what it is, when the push comes, to quit us like men and be strong—to feel all that is contained in that verse of Montgomery's (which has a reference to different seasons)—

"No : my soul, in God rejoice!
Thro' the gloom his light I see ;
In the silence hear his voice ;
And his hand is over me."

And now you may gather from this an answer to your question, " How I am." Father's health has been at times very indifferent. Providence seems to be weaning him, and fitting me. For what I am fitting, why should I inquire? Whatever may occur, whichever side of alternatives I contemplate, anxiety is before me, and I must of necessity leave the event, since I cannot foretell nor prevent it. Forgive me for dropping into this strain. I am too tired to rise above it; and so I will lay down my pen, and wait for the aid of the Sabbath—

> "That cheerful day in mercy given,
> That earth may look awhile like heaven."

August 20*th*. I had almost forgotten your inquiry about O'Reid, touching which, as I do not like to lay you under restrictions, I must rely on your discretion. It has not yet been reviewed, nor does it sell as I could wish, but the time of year is much against it. I have reason to be well satisfied with the opinions of both friends and strangers respecting it. I think I told you how Rev. Robert Hall, and Mr. Southey, old Charles Taylor, Dr. Smith, etc., had commended it. I do not, however, wish on any account to be known, especially by my *friends*, as a pamphleteer or author; I care less about strangers.

Well, I have heard the first four cantos, forming (I suppose) about half of the "World before the Flood," and a splendid poem it is! As it is not likely to be published this year at soonest, you will perhaps wish some account of it; but as the story is not fully unfolded, I must deal in generals. It is written in rhyming couplets of ten feet [syllables]. The action takes up about three days. The prominent character is Javan the minstrel, one of the descendants of Seth, who had been incited by a love of fame and curiosity to forsake the dwellings of the patriarchs, to roam amongst the

tribes of Cain ; but, unsatisfied, restless, and conscience-
smitten, he returns as a penitent, and is received by
Enoch as a pardoned prodigal. His love for Zillah
forms an interesting underplot. The catastrophe I
understand to be this : the chief of the tribes of Cain,
a Nimrod, having overrun the habitable world, draws up
his forces against the little remnant of the pious, with
the infernal resolve to extirpate them, and reign sole and
uncontrolled. The patriarchs are defeated in a battle ;
but at the moment he is proceeding to execute his bloody
resolves, the translation of Enoch takes place, in sight of
the whole camp. This, I understand from Parken, forms
one of the finest passages in modern poetry. The tyrant
is awe-struck, and afterwards is assassinated by his mis-
tress. Besides this, the Deluge is introduced in the form
of prophecy, and the Creation in that of an ode. The
fourth canto contains the narrative (by Enoch) of the
death of Adam, and is one of the most beautiful and
interesting passages I ever read. It is the conflict of
faith with the king of terrors, in the first sinner. I have
called it beautiful, but it should have been styled grand,
sublime. That sublimity too, which only the Christian
can *enjoy*, though the critic must *perceive* it ; such as
Montgomery, of all living poets, could alone, perhaps,
have attained to. Bloomfield's " Banks of the Wye" is
out, and is a *very pretty*, sparkling poem. It is, I think,
quite worthy of him. The author of " How d'ye do, and
Good b'ye" (Hon. W. Spencer) has sent out an octavo
of most exquisite *jeux d'esprit* and *vers de société*. Nothing, you see, but poetry. Mrs. More's " Practical
Piety" has reached, however, a fifth edition. Pray, have
you read Dr. Buchanan's " Christian Researches?"
Get it, if possible ; you will be highly interested in it.
And now I have exhausted my literary budget. I shall

be glad, in return, to hear from you whenever, as soon as, and as often as, you feel disposed. It is refreshing to get a grape now and then from Eshcol. It will do me good to hear from you that you are well and happy, as I hope you are; but do not write to me as a task. I thought I had many other things to say, but I fancy they were only feelings, not yet hatched into ideas; and I dare say they were not singing birds. The whole thirty unite in love to you. Father is, I am sorry to say, but very poorly. You will give our respects to your host and hostess; and my love to Devonshire. Now, once again, farewell, and God bless you. I am, dear Cousinette, yours affectionately,

JOSIAH CONDER,

Earl Myrtle, Baron O'Reid, Knight
of the Order of the Wreath, A.M.,
etc. But where my estates? A
castle in Ayrshire, and six feet near
the Artillery Ground!!

The paragraph about "O'Reid" in this letter refers to Mr. Conder's first separate publication, a pamphlet entitled "Reviewers Reviewed," published under the *nom de guerre* of Jno. Chas. O'Reid (an anagram for Josiah Conder). The Rev. Robert Hall observed, on reading it, that "he had always been of Mr. O'Reid's opinion touching the reviews; as to the *Edinburgh Review* (at that time, it is needless to say, very different in spirit from what it has since become), "it was worthy of a sanhedrim of hell!"

June 22, 1811.

XIX. . . . . And now I have exhausted my *topics*, what shall I employ my pen upon? As to myself, I have nothing to say. I am sorry that I cannot say Colchester began a new paragraph, but it was a delightful parenthesis. I was going to say, I *must* get rid of some of my anxieties; but as I do not see how this *must* depends on my own exertions, this would sound too much like saying what Providence *must* do for me. I am afraid to think that my mind and character would be the better for an external change, but certainly my feelings would be. What is before me I know not. I am only sailing on silently, but what land I am nearing, in what direction I am proceeding, I cannot tell, for I have no chart. I only hope to hold together for a few more leagues, and some shore I must arrive at. My father is very poorly this week. No sacrifice would be too great to disengage him from business, but it can only be done with sacrifices. This, however, is no pleasing subject; and you have cares enough of your own. I assure you I often think of them for a change; and then I sometimes feel a hope and a confidence as to you which react upon my mind, and make me feel resigned and patient for myself. I see how all the road to heaven is—difficulty. We only want to be quiet. We think, perhaps, we should be good enough without so much discipline—that we shall be well enough and strong enough without so rigid a diet, so frequent potions, and such hard exercise. We look at others who appear quite healthful and happy amid luxuries, or at least comforts, which we are fainting for. Is it not hard to say, "It is well?" "What I do, thou knowest not now!" If we did know, how joyfully should we submit to the mysterious conduct of our Master, and exclaim, "Not my feet only." We should do all, and bear all. And does not Peter's Lord and Saviour still preside over our lives? All here is mystery, but is it not mercy? Mysterious mercy, but mercy still. And though what He doth we know not now—oh, joyful and consoling thought!—we *shall* know hereafter.

After expressing thoughts like these one day to Olding, I said—" But, oh! Monday morning will be as difficult and overwhelming as ever! Of what use is this talking ?" " Not as much as ever," replied he : " there will be some difference; and if we can but acquire the habit of thus talking and feeling, we shall have done much, and gained that which must have a sensible influence on our conduct." With these views and this hope, I continue to write sentiments destitute of novelty, and to which my feelings very inadequately answer ; but the mind is the better for having thought a good thought, and the heart the better for every effort towards virtue. We will not, however, rest in either thoughts or feelings, but continue our work without fainting, and leave the clouds and the rain to do their part. We are not responsible for our own happiness, for it is not in our power. . . . . We must leave our father to pay our expenses to heaven,. while we only see to it that we are in the right road. In temporals and in spirituals we have only got to *act*, and we *must* learn to be happy, or at least comfortable, without success. And now, brethren, for the application. Ay, there's the rub. We will defer this to the next opportunity.

XX. Alas! we have no Urim and Thummim. Is it a vessel, or only a cloud, that specks the horizon? We have no glass to discover. But how foolish it is to be looking out at the door as if our eye would hasten the expected comer, till at last we are obliged to come in and calmly seat ourselves, and, what we might as well have done at first, wait. And then, how painful to hear step after step, nearer and louder, approaching, then pass by, and die away, while the suspended breath returns with a sigh. Better, then, to shut the door, and return to the needle or the spinning-wheel, and work away as if we had nothing to think of. What pretty, poetical, impracticable advice!

XXI. I am sincerely glad you think of setting about something, and I hope you will avail yourself of the opportunity to engage in it leisurely, but yet actively .... Is it not the case that you place a morbid dependence upon frames and feelings? Now, shall I confess to you that, in general, I consider all that is said about poetical inspiration and " comfortable opportunities," both literary and religious, as (I was going to say) half delusion and half indolence. Forgive me for using such terms, for I plead guilty myself to the implication. I think I know perfectly well the mood you describe, it is both the optative and the potential; but I believe the comparative excellence of the effusions of such hours would often be found far inferior to what we may at first conclude from the pleasurable feelings which accompanied them. Genius, I maintain, does not ebb and flow; it is only the spirits that vary, and we fancy our minds to be unempowered because they refuse to act. But mental activity and elasticity, that greatest of all intellectual blessings, and source of perennial enjoyment, is a *habit* to be acquired. I assure you I regret nothing more than the inertness of my own intellectual powers; but yet, if I may say it, I am better in this respect than you; perhaps for this reason, among others, that being of a more phlegmatic habit, and therefore less subject to those sunshine inspirations, those " angel visits, few and far between," than yourself, I have been compelled to do more without them, to work by the light of my own candle. And this I can assure you, that some of my brightest moments have been struck out, by dint of persevering mental effort, from a frame of flat and almost lethargic vacuity. I consider poetical exercises especially beneficial in this view. Very few of my poems, perhaps none of my best, have resulted from *frames*. I have written myself into a frame. I have been obliged to labour and to study, and found that there are enjoyments resulting from both. I think I have told you Montgomery's idea on this subject; that, as to the almost spontaneous flow of fancy which we sometimes enjoy, contrasted with the cold hours of barren thought, it will almost always appear on examination that the former were the unconscious result of the latter; that the previous labour bestowed on the subject which employed our seemingly fruitless thoughts prepared the mind for its subsequent free and vigorous exertion. I know *physical* effects are not to be reasoned against, but *mind* may do something even in curing these. *Do* not be at the mercy of accidents. He that observeth the winds shall not sow, and he that regardeth the clouds shall not reap. If the wind be adverse, or if there be no gale, let us take to the oars. It is not often that both wind and tide are against us. It is true that when a fog hides the landmarks, we may appear to make little progress; but still we are moving, and when the sun breaks out we shall find ourselves much further than we expected. We are not to judge of the usefulness of an hour by its actual, or rather apparent progress.' We can only judge by *average*. Is there not a sort of intellectual methodism? But we are to seek enjoyment, not as a preparation for exertion, but as the fruit of it: we are to obtain warmth from exercise. Your father wishes you to write for money, and so do I; but I am desirous that you should write for the sake of ascertaining your own strength, and promoting your own healthful enjoyment. Excuse this hortatory lecture; but as it is dictated by experience and prompted by sympathy, so it is as much addressed to myself as to you. I add with Burns—

> " And may you better reck the rede
> Than ever did th' adviser."

. . . . You render me impatient to see the " Scottish Chiefs," though I had almost vowed never to touch another novel. They intoxicate me. · I find my mind needs dieting, as well as constant exercise, to preserve it from morbid feelings. There are many poems which I dare to read only when I am rather flat, or very strong; for instance, some of Burns's and Campbell's. I have to gird up the loins of my mind and be sober, which is often no easy task for a poet of one-and-twenty.

XXII. I think we ought to dwell more on the guardianship, the shepherd-care, the providential government which Jesus Christ exercises over his people. It is an idea different from that which is annexed to God as the moral governor of the universe. The Divine Providence bears a special aspect to Christians under the administration of the Saviour, and it might often assist our faith and incite our hope to realize Him who bore the sorrows of humanity, and still retains its feelings—who came so near to man,* that He even suffered being tempted—as the King of kings, on whose shoulder the government is

---

* In the timidity of this expression, " came *so near* to man," there seems a trace of that morbid reaction against Socinianism, which made orthodox Christians, fifty years ago, fearful of dwelling on the real and complete humanity of the Lord Jesus. Socinianism, perhaps, did even more harm in the rebound than by its direct influence.

laid—as a tender Shepherd, who will never suffer us to want, but is Himself leading our steps through green pastures and beside the still waters.

. . . . . What a wonderful thought is it that we are encouraged to pray, not only for mercy for ourselves, but for blessings on others, that, peradventure, by "asking" we may sometimes "give a sinner life," and, much more, obtain for a friend happiness. Isaac was saying the other day, that perhaps it will form part of our delightful employment in the world of spirits to recall and mutually disclose the prayers we have offered for each other. Oh, that blessed world! Is it, indeed, a reality? Are we hastening to immortality? Is this life but the porch of existence, the prelude to eternity? Seeing, then, we look for such things, what manner of persons—oh! what different persons—ought we to be in our thoughts, and desires, and conversation!

XXIII. I dined with Dr. Collyer, at his house at Blackheath, last Wednesday, when he showed me the proofs of his new collection of 1000 hymns, designed as a supplement to, not substitute for, Dr. Watts. . . . . It will form a very interesting volume, and a powerful rival to Dr. Rippon. There are about 200 of Charles Wesley's, a poet of the first order. Those of his which the Doctor read possess a great deal of Addison's elegance, with Cowper's pathos, and Watts's seraphic fire. But to the point. I recollected the white book, and Dr. Collyer eagerly caught at the idea of anything of yours. My father, however, advised me to venture nothing without permission; and this note comes to request you would send me up your authority to let him insert in his collection that exquisite hymn of yours, "Oh, why this disconsolate frame," and, if you please, "Thou who didst for Peter's faith." .... The signature can be what you please: your name at length, as it is now so extensively known, and as it is desirable it should be, would, I think, be best. My motive in this suggestion and request is, of course, to do good. But, to speak more particularly, I wish others to receive that pleasure, to use the lowest word, from your hymns which I have; while at the same time, I may add to the value of Dr. Collyer's work, and oblige him too. There is, after all, so little good devotional poetry—scriptural rhymings, and metrical sermons, and textual paraphrases in rhyme, there are in abundance—that I esteem a genuine hymn a treasure. I have one in my possession, beginning " Come, my fond, fluttering heart," which *ought* to be published. It would be music to many a heart, because it contains feelings to which the heart responds, and which it is consolation to discover in another. I do not expect I shall ever gain permission of its timid author, from the mistaken idea (as it appears to me) that its publication would involve the disclosure of personal feelings. On reading a hymn, nobody inquires why it was written, or attributes the feelings it depicts to the poet's actual, or at any rate present, experience. Doubtless, in Cowper's pathetic effusions there are bound up many painful mental histories, many a mysterious experience, which are only to be even guessed at by those who have known something of the same. However, an anonymous publication could betray nothing; but I find I am pleading for what I have not ventured to ask.

I have given the Doctor my twenty-third Psalm, but do not know whether it will suit him. I have a little improved it. [Here follow several emendations.] I like thus to evangelize and Christianize the Psalms.

1812.

XXIV. . . . . There is this advantage in correspondence, that it leads us to spread out our minds before
our own inspection, in a way that we should hardly have
taken the trouble to have done for our mere selves. If
we are honest, it leads us to select those points of our
own character and circumstances which are the most
essential parts of *ourselves*, but which, in the bustle of
common thoughts, we are apt to lose sight of. . . . .
Minds such as mine are perpetually getting out of tune;
they sink a full note, after the world has been for some
time scraping upon them; and too often, for want of
leisure, I am obliged to keep playing on most discord-
antly to .myself, my thoughts out of unison. It is delightful to me at such times to have recourse to the key-
note, and tune my harp by that of a sister minstrel.

. . . . How apt are we to forget our own prayers—
wearied, if they appear unavailing; if answered, half
sceptic of their efficiency; or else disposed to rest on our
oars, insensible of our dependence and unmindful of our
duty! If you are disposed to ask me what led me to
this track of thought, I can only inform you that it came
of its own accord this evening into my mind, with the
conviction that my own heart was guilty; and I reflected,
too, how often a slavish and unchildlike sense of unworthiness, arising as much from a deficiency of love as from a
conviction of sin, had kept me back from the feeling of
gratitude—that wholesome, enlivening feeling. At other
times, so full are we of our wants and our burdens, that
we forget it is still our duty, *with thanksgiving*, to make
known our requests unto God. The temper of thankfulness is surely one of the greatest blessings we can enjoy;
it disarms misfortune of half its power. But it is truly
humiliating to find how much our gratitude depends on

nerves and spirits. To be thankful and anxious at the same time, thankful and poorly, and, worse still, thankful and ill-humoured, are next to impossibilities; and yet one might be more grateful, were it only for the peaceful, cheerful feeling which accompanies it. I believe one personal obstacle to the exercise of the specific duty is, that our self-love demands the mercies which lay claim to gratitude to wear some speciality of form in regard to ourselves, as though what we enjoyed in common with all called for return from none, otherwise than by the general cold assent of praise. In regard to other subjects of thanksgiving, such is the goodness of God, so immense, and by human reason so unaccountable, addressing itself rather to faith than to experience, that we are unable to realize it, or form our belief into a persuasion of its truth; so that we are content to reserve the song of praise for that world in which it shall be unfolded in all its fulness.

1813.

XXV. I am quite impatient of these long parentheses in our correspondence; but it is some satisfaction to know that they have been produced by circumstances, unforeseen and important, which have for the time held us apart—a new era in many respects to all of us—and not by any alteration *in us.* I do not like professions or promises; they are often ominous—the last effort of decaying affection, or the bright hour which precedes the devastating storm. But "life *shall not* do by us as it does by the rest of the world." Prosperity might make us forget each other; but on this side we have not much to fear, and in affliction we feel we are friends. . . . . I am persuaded, my dear friend, when you and I look back a year or two on our present circumstances, and the events of the few past years, we shall perceive a suitableness and harmony in the occurrences to which they have given birth. I do not presume to anticipate *your* future, or, so far as respects events, my own. There are, however, some apparent coincidences which one cannot help observing; they seem to hint out the designs of Providence. There is in the events of human life an orderly succession, a natural progress, which must be attended with changes. We lose little for which Providence does not present us with an equivalent; we gain little but at the expense of surrendering a something of enjoyment. We are apt unduly to regret the blossoms of the past, and to call the change of growth decay and devastation. But there is wisdom and goodness in the general order of our moral year. We are, I hope, too good husbandmen to look back; let us rather look forward to spring, and the next spring will be eternal.

Appended to the letter from which the foregoing extract is made is a copy of birthday verses addressed to Mr. Montgomery, which may fitly be inserted here, as a simple but graceful memorial of one of the author's earliest, most valued, and most enduring friendships.

TO JAMES MONTGOMERY,

NOVEMBER 4, 1812.

It was a fiction wild but sweet,
  By ancient bards related:
They held that on our erring feet
  A guardian spirit waited;
That every mortal from his birth
Was thus, through all the ills of earth,
  By genie, fay, or heavenly power attended—
    The secret lover of his soul,.
    Who, with unseen, unfelt control,
Watched o'er his mind, and all his steps befriended.

It was a solemn, soothing thought
  To minds of pensive sadness;
In hours of lonely woe it wrought,
  And turned the gloom to gladness.
This shadowy partner of the mind,
With awe mysterious and refined,
Was loved and worshipped, feared and cherished.
  Its voice, in inward converse heard,
  Courage, and faith, and hope conferred,
Or whispered peace, when hope had perished.

And is there not some shadowy power,
  Which rules in secret o'er us,
And oft, in Feeling's twilight hour,
  Stands half-revealed before us?
Thy guardian friend is hallowed Fame;
She fires thy mind and loves thy name;
Hers is the voice that haunts thy slumbers.
  A gentle power my path pursues,
  Friendship, my angel-guide—the muse
Who first inspired my simple numbers.

I have a harp of many strings,
  Such mystic powers invest it,
On certain days it murmuring rings,
  Although no hand hath pressed it.
I start, and listen: floating near
Responsive notes arrest my ear,
And she, my spirit friend, appeareth;
  Geranium blossoms intertwined,
  With violet and myrtle bind
Her brow, and near her heart a rose she weareth.

And thus, with flower and evergreen
  Her virgin brow adorning,
The gentle sprite, with pensive mien,
  Appeared this hallowed morning.
November's chill and sullen blast
Melted to music as she past,

And to my lyre a thousand lyres replied.
I saw the heavenly gates unfold;
There thrones were set, and harps of gold;
And Friendship stood exultant Fame beside.

Another early and dear friend was the Rev. Henry March, now of Newbury, in those years a student at Homerton College. The friendship then commenced survived the changes of more than forty years, strengthened and hallowed by the assured hope of its being perpetuated in a happier world. The letters addressed to this highly valued friend naturally embody many of their writer's views on religious, theological, and public topics. The first bears date August 12, 1813.

XXVI. MY DEAR FRIEND,—Your letter, which I still consider unanswered, is simply dated "Saturday." Was this considerately done, that the lapse of weeks since I received it might not reproach me, in case of my not being able to reply to it so early as I wished? I have often looked at it, and promised myself some pleasure in going over it with my pen in hand; but opportunity is with me always future. The angel visits of leisure are indeed "few and far between." The chariot of time is generally driven by his ill-favoured charioteer, necessity; and its course is only visible by the dust it throws up in its progress over the dull high-road of life. Excuse this metaphor. The fact is, I feel as if I should like to take a ride exceedingly this evening, and taste the free breeze; from which idea, perhaps, it arose that I got astride a simile which had well-nigh ran away with me. Oh, the country, the country! I long to revisit it as ardently as ever fond lover longed to embrace his chosen one. My mind is kept awake so constantly by the din of the world, that it seems as if it required, like the body, an interval of slumber, and the solace of dreams—not only to repose from exertion, but to forget all of itself but the past and the future, of which the dreams of fancy and remembrance are framed. Let this be my apology for the real difficulty I feel in improving the brief minutes of leisure, so as to render this letter, by any intellectual exertion, at all worth your reception. There are a hundred topics which it would be delightful for me to talk over with you in Somersetshire, but which now it fatigues me to think of. But I will no longer defer writing to you.

You apologise for egotism, and yet without it how are we to know each other? It constitutes the individuality of a letter, which forms its interest. I regret that we know no more of each other; but when we have met in person there has seemed to exist an awkwardness somewhere, which has prevented our minds coming into contact.* The language of friendship is so arbitrary and idiomatic, that it requires habit before we can converse with fluency in its various dialects. But I am sure on most points we should sympathise. Our feelings are set pretty nearly in the same key; it is in our habits of thought we are different. In regard to the discourage-, ment which arises from the illimitable nature of knowledge, and the imperfection of the intellectual powers, it is a subject which has often pressed upon my attention; and I have been disposed to believe that we ought to regard knowledge itself as a mere means—a moral means in subservience to our education for a higher state of being. The greater part of that which we dignify by this name, and which is certainly essential to certain temporary purposes of life, is so entirely unconnected with the permanent realities of the soul, that its use and remembrance will terminate with the dream of life. " As for

* " We had known each other then but a few months.—H. M."

knowledge, it shall vanish away." I certainly would not
remain willingly ignorant of any of the wonders of natural
science or human wisdom; I would not part with the
thirst for knowledge, which is as essential a concomitant
of mental health, as the appetites are of physical vigour.
But shut out as the greater part of society are from intellectual pursuits, often being compelled to sacrifice
them to the considerations of duty, it would be discouraging to think that on this account they should suffer
any material loss. It certainly is humbling, and designed
to humble us, to find what long and patient labour is
requisite for the attainment of the first principles of
science; but we ought not always to estimate the result
of our day's labour by the sum of our acquired knowledge.
If the mind has been exercised, a process has been going
forward, by which the most valuable ends of knowledge
are subserved. It is thus I console myself. I find I
must remain ignorant for life on many classes of subjects,
for want of leisure to pursue them; and must suffer
under an erroneous judgment, perhaps, on several points,
in consequence of this ignorance (for the chief end of
knowledge is the correction of error). I believe that the
power of being great or distinguished is denied me by an
all-wise Providence, because the very means are withheld.
Still, I have the moral means of improving my faculties,
by directing them to the real objects of life, by maintain-
ing that simplicity in my motives and endeavours which
is essential to intellectual advancement, and by cultivat-
ing habits of attention to the principles and necessary
relations of truths and of actions, which form the basis
of wisdom. With these views, what an infinite advantage has the simple Christian over the philosopher, because he *is* simple! With the Bible in his hand, he has
the key to half the problems which engage the other's

life-long studies; and in the disposition to receive and delight in truth, he already possesses the best fruit of knowledge. And what a prospect is unfolded, so soon as the initiatory term of his existence shall be completed! In what strange and surpassing sense shall we then " know as we are known !" What new objects will then engage all the energies of thought—objects not of form and shadow—the modes, and accidents, and names of things—but realities, seen in their essence and necessary relation to each other, and to the Great Cause of all things! Knowledge there will no longer be a distinction, a laborious acquirement, but an element and an instinct. Heaven will be a region of intellect, but a state of action too; and the perfection of our powers will be accompanied with the determination of our affections towards their true centre: and in this consists the harmony of being.

I have lately been reading a little work which you are, perhaps, no stranger to—" Scougal's Life of God in the Soul of Man." I am delighted with it beyond everything. It is the very marrow of divinity and philosophy. One sentence especially is to me a golden one—the love of God " is an affectionate and delightful sense of the Divine perfections." It is only this that we want to make us happy and truly great, in possessing the image of God. In ourselves we have only sources of discouragement, but we are not " straitened in Him," nor have any reason to fear that we shall find ourselves inadequate to any service to which He has called us, if we go forward in his strength.

What a relief it is to the mind to turn to such subjects as these when sick of the emptiness of life! The world is, indeed, " a tiresome place." Its best goods are scarcely worth the purchase. Disappointment and care.

is our alternative discipline ; it matters little what form they assume. " The heart knoweth its own bitterness." It is your privilege that the path you have chosen exempts you from much to which others are exposed, whose daily converse and efforts must necessarily respect low and selfish objects. The fewer and the higher our secondary objects, the better for our peace. The nearer they are to our ultimate object, the more secure are our enjoyments. But I must break off here. I hope to hear the country has set you up in health. . . . . Pray remember me very respectfully to Mr. Gunn.—I am, dear March, yours affectionately,

JOSIAH CONDER.

To the same date with the foregoing belong the following extracts from his correspondence with his youngest sister :—

Oct. 20, 1813.

XXVII. . . . . The tone of your last letter delighted us all, and relieved me of some anxiety. Your first made us feel for your plight, when you found yourself two miles beyond N——!! But as it ended well I was not sorry for it, nor should I be for anything in the shape of adventure or peril that may end in safety. One is always the better for having undergone them. In fact, there is nothing of any *consequence* except *consequences;* and it is consequences of a moral nature which are chiefly to be regarded. I give you credit—whether I am right or wrong will be seen from your future life— for a great portion of *latent* energy. You have yet to learn the strength of your own mind. Till a person has been placed in situations in which he has to act for himself, and to take a part in life as an individual being, he has no opportunity of ascertaining either his strength or his weakness. Your mind at home was in considerable danger of stagnation; there is nothing here of strong excitement to stir up your feelings; there is no object— and we all must have an object—to employ your efforts. I am quite sure that though we might, without much moral discipline, become amiable domestic animals, and be quite content with a warm hearth, to be capable of *happiness* it is absolutely necessary that we should do a great deal for ourselves, and that a great deal should be done for us. Happiness is a fortune to which none of us are born: we must go to school to Industry, and then serve an apprenticeship to Experience; and then we must set up for ourselves on the borrowed capital of affection, added to our private stock of integrity. By the help of diligence and good management, we may thus *make our minds and circumstances meet*, which is as good a definition of happiness as can, perhaps, be given. Depend upon it, we must make our minds work hard, which they do not like, to be, or to deserve to be, happy. Mankind in general are half asleep; their "drowsy powers," as Dr. Watts calls them, can only half see and half feel. They walk as in a dream, and hear neither the whispers of Duty nor the warnings of Conscience. "Indolence is the half of vice," in most cases: it is not the indolence of the saunterer or the lounger that is meant, but intellectual inertness. Men are incapable of being happy, because they love ease, and rest, and pleasure; and it is not till they have been successively deprived of these by affliction, by necessity, or by that sense of duty which does the work of necessity and affliction by self-denial, that they learn what happiness means. To renounce ourselves—as respects God, by humble obedience and submission, and the self-renunciation of faith—and, as respects our fellow-creatures, by meekness and love—this is the great lesson of life, and the secret of that true self-possession which makes us equal to all circumstances as to our duties, and superior to them as to our enjoyments. . . . . We come into the world to *act*, not to enjoy. I am just beginning to have something of an habitual persuasion of this truth, and with much, very much, to engage my affections and my hopes, as you well know, and to promise what is called happiness. . . . . I am yet convinced that I shall never find any solid or sufficient happiness from anything but God; that friends can *only*, or at least that they *principally*, promote our happiness by allowing us to make them happy, and thus calling out the best affections of the heart; or by imparting to our minds the transforming reflection of their excellences. But if we live upon our friends in any way we are doing wrong, and they will be made disappointment and care to us. It is selfishness too often, or the mere instincts of our nature, which make us cling to them. We shrink back, like the infant in the nurse's arm, from the stranger world; but when we cease to be children, we must put away childish things and childish feelings.

> " The shadow of *thy* wings
> My soul in safety keeps,
> I'll follow where my Father leads,
> For He directs my steps,"

is a verse I have again and again repeated to myself. To realize its truth, and rely on it, is all we need. Or shall I give you a verse from another favourite poet of ours?

(ADDRESSED TO THE DAWNING HOUR OF DAY.)

> " What if a day of sun,
> Which has in clouds begun,—
> Thou canst not promise to be ever sparkling,—
> Show that thy doubtful sign
> Can calm with storm combine,
> And temper with clear rays the shadows darkling.

> Tell of the tempest wild,
> That leaves the air more mild ;
> Of chills which tend the *ripening* term to lengthen ;
> Of showers that serve to show
> The brightness of the bow ;
> And winds that try the roots they do but strengthen."

I have given you rather a long sermon ; this must serve as the hymn. I will conclude with a short but emphatic prayer, when it is really meant as now—God bless you.

December 21, 1813.

XXVIII. . . . . The principal use of birthdays is, in the case of absent friends, to have a set time to remember them *specially*. You are seldom, indeed, forgotten by me, any more than by any other member of your family. But I see you in the midst of a crowd, and though, if you could but see it, I now and then give you a nod and a smile, I have not time often to single you out for more particular attention. If you were at home it would be the same ; for I am speaking of the things which employ my mind. Often what is passing before me with such rapidity seems but a dream—the things I see appear the most unreal—and I long to wake, that I may command my own thoughts, and look at the objects I love best. Perhaps all this will appear strange, if not unintelligible to you. Perhaps the plain English would run thus :—That I live in such a bustle, have so much to do and to think of, and am drawn and driven so many ways, that I sometimes am absolutely giddy with the whirl, and fall down almost spent. . . . . .

Now, do you want to know what I have been so much occupied with ? I look back, and cannot tell you ; for though Time, as he advanced, appeared at the head of such a multitude of duties, businesses, and clamorous engagements, and the sound of their trampling almost stunned me as they passed, yet it was upon the sands that they were treading, and they have left no footsteps behind. I have picked up, indeed, a few things which dropped from them, but they are trifling mementoes, of no use but to the finder. " And this is life! Ah, fleeting vapour!"

.... I calculated upon your getting much good from this visit, and, I dare say, I shall not be found materially out in my calculations. At home, your mind is pent up, and has not breathing-room. It has been so, in great measure, with mine; and if it had not been for *my trials*, for circumstances which obliged me to *act* and made me *feel*, it would have been much more so. The conviction it has wrought in my mind is this :—That our happiness is always promoted by the circumstances which tend to our improvement; and that it is our *character*, *not* our circumstances, on which it essentially depends. Nothing but *character* is an object deserving our solicitude. At this moment I have a thousand anxieties pressing upon me, of various kinds, but I am the better for them all, because they are anxieties which connect themselves with persons and things which I value, *not so much* as conducive to my happiness, as because they have had a beneficial influence on my mind and my affections.

.... There is little in the past worth looking at, except our failings ; and ever since Lot's wife, it has been the safest to look forward. Perhaps you may see some dark clouds behind you, but remember you are meeting the wind, and they have passed over. However, there are some things which are not to be forgotten. The past has been rich in mercies, mercies which shine all the brighter out of the clouds. As to the future, we cannot discern much, because we are climbing an ascent, and

shall be all our lives, so that we can only look down on what
we have passed.   But, oh, what a prospect shall we have
from the top!

(To Mrs. Gilbert.)

Axminster, Feb. 1, 1814.

XXIX. My dear Friend,—This is a part of your
style and title which I hope does not admit of change,
but one which, without Act of Parliament, you may continue to wear, in addition to whatever names and honours
you may succeed to, and this both in right of yourself
and of your husband. . . . . The scenes of life pass on
and shift, without, in general, exciting much surprise by
the abruptness of the change.   The actors remain much
the same, though the situations vary ; and the business
of the drama proceeds in natural and gradual succession.
But now and then there is an evident transition, which,
without consulting any prompter's book, we may call a
new act : a definite point is attained in our existence,
from which a new series of circumstances and actions
commences, arising from the unforeseen change. A new
vista is opened, a new horizon formed ; and it seems that
our individual self is composed (as you once said) of successive, rather than continuous being.   It is more than
interesting, it is of important advantage, when we find
ourselves suddenly set down on a point of life which,
when only seen in distant imagination, appeared the
highest and brightest in the prospect, to recollect all
the ideas which the anticipation awakened; and trans-
migrating for a moment into the reanimated form of our
former self, to look up at its successor, reposing on the
Present.   One important circumstance, however, which
enters into that Present, we could not from any previous
point anticipate ; and that is, the aspect of the Future
from thence.   If we could, by any power of imagination,

transport ourselves into the indefinite form of what we shall be, and look at the *now* we occupy on the *other side*, we should then be better enabled to appreciate, and perhaps to improve it. Some such knowledge of the future is perhaps necessary to our complete enjoyment of to-day. . . . .

" To-day, with all its bliss, be mine !" said the minstrel. My dear friend, I am happy I can congratulate you on your *to-day*. I do not know whether I should add, " with all its bliss," for that is a word which seems to speak too much for modest prose ; and after thirty we drop it from our vocabulary, from finding no object which it will fit. I may congratulate you, however, on the possession of that rational happiness, or the means of that happiness, which, if less brilliant than the dream of Fancy, is more real and permanent. And after all, when the cause is fairly tried, I am disposed, for one, to think that the solid goods of life, the real sum of enjoyment (in spite of the cares and ills which spring up with our blessings) which forms the common lot, rather differ in their nature from the anticipations of youthful hope, than yield to them in degree. If I have taken a favourable moment for the estimation of life from my own experience, it is one when the pressure of solicitude and care is by no means unfelt, and when circumstances call for particular anxiety. I need all the elasticity of hope, and all the assurance of gratitude, and all the confidence of trust, to nerve me for the ascent on which I have entered. . . . .

I shall add a P.S. to this, I dare say, when I get to London, which I left for one day, and have not now seen for three weeks. Like John Gilpin, I rode much further than I expected, for I thought only of meeting my friends at Salisbury ; but after being shut up there a week by the snow, I contrived to escape here, where I have passed almost a fortnight, which has well repaid me for the perils of the way. I do not know whether my adventures have found their way into the papers yet; but I think of publishing a quarto volume when I return, dedicated to Sir John Carr: the frontispiece, Letton Heath. at midnight, the mail overturned in a deep snow, and a high gale. But I will not anticipate its contents.

The following is to his friend, Henry March: —

1815.

XXX. The receipt of your letter gave me pleasure before I opened it. The mere direction of a letter in the handwriting of a friend is interesting; and it matters comparatively little what are its contents, if it tells us he is well. But the contents of yours were such as to make a letter valuable, by stirring up one's better feelings, and rekindling those sympathies which the world continually tends to extinguish. The friendship, or virtue, or feeling, that has no deeper root than in *sentiment*, will most assuredly be blighted and withered by the realities of life: for sentiment itself can only exist in the mind when the thoughts have room to expand, and there is leisure for the operation. Sentiment is the blossoming of the thoughts; or rather it is the thoughts running to seed, out of which fresh thoughts are to spring up. But when the quiet leisure of youth—the time for laying in thoughts and feelings, for talking of what we would or will do, and singing of what we have done—is past; when the *present* call for action incessantly occupies the whole mind, and we are obliged to act according to what we are, rather than from what we feel; then principles, not sentiments, habits produced by feeling, rather than feeling, will constitute the only basis of virtue and friendship. I do not know whether you ever read Butler's admirable section (in his "Analogy") on the law of our nature by which passive impressions become weakened by repetition, while active habits strengthen. It is wisely constituted that it should be so; and although we do not like the idea of resigning any portion of our youthful *impressibility*, we soon learn that solid happiness, as well as virtue, consists in the exercise of the affections and the active powers of the mind—in benevolence rather than in sensibility.

I scarcely know what has led me into this train of thought; but I have had a little experience, by this time, of the effects of the world upon my mind. I think I can say I watch with jealousy every shade of change which it undergoes in the process of daily action. I am anxious to approve myself to my friends as the identical person they expected me to be; the legitimate heir and successor of my former self. Your letter put me upon thinking whether I had given you all that portion of my time, thoughts, and affections to which you were entitled —whether I had discharged all the duties of friendship. The expressions in your letter seemed to evince that I undeservedly occupy a larger place in your mind as a distinct object of interest than I am able to allot to any one of the few friends whom I esteem so highly. It is not that love, real love, is a narrower of the heart; for if, when any particular object is once brought under the focus of our thoughts, we feel towards that object all we ever did, although those feelings may often lie dormant, we may allow ourselves to believe that our heart is not narrowed because our mind is occupied with all that is tender in affection and holy in duty. I often think how Isaac and I are now separated, who used to be as friends so much to each other. I believe we are in affection and sentiment the same; but our friendship has become a transaction of the past. Finite beings can only exist in time and place; they can only think in succession; the eye, though it appears by the rapidity of its movements to take in sometimes the whole horizon at a glance, really can only receive the impression of an inconceivably small portion of an object at once. In like manner, the mind can only by successive operations embrace an extent or variety of interests, by shifting, as it were, the focus of affection; and while it is fixed to any particular point, all the rest is fancy or memory.

I do not know how it is, that when we meet—whether through your fault, or mine, or both—we often chat about nothings, instead of pursuing such a subject, for instance as this—something real, relating to our internal selves. I believe it is, that we see so little of each other, that we hardly think it worth while to begin. But we ought not to suffer this. I was going on to say, that in reference particularly to intercessory prayer, I wish to satisfy myself as to what portion should be devoted to the office and expression of friendship. I have often thought much on this subject. The mind is sometimes distracted with the variety of its cares and interests, as it is at others painfully engrossed by those which immediately press upon it. A formal discharge of any supposed duty of the kind would obviously be inefficacious, either for the purposes of prayer, or even for exciting the feeling of affectionate sympathy towards the subject of our prayers. General sweeping clauses of intercession always sound to me like unmeaning compliments. The heart is, I know, the best arbiter and casuist in these matters; but still, as you allude to the subject, I should like to have your sentiments a little more distinctly upon it. . . . .

[In reference to the last topic, it may be remarked,

that while mere general petitions are worthless indeed, if the mind rests in the vague generality, yet the form may be general, while the thought in the mind is specific. In a prayer offered aloud for others to join in, much will depend on the tone in which the words are spoken; for tones are the language of emotion, as words of thought. "Thought is quick;" and such a brief general expression as "Our dear friends," spoken in a tone of genuine feeling, may, in a momentary pause, be interpreted and applied in thought to a multitude of individual cases and special interests. Yet, is there not room to fear that the duty of special intercession for one another is often too much neglected by Christians?]

In the interval between the dates of the two last letters, a momentous and happy change had come about in their writer's circumstances. The prematurely sad and sombre views of life conveyed in some of his earlier letters had been happily contradicted, or at least modified, by the fulfilment of a hope entertained through anxious years, when its fulfilment seemed at first impossible, and afterwards uncertain. Poetic dreams had become sober certainty. Even the drudgery of business had acquired a new and inspiring motive; it was no longer for himself he worked. The scene of daily care and toil had become Home; for a bachelor may have a house, but he has no home. So, at least, thought the writer of these lines, penned two years earlier:—

> That is not home, where day by day
> I wear the busy hours away.
> That is not home, where lonely night
> Prepares me for the toils of light.
> 'Tis hope, and joy, and memory, give
> A home in which the heart can live.

These walls no lingering hopes endear;
No fond remembrance chains me here.
Cheerless I heave the lonely sigh—
ELIZA, need I tell thee why?
'Tis where thou art is home to me,
And home without thee cannot be.*

On the 8th of February, 1815, Mr Conder married
the lady addressed in these lines, the second daughter
of Roger Thomas, Esq., of Southgate, in Middlesex (deceased many years previously), and granddaughter, on her
mother's side, of Louis Francis Roubiliac, the sculptor.
How fitted she was—to use his own words—" to make
the poetry of his life," if the biographical pen were held
in some other hand, this might be no unfitting place to
say. But it has been already intimated that it is not
intended to occupy these pages with private details of
domestic life, interesting only or chiefly to intimate personal friends. It is enough to say, that it would be hard
and rare to find a union in which a more perfect adaptation alike of character, taste, heart, and intellect existed;
or which could afford, through forty years, a larger
amount of pure and hallowed earthly happiness.

The new home was in St. Paul's Churchyard, Number
Eighteen, to which Mr. Conder had removed his publishing business, and where he continued to carry it on for
five years, till within a few weeks of the time when the
great bell tolled out the close of the longest reign in
English history, and old George the Third, under whose
troubled rule the events recorded in these three chapters
took place, slept with his fathers. The events of these
five years do not need any elaborate chronicle. Literary
labours went hand in hand with the cares of business.
New literary friendships were formed, and schemes pro-

* ".Star in the East," etc., page 101.

jected; and the career of authorship fairly entered upon. London and the ledger grew less and less tolerable; and country quiet and literature more and more inviting. Family joys brought with them the cares which are their usual attendants, and the sorrows which are their seldom absent shadows. Twice the eldest born was left the only son; and the precious remains of the second and third were laid to rest in the family grave, in the old Nonconformist burial-ground of Bunhill Fields. The following extracts are from the correspondence of these years :—

XXXI. . . . . And so we have, many of us, become fathers and mothers, and are actually in the way to occupy the names and seats, and then the graves, of those who were our parents, and fondled *us*, and talked of what we should be. And now we begin to perceive that what appeared in our early days to be a plane, because we were intent upon going onward, is in reality a sphere, on which, beyond a certain point, we begin to descend. And now we seem to be on the central spot, on which the clouds of infancy and the shades of age form the boundary of either prospect. Yet life itself is a beautiful process; and this world itself, with all its frosts and storms, with eternity beyond, is like a clear winter's day with sunshine—beautiful and cheerful still. And what a lesson does it afford whenever the sun goes in—familiar as the occurrence is—and leaves the scene cold. But I am undesignedly beginning to sentimentalize, as I did before I had so much call for thoughts, and actions, and feelings of a busier and deeper kind than sentiment knows of. It is the first time I have moralized on becoming a father; nor have I written a *poem* on the occasion.

XXXII. . . . . Your letters are always interesting because they are full of character. I congratulate you most heartily on having attained this point; that you have tried on your armour, and gone through the manœuvres of theological exercise, preparatory to taking the field in earnest. Seven times a week, however, would soon wear out a veteran, and you must therefore allow me to charge you with great imprudence in putting your bodily strength to so severe a trial. I do anticipate, March, *much* good, should Providence favour you with competent health, from that sincere application of the whole force of your mind and character which you will bring to the ministerial office. How rarely, I fear, does a young minister commence his career with the ardour inspired by simple motives, and in the strength of devotion! It is not simply as your friend that I feel interested in the event. I have told you before, that it is with more than ordinary sympathy I contemplate your devoting yourself to that work in which I sometimes think, had not Providence so clearly appointed me to other duties, I could have found the employment most congenial to my character. I think there is that degree of similarity between us, that may allow me to feel as if you were about to realize the very part I should have wished to sustain. This, however, is my post, and, as Milton beautifully says—

"They also serve who only stand and wait."

The discipline of mind which I have undergone, and which I must still undergo in business, is, I am deeply convinced, of the most salutary kind. The *responsibilities* of business, the incessant activity, the degree of foresight it requires, the feeling of dependence on others, the necessity of self-command and caution, and a measured tone and manner, which attach to the situation of a trades-man, are all calculated to have a maturing influence on the character, considered as an educational process. But the world is, in this form, a severe schoolmaster; it is well if he teaches us the lesson of Christ. I know I have still so much indolence of mind left, so much of the atheistical pride of independence, and so much love for the world, in the form of refined luxury, that I may need to be kept under by the discipline of anxious carefulness. But it is hard, very hard, to be quite resigned, cheerfully and implicitly resigned, to the appointments of Provi-dence, under circumstances which leave little pause for collected thought and for the quiet acts of faith and gratitude, which fritter away the mind by a succession of insect attacks.

You see that I am availing myself of your invitation to deviate into a strain of egotism, in which, the older I grow the less disposed I am to indulge. It is difficult to make one's self understood. One does not want to be encountered by some religious truism, which, however applicable to the case, may be wholly inefficient as a pre-scription to the feelings. You will not, I think, have misunderstood what I have written as dictated by the morbid spirit of complaint. I have nothing to complain of but myself; but the hurry, the exhaustion of mind, the petty vexations to which I am subject, make me pant, sometimes too impatiently perhaps, for some more quiet, more retired sphere. London is a hateful place; and the loss of such friends as Benjamin Neal makes it appear still less endurable. But what I most feel is, that I can so seldom sit down in my dear home, and enjoy the sweet sunshine of love, in its purest earthly form, in tranquillity. How contemptible as an *object*, how all-essential as a

means, does money then seem! These are trials and
temptations, March, which, if your talents do but introduce you into a situation of *competence*, it is probable you
will never realize. You will, doubtless, have others,
adapted to your character; you have had others. Loss
of health is, I am convinced, one that is often lightly
depreciated: it is a great mercy to enjoy animal life.
Nothing affects my constitutional cheerfulness, scarcely
anything, but the physical frame's suffering from anxiety
or want of proper circulation. When this is the case, I
am not without misgivings that I am not invulnerably
strong. We do not know what we are reserved for, or
what is reserved for us. But whichsoever of us has the
shortest task to fulfil, the least arduous warfare to discharge, may we but at length obtain the free gift we cannot merit!

> "There is a home, there is a rest,
> There is a heaven in view."

But how much easier is it to be tired of earth, than
to be heavenly-minded! I have many, and strong, and
tender ties to earth, which make me love life. It is
a burden I should, doubtless, fear to lay down. In every
form, futurity is awful. Oh, to be kept, and guided,
and sustained by Omnipotent Mercy *unto salvation!*

I have no room for other topics. As to Dissent, in
my most solemn moments I think I *most* deeply feel the
importance of the principles on which it rests. Do not
hold them loosely.

October, 1818.

XXXIII. . . . . I rejoice most unfeignedly in the animating prospect of usefulness which has unfolded before
you, and I feel the more interest in it, as I fancy yours is
precisely the kind of situation which I should delight to

occupy. Not that I indulge a wish of this kind. I am satisfied that I am where I am *placed*, and any change that appears to me desirable, I wish to be made *for* me rather than by myself. The tranquillity of the country, however, *is* a good, and when it can be enjoyed in connection ,with active usefulness, and an occupation favourable to spirituality of character, it presents certainly the circumstantial means of happiness. You have doubtless some alloy, some secret bitterness; discipline must be going forward. I do not ask what it is, but I believe there must be something of trial mixed with every dispensation of mercy, in order that the work of sanctification may still be going on. And if the external is all calm and serene, the fears, and doubts, and corruptions of the heart turn against a man, and these become his trial. In choosing or changing for ourselves, we cannot know what we take as the encumbrances of the new situation; but we may be sure there is some mortgage to Care or Sorrow upon it. It is the only safe way to take what is given us; and you have the satisfaction of having acted thus, and have therefore the assurance that you are well provided for.

. . . . You are to tell me what you think of my book. As I expected, some of the statements have excited discussion. Bishop, of Ringwood, has written to me upon some points which he deemed exceptionable. They relate to the nature of the visible Church, the terms of communion, etc. Dr. Winter advanced some positions on the subject, in accordance with my views, in the last monthly meeting sermon (which I suppose will be printed), and your tutor, Dr. S., found fault with them, as well as (I believe) some others. Dissenters want to have their minds brushed up and cleared from the cobwebs in many respects.

The work here referred to was Mr. Conder's first considerable original publication, a treatise "On Protest-ant Nonconformity," in two octavo volumes, printed in 1818. The second edition, in one volume 12mo, was published in 1822. The work had been for some years in preparation, and is thus referred to in a letter written about two years before its issuing from the press :—" I am fearful that I shall not be able to supply a work of the exact description you mention—a 'vade mecum, or text-book of principles, calculated for constant and easy reference.' Robert Robinson would have been the man to furnish a book of this kind, and it would require a pen not less vigorous than his to compose lectures upon Nonconformity deserving of constant reference. I hope I may do some good by supplying an argumentative treatise on the fundamental principles of Nonconformity, which, as a whole, may serve to show that those principles are deducible from the nature of religion, the design of Christianity, the laws of moral agency, and the declarations of the New Testament."

At the close of the year 1819 (considerable part of the autumn of which was spent at Hastings, for the benefit of Mrs. Conder's health), Mr. Conder disposed of his business to Messrs. Holdsworth and Ball, and removed to the neighbourhood of St. Albans, Hertfordshire, devoting himself thenceforward to the pursuit of literature as a profession.

The following brief private memoranda show that so important and decisive a step was not adopted but after much anxiety, and with earnest prayer for Divine guidance :—

Dec. 27, 1818.—Mem. Make more a conscience of prayer-meetings, and interceding for the church and its pastor. I have been deficient in this. Improve what I have, as I would secure higher privileges in the event of a removal.

I am closing a year of many trials, but all tempered by mercy. Dear Charles, how easy and beautiful his death! How my dear wife was sustained and endeared to me! The robbery—how much worse it might have been! And so of E——'s illness, and my father's; and so of this last trial in the dear babe; and so of pecuniary losses and difficulties.

Need I fear intrusting my all to the same all-wise and merciful disposal? GOD IS LOVE. Oh, to feel this at heart!

Still I must wait till the cloud moves forward. I have no longer any wish, I believe, as respects either town or country; but only, if it be the will of God, to enjoy more leisure and serenity of mind by being made easier in my business, and saved from anxieties on the score of characters. I trust this will be given me, if it be for my good. "Show me the way wherein I should walk, for I lift up my soul unto Thee."

I believe I am not above my business, though friends represent that it is a pity I should be so employed; but God has put me to it—He must remove me. Yet the growing feeling of unfitness is very discouraging—unfitness from circumstances which discourage me; the want of requisite assistance; continued perplexity.

Oh, for more grace! Be this my daily prayer; and that the design of the present may be fulfilled in me, as the best preparation for the future. I commit my way to Thee. If I am thine, blessed Lord, Thou wilt provide for me.

Homerton, July 4, 1819.—The Lord has heard me, and delivered me from the burden, and made the path clear. Oh, that the depth and permanence of my gratitude might bear some proportion to the earnestness of my supplications. Let me remember, "*Were there not ten cleansed?*"

How shall I praise Him? By a frequent review of the way He has led me, the interpositions He has wrought for me; by caring more for the things of the Lord, now I am less burdened with worldly carefulness; by trusting Him more implicitly; by walking with Him in purity and spirituality; by setting apart more time for the closet. Lord, help me!

Lord, thou knowest that I have besought Thee with tears, that this change, if ever realized, might conduce to my spiritual advantage and my usefulness; but hitherto my mind has been confused, hurried, and worldly. Oh, make me to feel thy love in the bestowment of the prayed-for blessing. Thou hast been nigh in trouble, be not now far from me. Let not unbelief or a careless worldly frame spoil all the good Thou designest me; let me not have in the prayed-for blessing less than I prayed for, through the withdrawment of thy grace.

I am not my own. This day I have been again recognising that blessed truth. I am bought with a price. Infinite love is asserting its claims to my whole being.

> "Thou hast dearly bought my soul,
> Lord, accept and claim the whole!
> Come, and make thy blest abode
> In my heart, thou Son of God!"

Oh, may I feel the Great Inhabitant within me, and feel myself more, though worthless and vile in myself, a consecrated thing!

May I be more awake to the grand conflict! What am I doing for the kingdom that shall come? Am I fighting for Christ? How would love to Him set all right within me?

O God, with my whole heart have I sought Thee, let me not wander from thy commandments. Blessed Saviour, pray for me, that my faith fail not, and let thy grace be sufficient for me. Oh, that I may find the circumstances in which I am now placed more congenial, not simply to my taste, to my native character, but to the tendencies of thy grace within me.

Sept. 5, 1819.—Read La Fléchier's Life with different impressions from those produced by a former perusal. Yes: such would I be. This book, and the "Memoirs of Martyn," have given me new ideas of living Christianity. It is with such men I want to come in contact. How do our associations, owing to the low tone of religion among us, dwarf our characters! It is my earnest prayer that, in removing, I may be directed to the neighbourhood of some simple Christians, with whom I may delight in going to the house of prayer in company, not on the Lord's day only, but on other days.

There is no satisfaction in religion if it is not the *everything* with us, the source of our daily pleasure as well as strength; if in circumstances of comfort, no less than in seasons of trial, we are not looking to prayer, and faith, and communion with God, to make up the main happiness of the day, and viewing other things as subsidiary comforts. This is the only solid, secure ground of dependence. "In the world, tribulation; in Me, peace." As Leighton says, a blessed legacy, taken altogether.

"*Let him deny himself.*" In what do I deny myself? Literally, nothing. I have every comfort.

" How do thy mercies close me round!
    For ever be thy name adored!
  I blush in all things to abound:
    The servant is above his Lord."

(Wesley, 220.)

I seem to have this sign of my Christianity to seek. And
yet, is there no scope for self-denial in the conduct of my
thoughts, in reference to sloth, vanity, carnality? No;
Christ *cannot* be followed without self-denial under any
circumstances; the imitation of his holy example involves a perpetual denial of self; and self cannot be
denied otherwise than by supernatural strength. It
must be because I do not follow Christ that I do not
know more of what is implied by self-denial. Lord, call
me, that I may follow Thee with a perfect heart!

I contemplate the ministerial work with very different
feelings from what I have done. I see' and feel that I
want the first requisite—a heart overflowing with Divine
love towards sinners. I want other requisites of the
nature of habit; but this is the chief. It would be irksome beyond endurance without this change in my
character, unless I sank down into the mechanical performance of the function. In the one case, one would
have to pump up motive to the work; in the other case,
habit is having the water laid on. But neither will do:
it must come from the well-spring of devout feeling.*

I have no plans, no wishes for the future, but sometimes a sinful dread of the great trials which I imagine

---

* Later years, and growing acquaintance with human nature, would
probably have modified this remark; as practical experience of the ministry could hardly have failed to do. The deepest feelings are not always
overflowing. The founts of emotion are often like those ebbing and
flowing wells, which have perhaps sunk out of reach when the thirsty
pilgrim comes to dip his pitcher; and anon are idly brimming over in

my character needs. But this is to limit the wisdom and to distrust the love and sufficiency of God. Yet, O Lord, I know and assuredly believe that Thou art all-sufficient, and that by thy grace there are no possible evils in which I might not be made to feel this. I only tremble at being stripped of earthly goods, without having faith to embrace the infinite equivalent. Jesus, have mercy on my imbecility and infirmity, and spare me the light of, my eyes! " Fit me to serve or suffer." Help me to obey and to trust.

Let me think, " I will look at God only to make me happy to-day;" and then, " I will look to God to provide for to-morrow." I am wondering where our home will be. It is fixed. He knows it. Is not that enough ? Oh, how much greater things hath He done for me than find me a house! We are astonished at the incurable distrust of the disciples, after witnessing successive miracles wrought for their safety or deliverance; but it is the human heart, and I find it to be so. But would not perfect love cast out this unchild-like fear ? A consciousness of guilt and unbelief are the *only* sources of such unworthy solicitude.

Dec. 19.—He hath found us a house, one in every respect to our taste; and now I am ready to ask, How long am I to stay here ? Oh, incurable imbecility! Here is a fresh tie to earth—a larger portion of worldly good introduced into my affections. Will their healthful action suffer no abatement from the subtile poison ? Will there need no neutralizing ingredient ? Will there be

solitude with wasted affluence. Only the still silent depths of conviction, the hidden reservoir into which the showers of heaven have slowly filtered, keeping it ever unexhausted, can feed and fill the channels of action with motives ever fresh, and pure, and strong, and adequate to all the exhausting demands of daily duty.

no earthy tincture, as the effect of so much more of earth absorbed into one's self? "If any man hate not *house,*" etc., "for my sake." This is a part of what I must be ready to resign at once for Christ. Oh, let me hold it loosely, unanxiously! It is not home; not meant for our rest. The glory of the second Temple was the presence of Christ; and what can be the beauty of an earthly residence but his presence? How easily might this fair scene be transcendently surpassed by a darksome comfortless cottage, where there was the felt and visible manifestation of God! But yet, this is the house to which his gracious Providence has brought me; and I trust in Him to make it a scene of happy hours. And it must be always right, and always safe, to praise Him for all He does, and to trust Him for all He has promised. Distrust and ingratitude always go together: Oh, to be delivered from them!

CHAPTER IV.

" THE *Eclectic Review* was commenced, in 1805, by a number of gentlemen who were solicitous to rescue the literature of their country from the dogmatism of superficial critics, and the irreligious influence of a semi-infidel party." A new series was commenced in 1814, " published by Josiah Conder, 18, St. Paul's Churchyard." After some changes of editorship, during which he had occasionally to edit the *Review* himself, Mr. Conder became its stated editor, as well as proprietor. In his address on the commencement of a Third Series, fifteen years afterwards, he says :—

With regard to the principles of the work, they are too well known to require avowal, except for the purpose of showing that they cannot be abandoned. The original design of the proprietors has never been lost sight of, which was to reconcile those long-divorced parties, Religion and Literature—to create or cherish the love of literature in the Christian world, and to watch over the interests of religion as implicated in our literature. It rests its claim to public support on being the *only Critical Journal* embracing the wide range of general literature, which is conducted with this view, and explicitly upon evangelical principles. It may also be affirmed, without disparaging the merit or usefulness of other periodicals, that in the pages of no other journal will there be found a record of the various productions and progress of literature in England during the past four-and-twenty years, to which the Christian scholar will be able to refer with equal confidence and satisfaction. This assertion is made in reference chiefly to the plan and principles of the Journal, although there is no occasion for affecting to shrink from any comparison as to the general character of its articles. As Editor, how inadequately soever I may feel to have discharged the office, during the years that it has devolved upon me, I can take no lower ground in speaking of the writers. . . . . With regard to the minor differences which divide the Christian world, they never have been, they never shall be, suffered to intrude into the region of literature so as to influence a critical decision. There exists an anxious wish to merge those differences, so far as is compatible with a firm maintenance of the principles of religious liberty, and the honest discharge of the duties imposed upon a reviewer, in reference to questions of biblical criticism, ecclesiastical history, and biblical theology. In reference to these subjects, a negative opinion, or a silent one, would involve a dereliction of principle, by which not even the interests of charity could be subserved.

If, from the known sentiments of writers whom I am proud to rank among my friends and contributors, the *Eclectic Review* should be deemed the organ or the advocate of any denomination or religious party, I can only say that nothing can be more unfettered by any ties of interest or obligation than the conduct of this Journal. With regard to any such connection, I must be permitted to reply, in the language of the illustrious Colonel Hutchinson, I have not chosen the party, but the principles they profess ; and I am not therefore so unreasonable as to expect their gratitude for services and sacrifices which they might be more ready to claim as their due, than kindly to appreciate.

Mr. Conder continued to conduct the *Review* for a period of twenty years, often contributing largely to its pages. Among the stated or occasional contributors, were some whose names have since risen to the highest rank in literature ; others, of accomplished scholarship, elegant taste, and scarcely inferior intellectual power, yet who never made themselves a name, but were content to fight the battle of knowledge and of progress in the ranks of that great army of anonymous writers, to whom the world has been so much indebted, from the days of Job of Uz, to the days of steam-printing and penny literature. It is a curious topic of reflection, how much of

the current gold of human thought and speech has come
down with no image or superscription upon it; how many
strong and stirring, wise and pointed, or sweet and tender
sayings, that have become immortal, were uttered by unknown or forgotten lips. It would be somewhat melancholy to think of so much hard, faithful, fruitful labour,
wrought in obscurity, and flung into the world's treasury
without the grace of a single acknowledgment, did one
not remember that literary fame is, after all—the giants
excepted—but a tardier oblivion; and, on the other hand,
that no true work can perish, no fruitful labour can be
vain, and though the world may forget it, "the Day shall
reveal it."

Mr. Conder's connection with the *Eclectic* no doubt
exercised a powerful influence both on his mind and on his
career. It seems to have been the chief link between his
London life as a man of business, and his country life as
a man of literature. It tended powerfully to form his
style as a prose writer; to develope the critical and analytical faculties of his mind, perhaps at the expense of the
poetical; and to render him at home and well informed
in a vast and miscellaneous range of subjects, rather than
profound and erudite in any one. It may be said that
his natural powers were so equally balanced as to have
been capable of receiving a strong impulse in several distinct directions: his labours as a Reviewer, and afterwards
as a Compiler, rendered criticism, analysis, and interpretation the most prominent and powerful of his intellectual
habits. The proprietorship and editorship of the *Review*,
moreover, naturally led to the formation of many literary
friendships. Even a brief memoir of his literary career,
would seem scarcely complete, without the side-light
shed upon it from the letters of some of his most distinguished literary friends. The materials of the present

chapter, therefore, are selected from those portions of this correspondence which appear the most worth giving to the public; and they will be read with lively interest for their own sake, apart from their connection with the present memoir. Those of Mr. Montgomery and Mr. Foster are selected from a mass sufficient to form a volume. They would, no doubt, have been handed over to the biographers of those eminent men, but that they were at the time out of reach. Mr. Hall's letters, of which one or two are here given, are brief and few, the illegible penmanship and occasional errors plainly showing how irksome was the use of the pen to the great preacher; but they are not without characteristic touches worth preserving. Southey's letters are thoroughly characteristic; and the contrast which they present to Montgomery's is very striking and suggestive. The remarkable and touching letter from Ebenezer Elliott, " the Corn-law Rhymer," was not addressed to Mr. Conder, but forwarded to him by Dr. Pye Smith, with the hope that the *Eclectic* might aid the almost despairing poet in his struggle up the steep path of fame. It possesses such a profound and affecting interest, that it deserves not to be lost. Yet the Editor would not venture to print it, but in the belief that it will be read, not with cold curiosity, but with deep sympathy for the passionate inward conflict of a proud and gifted spirit, wrestling fiercely with difficulties to which a feebler nature would have succumbed.

FROM JAMES MONTGOMERY, ESQ.

Sheffield, Dec. 13, 1808.

I. DEAR SIR,—I recollect that I promised to tell you how I liked the " Original Poems for Infant Minds," when I had read them. Criticism is to me such dry and dreadful work, that I shall say in as few words as possible, just to redeem my promise, that I have been much better pleased with them than with many more ostentatious volumes, written for infants of larger growth than these Lilliputian pieces, which have very extraordinary merit (and the greater merit, because it required so much self-denial, where there was both talent and temptation to go gloriously astray). They are composed precisely to the standard of the capacities to which they are addressed ; yet have ingenuity and elegance enough to delight, minds of any standard above idiotism, and below the intelligence of angels. There is a vein of originality that flows through them—originality from the purest and most inexhaustible source, actual observation, and genuine feeling. Fiction has been *supposed*, merely because it has been *said* (at least, I know no other reason for it) to be essential to poetry. I deny it. Truth is the very soul of poetry, and poetry is the very body of truth ; every feeling, every sentiment, every description in poetry, to please,*must* be true; and all are agreed on this point, who are agreed on nothing else concerning poetry, that it is its first and most indispensable requisite to please. Now I appeal to your own heart whether (as far as you are sure that your taste is sound, and that you do not mistake factitious feelings for real ones) you are ever delighted with anything in poetry that is false—false imagery, false thoughts, false character, false feelings ? No, surely; and why are you so much more charmed with these unpretending little pieces than with thousands of great ones, more swelling in style, and more laboured in subject ? Because the former are all breathing with truth, the latter dull, dead, and detestable affectation— and what is affectation but fiction ? Fiction is allowable

K

in the form of poetry—that is, rather, the form of fiction is allowable in poetry; for still the soul of the poetry is truth, and fiction stands in the place of truth, not to deceive, but to attract greater reverence and attention from volatile and capricious man. Fiction, you observe, in these cases is not *opposed* to truth as a rival, but *at her side* as a handmaid; or, to change the metaphor, fiction here is a mask which truth puts on, to make her lovers desire the more to see her countenance. But I must have done with this. I am glad I have no room left to find fault with these poems, that have afforded me such simple, yet high gratification. I think the verse is sometimes too harsh; the anapæstic pieces, in particular, are very ruggedly written, and there are now and then rhymes that box my ears, such as vol. i. p. 97, *moon* and *gloom;* vol. ii., *Miser* and *Eliza!* Fie!

When I met you at Mr. Gregory's, I remember speaking very disrespectfully—I often say very rash things from mere impulse—of Pope's simile, "Alps rise on Alps," etc., which you, I think, had been praising. I did not condemn the comparison or depreciate it, but I said it was stolen. I was sorry afterwards, because I could not then prove my words; and it was too much to expect that you would take them, in such a case, for granted. I knew that I had met with something resembling that famous simile in one of our old poets; but on ransacking my memory while I was in London, I despaired of finding out in whom I had seen it. I found the passage accidentally the other day, which I had in the general idea when I was at Woolwich, but could not then quote a word of it. It is in Drummond's Poems (of Hawthornden). The whole passage is transcendently beautiful. Here it is :—

" Great Architect! Lord of this universe!
    That sight is blinded would thy greatness pierce.
    Ah! as a pilgrim who the Alps doth pass,
    Or Atlas' temples, crowned with winter-glass,
    The airy Caucasus, the Apennine,
    Pyrenees' clifts, where sun doth never shine,
    When he some craggy hills hath overwent,
    Begins to think on rest, his journey spent,
    Till, mounting some tall mountain, he doth find
    More heights before him than he left behind :
    With halting pace, so while I would me raise
    To the unbounded limits of thy praise,
    Some part of way I thought to have o'errun,
    But now I see how scarce I have begun.
    With wonders new my spirits range possest,
    And wandering wayless, in a maze them rest."
                Hymn on the Fairest Fair.

I do not know that this original of Pope's admired
and admirable simile has been pointed out by any of his
commentators—most probably it has ; and perhaps the
image itself might be traced to antiquity, it is so striking
and beautiful.   I have read Smyth's Poems with all the
delight that they are calculated to inspire in some places,
and with all the indifference that others inevitably induce
over such dull souls as mine.   He is never so much a
poet as when he speaks of himself as one.   Then, indeed,
the poet breaks through the cloud of the man, and shines
in "the heaven of invention."   I feel all his warmth, I
lie down in his beams, and existence is enjoyment.   In
his love pieces, too, he is often exquisitely tender, and
impassioned almost to ecstasy, without being licentious.
On other subjects he is really to me very frequently
heavy, obscure, and pedantic.   This is bold criticism ; I
fear there is more sincerity than prudence in my thus
venturing to sit in judgment on a living author.   Is he
not a man and a brother?   Yes, truly, and he has the

faults of both, or he is no man and no brother of mine.
The stanzas "To Laura" are, in my poor estimation, in-
comparably the finest in the volume; I know nothing in
Collins superior to them. I have not a line left to
criticise your own verses; I saw some in the last
Athenæum. They were worthy of you; will you take a
poet's hint? *Always* write your *best*, and every time you
will write *better*. Remember me respectfully to your
father and family. Be assured yourself of my sincere
esteem and my earnest wishes for your [welfare, as one
who would be immortal both in this world and in that
which is to come. Farewell. I am truly your friend
and servant,

J. MONTGOMERY.

Sheffield, July 25, 1809.

II. . . . . I find that if I wait for leisure and disposition to write to you, I may never write at all. I therefore sit down, at the close of a newspaper day, to address
you in such terms as may come without invoking the
epistolary Muse, if there be such a lady, though I am unacquainted with her; yet in such terms as will not fail
to please, because they will be the language of simplicity
and truth. . . . The poem to "Fancy" is more airy and
elegant in thought, than either in expression or versification; that is, it is best in what is best, and fails only
in what is of secondary importance. Such as it is, I have
no doubt that ere now it has been read with rapture by
Robin Goodfellow to Queen Mab and her maids of
honour under a tuft of cowslips, while the summer moon-
light slept upon the ground. Thank you for the Nursery
Rhymes. My opinion of them I presume you saw in the
Iris, which I sent you, containing a specimen, with a note
of recommendation. I think this Lilliputian volume in

every respect worthy of the fair and truly ingenious authors of the "Original Poems." You certainly have as good a title to the "Alps" as either Drummond or Pope, and your Muse did right to mould them into a new-year simile of her own. At the same time, I dare not swear that the critics would not condemn it as contraband, though Pope's is more plainly a plagiarism than yours can fairly be deemed. . . . . I was greatly pleased and interested in the account which you give of the circumstances that awakened and have cherished poetical feelings in your breast. Their delightful and exhilarating influence you seem to have enjoyed; may you continue to enjoy it; but remember that they must be kept in subjection to duty, conscience, and self-interest—self-interest rightly understood, which prompts us to seek present and eternal happiness only in the ways of wisdom and the paths of peace. O if ever you slacken the reins of these fiery and impetuous feelings (which under due government will carry you round heaven and earth in the chariot of Poesy), your fate will be as deplorable as that of Phaeton, when he attempted to drive the horses of the sun, slipped, and made an anti-climax of his neck. I have been forced to let myself down by this unlucky anti-climax from the height of the foregoing simile, in the middle of which I was interrupted, and at the end of two days have not patience—even if I had time and space, though both are wanting—to work myself up into the sublime mood, in which I was dictating poetic oracles to you on Tuesday evening. I shall lose this post if I do not make haste; and as I am all in a hurry of preparation to leave Sheffield to go for a month to Scarborough, I am determined to hold Time by the heel, for I cannot get at his forelock, while I run my eye over the margin of your MS. poem on "Silence," and just pen down one or two of the ill-natured things that I have written on it in short-hand. Imprimis, a poem on silence is a poem on *nothing* : silence is a *negative*. This is not carping, or even *Eclectic* criticism, which you seem to dread so much ; it is a *solid* ground of objection against a poem cast on your plan. You have displayed powers of imagination far beyond anything I had expected of your genius, highly as I thought of it before ; yet you have failed— and an archangel would fail in the same way, though, perhaps, not in the same degree—to make silence a *distinct* and *consistent* being. The thing is impossible, and therefore be not discouraged by this harsh (only apparently harsh) condemnation. Whatever actions or attributes you may give to silence personified, you might give to a hundred other imaginary personages. For example, to confine myself to your first and second paragraphs. Is Silence *more* the sister of Chaos than *night* or *uproar* might be styled ? Does Silence " *sit* at the feet of Deity," "*walk* on the revolving spheres," "*look down* from the skies" upon the earth, or *dwell* among the Alps, where a breath may bring down an avalanche, and scare away the goddess ? All this might do well in *metaphor*, but it is incongruous in extended *allegory*. The fault I find, if I can make myself understood, is, that none of these things are *characteristic of her, and of her alone ;* for in truth Silence has only one characteristic—and that I confess sufficiently striking to distinguish her from all her sex—*holding her tongue !* The moment she speaks, or hears, or moves, she vanishes into nonentity, and no charm of poetry can possibly hold her. . . . . My time is expired, as well as my paper and my strength exhausted. I have a pain in my breast so severe when I lean an hour over a desk, as to make me very low indeed. This alone ought to exonerate me for twelve months, if I live so long, from answering the kindest letters. I will only add, that your poem on "Silence" has more beauties than I could number and describe, had I this whole sheet unoccupied before me. Therefore do not imagine that I am sensible only of its radical defect.

Sheffield, Jan. 19, 1810.

III. I take a large sheet of paper, because I intend to write a short letter; and it frequently happens with me, that when I sit down with that determination, the thoughts come so thick upon me towards the close, that I am forced to crowd more into the last ten lines than would eke out three pages in a fair round hand; a circumstance prodigiously provoking when one is inditing a random scrawl on the very back of Time, between his wings, and while he flies full speed after his unapproachable forelock. Now, as I am almost persuaded that these malicious thoughts lie in ambush in the brain, and watch the opportunity to rush upon me the moment they see that there is no room left for them, I am resolved to be beforehand with them on this occasion at least; and as I really have almost nothing to say, and not a minute to waste in saying less than nothing—that is, such stuff as this preamble is made of—I will, as briefly as may be, answer the main points of your two last obliging letters; and this I hope to do before I get to that part of the paper when ideas light like a swarm of hornets on my head, and sting me to distraction for want of a place to shake them off. The precious extract from Miss T——'s letter respecting the intended volume of the Band of Minstrels, was very refreshing to one whose spirits at that time were struggling with unprecedented difficulties, and *sore discouragements from other friends,* in the composition of that long poem with which I have secretly threatened the public. I finished it on the last Saturday

of the, old year, and have been *learning* to breathe ever
since. While this growing mountain lay on my breast
for seven months with increasing pressure, I scarcely could
draw a peaceful breath, but gasped like a fish which has
leaped upon the leaf of a water-lily, and cannot return
into. its element without falling into the jaws of a pursuing pike. But though this tremendous work is thus
completed—save the bitter penance of revisal—I know
not whether I shall publish it this season or no, as Mr.
Bowyer, for ever varying his plans and perplexing me
with his delays, has lately| made some proposals which
will, perhaps, issue in my publishing the "West Indies"
as the leading piece of my next volume, instead of the
" World before the Flood."

. . . I am well pleased with the alterations which
you quote from your amended poem of "Silence." I
knew that if you merely sat down to transcribe, you
would greatly improve and enrich it with new graces and
expressions, that would spontaneously sparkle out of the
subject. The altered stanza in your poem to "Fancy" is
very lovely in itself; and whether you intended it or no,
contains a most exquisite allusion to Orpheus in the
Shades, redeeming his lost Eurydice by the enchantment
of his lyre. Your motto, it seems, is from Hurdis: I
have no objection to make against either the poetry or the
application of it; I only notice it to say that Hurdis is
no favourite of mine. Both his sublimity and his humour
are equally forced; plants of Parnassus they were, I acknowledge, but raised in the hothouse of Cambridge.
There is, however, sometimes a mingled touch of plea-
santry and pathos in his pieces that is instantaneously
and permanently affecting—an unquestionable proof of
the power of genius, paralysed by pedantry and bad taste,
it generally appears to me. You, however, may like him

as much as you please, only *do not make him your model*, even in his best moods and most becoming apparel. The form of dedication which you propose pleases me exceedingly, and will honour me more than twenty pages filled with all the eloquences of eulogium by which Dryden was at once distinguished and disgraced.

Sheffield, May 6, 1810.

IV. . . . . I believe I ought to acknowledge the honour which the " Associate Minstrels" have done me, by their graceful dedication, in a congratulatory ode, recounting their merits and foretelling their future glories. But I am so entirely unaccustomed to write panegyrical or even complimentary verses, that I must, in plain prose and in plain truth, tell them, through you, that I most sincerely and fervently thank them for the most pleasing and elegant token of unbribed and unexpected approbation which I have yet received in public for the labours of my Muse. Thank them, therefore, individually, and thank them collectively; their kindness is not the less estimable because, except yourself, they are all unknown; though I suspect T. to be your father, whom I will not permit to remain quite a stranger; therefore present him with my cordial remembrance, and tell him he need not be ashamed of being caught, in his old age, dancing with his " old woman" in a circle of young minstrels. Youth looks more lovely, and age more venerable, when associated together in innocent pastime. Horace tells us, that when he was a boy, slumbering on a mountain, the ring-doves of Venus (*fabulosæ palumbes*—doves of renown), covered him with fresh leaves of laurel and myrtle, so that he slept safely amidst serpents and wild beasts—" Non sine dîs animosus infans." Now, though I am no more a boy than I am a Horace, I find myself covered with foliage more fragrant and flowering than myrtles and laurels, which unseen beings—not the fabled doves of Cytherea, nor the fairy bands of Queen Mab—have scattered upon me, and which perhaps will render me less vulnerable, though, alas! not secure, from the bears and vipers of criticism. By these I expect to be worried and stung from month to month, without mercy and without measure; for since I was stricken by the Hunter of the North, every ass can turn up his heels at me. You are right in your judgment of the motives that influenced the writer in the *Christian Observer*, if I have any discernment, or am not utterly blinded by the sense of wrong which he has done me. I have borne with patience, almost with disdain, the flippant and dogmatic reproaches which have been cast upon my *prosopopœia* (which is not an embodied and visible *personification*) of "the grave." I do not know that I shall ever be provoked to answer them, otherwise than by retaining the passage without any concession. You say truly, that the Bible would offer a fine field for such reviewers to display their wit and acumen. . . . .

I return to a much more delightful subject—the volume of the "Associate Minstrels." Your "Silence" is so much improved from its first form, that I am not disposed to find one fault in it here; but remember what I tell you now: when you are ten years older, you will see more defects in it than I have heretofore pointed out; but you will never need to blush for it; it is the promise of something so much greater than itself, that you must beware not to disappoint the expectations of your friends —shall I say, of the world?—by negligence or precipitancy. You ought now never to write on a mean or insipid subject, nor ever to do worse than your best, whatever be your theme. I speak more confidently of your talents to your face, because I spoke highly, romantically, of them before I saw your face or knew your name. This is a pledge, both to you and to me, that my commendations are sincere; and you cannot deny that my criticisms are the same.

Of your companions, I have only space to say little—and I am glad; because it will compel me to speak out and to speak warmly, leaving me no refuge for qualifying and neutralizing my honest praises. " A." is, in my mind, the queen of the assembly. She is a poet of a high order, the first, unquestionably, of those who write for children, and not the last, by hundreds, among those who write for men. The " Maniac's Song" has not only the " melancholy madness," but the " inspiration of poetry" also. The simile, page 97, is wonderfully fine, and I apprehend perfectly original. The two stanzas that contain it are as lovely as the stars they celebrate. " J." is very delicate and sprightly; there is a tender playfulness in her best manner that is truly fascinating. Your favourite, " E.," has a splendid imagination, and excels in description; her colouring is, like that of nature, glowing, and her pictures, like those of nature, harmonious; but she must travel a little wider, and vary her scenery more, lest she should lose the benefit of her other powers, which she has not yet discovered in herself, for lack of an opportunity of exercising them. " S." is a new signature to me; the lines, page 187, are peculiarly impressive; the *reality* of the subject (one which an author could scarcely have invented) gives them an affecting and awful interest. The lyre of S. does not disgrace the concert of the "Associate Minstrels." Of T.'s verses I have already spoken. I hope J.'s " reply" will induce him to take his harp from the willow, and tune it to the songs of Zion. On turning over the leaves to count the signatures, I find your good father signs " C., sen^r." (it had run in my foolish head, that T. was his mark, and that it was affixed to the " Farewell to the Muse"). I am therefore in the dark about " T." But after all these encomiums, you will very plausibly suspect that I am flattering you round, since I have not found any fault with any one of you! There may be room enough to find fault in your volume, but you see there is not room enough in my letter; therefore you must excuse me that trouble, especially as I have no doubt that you are all aware of more motes in your eyes than I can see, for the beam in mine. To the best of you I would say—Do better, and better still, to the end of your career. . . . . I can't say another word here, but God bless you.

V. . . . The " Ode to Cheerfulness" is certainly one of your most spirited pieces, and I do not wonder that it is a favourite with yourself; yet I am not sure that readers in general will be particularly delighted with it, because few can sympathise with the emotions that inspired it, and still fewer will take the pains to understand the allegories that adorn yet obscure every paragraph. It is quite a hieroglyphic piece of writing; it has the general fault of your poetry—a splendid fault, I acknowledge, and it has that fault in the utmost excess —more light than fire, more imagination than passion; it is as much painting as verse, and is addressed more to the eye than to the heart. I tell you these things freely, because I do not fear offending you, and it may do you good to know the impression which your compositions make on other minds than your own, and those of your immediate and most intimate friends, who have, in their various degrees, the same genius and taste as yourself.

Sheffield, Nov. 5, 1810.

VI. DEAR FRIEND,—I am at all times so far in arrears with my correspondents, that you must not wonder if I write to you much less, as well as much seldomer than you deserve. There is nothing that I desire so much as to receive, and nothing that I dread more than to write, letters from and to the friends that I esteem and love; of this number be assured you are one, whether I tell you so once a month, or once in seven years. . . . .

With respect to your exposition and vindication of the figurative form of your poetry, I can only thank you for it, and acknowledge it to be as ingenious as it is candid. If I were with you, I might talk you to stupefaction on this subject, but really I must forbear entering upon it otherwise than casually and lightly by letter. One may talk spontaneously with great interest and animation on such a flowery and fertile theme, either of argument or illustration; but I could not pretend to *write* upon it without more expense of thought than I can afford at present. I must therefore leave it till we meet, with this remark, which I believe your own observation will justify, that I myself am the most metaphysical poet of the age, if I deserve the name of poet in the age of Campbell, and Southey, and Scott. . . .

You must not be too impatient to be put out of your misery (the misery of suspense) by the reviewers. Those gentry praise or censure to suit their own time and convenience; and poor authors destined either for the laurel or the cudgel must wait for their turn, which comes soon enough, I assure you, when it comes at all, especially if it be a hard turn. Can anything be imagined more unreasonable than the impatience of eels to be skinned, or lobsters to be boiled alive? Nothing, truly, except the *immense desire* of a poet to be reviewed. Yet it is a very natural and very tormenting desire. I feel it almost as irksome at this time, as if I were still a fresh-water author, and had never been thrown headlong, and sunk lower than ever plummet sounded, in the black sea of criticism, to be devoured by sharks and sword-fishes. I was astonished last month, not at the clemency (which was the utmost I expected from that reverend quarter), but at the prodigality of the *British Critic*, in praising my "West Indies;" but it only makes me tremble more at the apprehension of tortures yet to come from other judges and tribunals. I have not the remotest means of conjecturing whether the Edinburgh savages will bind me to the stake again, to endure their exquisite cruelties, or whether they will condescend to overlook me altogether. . . . .

I shall expect almost unprecedented excellence in Southey's new poem; but I do not like the name, for I do not know how to pronounce it. This may appear a frivolous objection; it is, however, the most serious that I can yet urge against his poem. When I have seen it, this will, of course, be done away ; and I wish I may not be able to find another fault about it.

June 11, 1811.

VII. MY DEAR FRIEND,—Three of your unacknowledged favours lie open before me; I have just now re-perused them, and in order to pacify my conscience, I thank you at once, and with my whole heart, for these affectionate tokens of your unwearied kindness to one who so often puts your friendship to a test which proves its purity and disinterestedness ; the small and slow returns that my poverty of spirit enables me to make for your frequent and liberal communications will, however, be accepted by you with an indulgence which will not fail to lay me under yet deeper obligations. . . .

I thank you particularly for the ingenious pamphlet on the subject of Reviews, which, a few passages excepted, I have read with great pleasure and entire approbation. . . . . I wish that all the writers and readers, critics and poets especially, in the kingdom would peruse your friend's essay as diligently as I have done; and if they found as much pleasure in it, they would think themselves well repaid. I do not choose to acknowledge that I have felt rebuked, or that I shall be profited, by any passage referring to criticism. So far as the author has condescended to notice me as a poet, I felt that I ought to be humbled by the honour which he has conferred upon me; but I fear that I have not to quarrel with him, but with you, for dragging me before the public as a suspected critic. Even the indiscreet zeal of friendship, which may have induced you to proclaim me an *Eclectic* reviewer, can scarcely be admitted as a justificatory plea for placing me in a most invidious situation. I forgive you, because you are too young and too warm-hearted to know any better. But, my dear friend, I have no ambition to shine as a critic; and I am weak enough to be ashamed to be known as one, for reasons that are too complicated and perhaps too delicate to be exhibited in the "tangible shape" of written words. But I do not mean to shrink from any responsibility which may attach to me for my presumed connection with the *Eclectic Review;* nor will I hesitate *now*, since I am braved to it, to acknowledge that I have at different times contributed articles to the work. It is not probable, however, that I shall in future be answerable either for its defects or its excellences in any degree, unless some unforeseen circumstance should make me feel it my duty to assume the mask of Aristarchus. The exposure of my name in your friend's pages is, I assure you most conscientiously, a sufficient punishment for all the 'critical crimes that I have committed; and if you knew how many temptations to commit more I have resisted and overcome, you would perhaps think that I ought to have been freely forgiven the sins that I did, for the sake of those that I did not. While I am talking about the *Eclectic*, I am naturally reminded of your vehement censure of the critic of "Kehama." I do not think so harshly of the article as you seem to do; it is written with great power, though not with much vigour or address. I have no idea who the author is, and therefore I can speak impartially between the reviewer and the poet; but if I were inclined to say that the latter had ever deserved the anathemas of the former, I would add, that the former ought not to have bestowed them so heartily and heavily as he has done—perhaps only from want of ability to lay them on lighter. I have not yet read the poem through. About a month ago I had an opportunity of looking into it, and I *ran a-muck*, if I may use the expression, through about two-thirds of it; and I may say that it pleased and provoked me more than any work of Southey's had done before. Its merits are above my praise; of its faults I am not disposed to speak. When Southey excels all living poets, and equals the greatest of the dead, it is *because he cannot help it;* when he falls and grovels, it is *on purpose*. The buoyancy of genius carries him, by its own irresistible impulse, into the highest heaven of invention; but by headlong violence done to himself, he sometimes descends into a gross and earthly atmosphere, in which he can neither breathe nor fly with freedom. But in "Kehama" I do not mean to blame him so much for degrading, as for misapplying his talents. This subject is, however, too copious for a letter; we will talk about it when we meet, as I said before of other equally prolific subjects.

I have not seen Mr. S. in Sheffield during the spring, as I was tempted to hope from your hint concerning his journey to town. But who am I, that I should think of him turning aside even for a moment to look at me? Well, I am as proud a man, if I am not as great a poet, as he is: if the mountain will not come to Mahomet, Mahomet will not go to the mountain! He is the superior, and therefore, if we meet, he must take the first step; and then I will take two, three, twenty, to "kiss the shadow of his shoe-tie."

You will give me credit for having been duly enraged at first, and most magnanimously indifferent afterwards, at the miserable splenetic attack of the monthly reviewer on the "Associate Minstrels." Even in that work I never saw anything more pitiful. But yet this important critic happens to be placed on such an eminence, that he can amuse himself with breaking the heads of giants below, by dropping pebbles upon them as they pass. It is the height from which they fall, and not the strength of the arm that hurls them, which makes them fatal.

. . . . Reversing the terms of the saying of Socrates, I would observe of Southey, that the Reviewers may *hurt* him, but they cannot *kill* him. This reminds me of the sneer of the Edinburgh Reviewers at Bloomfield and myself in their critique on "Kehama." I am afraid that this has been thrown out as the signal of a broadside attack from that quarter on my last volume. I must bear it if it comes. I am far from being ashamed of being classed with Bloomfield, who is a true poet, or he never could have outlived the praises of Capel Lofft, which would have suffocated any earth-born muse.

L

" I would not for a world of gold
That Nature's lovely face should tire."

Should these two simple lines of Robert Bloomfield's be preserved alone of all his writings to the hundredth generation of posterity, as a quotation in some immortal work, these two lines alone will satisfy the age to come that their author was a poet of exquisite feeling. Remember me most kindly to him, and say that I long to see the " Banks of the Wye."

September 13, 1811.

VIII. If you are not alarmed at the size of this sheet of paper, I am; and I shall reduce its blank immensity with all possible expedition, thereby probably increasing your consternation as I diminish my own. But really if I have patience to fill these formidable pages with common sense in common English, I think you may find courage to read them. Last Thursday evening I sat down seriously to write to you; but when I had re-perused your late letters, and repeatedly conned over the verses without a name, I was interrupted, and compelled to postpone my design; however, to convince you that I had been heartily thinking of you at that time, I despatched my messenger *Iris* by that night's post to intimate that I should soon follow her in due epistolary form; and I doubt not that she was as welcome to you as ever, in the days of her divinity, she was to any favourite of Saturnian Juno on an errand of mischief. In my service I trust she is better employed, though no longer " *Iris de cœlo*," but a true *terræ filia*. . . . .

First, the verses headed by Adrian's address to his soul, of which you are very naturally as fond as he was of it, and apparently not less anxious concerning their future welfare; for you have thrice challenged me to prove their mortality if I could; after I had twice failed to do this, you ought to have been satisfied, and "*Io triumphe!*" sung with all your might. Indeed, unless I descend to verbal criticism, I cannot find another fault in them than I have already found, and you have disproved. I have stated that they want compression, to which you have replied, victoriously, "Want compression, when I have just added four new verses to them!" Perhaps, I ought either to have said that they want *perspicuity*, which, in my opinion, would be the *effect of compression*. I would not have a thought less—they have not a thought to spare, for all the thoughts are good; but I should like to see them in half the compass of words, because they would then appear with twice the advantage. This you know in theory, and in criticising the second canto of my "World before the Flood," you can preach it to me most eloquently and unanswerably, tracing it even to one of its causes—the employment of *rhyme* but you have to learn it in practice; and it will not serve you to plead that I am as great a sinner as yourself; for grant that, what follows? We can both teach what we do not know; for to *know* what is right is to *do* it; to *say* it is neither. A parrot may say, "Lord, bless me!" or . . . but can a parrot either pray or swear?

. . . The piece turns on two ideas—the possibility of spiritual communion in absence and in the body, and the future state of the soul. Few, I fear, of your readers will nicely distinguish these points, or clearly comprehend to *which* you allude, or even to *what* you allude, in some of the verses. This is my main objection to the piece; and as its truth must rest on fact, and not on argument, I leave it to you to prove, by making experiments on your friends with the poem itself. If it leaves a distinct and lively impression *of your views* upon their minds, in the order in which you have exhibited those views, then I am mistaken, and your poem is as immortal as the soul of Adrian, or at least it will live as long as his dying speech.

With regard to the trochaic rhymes, I answer, that where they are happily employed their effect is exquisite; but wherever they surprise by their novelty, the effect is either harsh or ludicrous. (On reading over my letter, I recollect that I wrote a valentine last February, with trochaic rhymes; if I had room I would send it, that you might have your revenge.) Our language is deficient of these, or rather deficient of variety in the terminations of these; for you may rhyme double from A to Z in Johnson's Dictionary, by taking the participles of verbs; but these soon weary the ear, and though they must be frequently used, they should be mingled at due distances with others. Rhyme in verse ought to have a *general,* not a *particular* effect. It is most enchantingly felt where it is least obtrusive, either by its harshness or singularity. Uncommon rhymes, even iambics, almost inevitably dissolve the charm of a sublime or affecting passage; and it is the misfortune of trochaics in our language, that the rhymes must either be so common as to be despised, or so uncommon as to be strange; in each case they are made too prominent, and betray the artifice of the poet and the poverty of his art. To conceal the latter is the acme of his skill, and to conceal himself is almost as difficult; but he must do both to captivate his reader, and move and melt, and raise him at his will.

At first sight it appears extraordinary that there should be so few rhymes, either iambic or trochaic, in liberal use among our best poets; and one would imagine that the ear would be quite disgusted with the perpetual recurrence of the same endings in any hundred verses of any poem that is published. Now, this would assuredly be the case if the rhymes were always emphatical, or in any considerable degree more striking than the other syllables of the line; but their sweet correspondence, and the momentary suspension of the breath after uttering them, have no other effect in good poetry than that of binding and harmonizing the whole, and prevailing throughout like the key-note and its chord in a strain of music. In truth, we are no more offended by the frequent return of the same rhymes, than we are with the everlasting repetition of those particles that occur in every sentence, such as *and, if, but;* which proves that rhymes ought not to be emphatical, or so uncommon as to strike. I cannot expatiate further on the subject; we will renew it when we meet. I will only, lest I should forget it hereafter, in reply to a question in your last note, say, that I do *not* "concede that rhyme tempts to diffuseness;" and to convince you by a greater authority than my own, I refer you to what Pope says in his introduction to the "Essay on Man:"—"I chose verse, and *even rhyme,* because I could express [my principles] more shortly this way than in prose itself." And he exemplified it, for I know nothing in our language so clear and concise as the best passages in that essay. At the same time, I acknowledge that those who write in rhyme may be diffuse if they please; the wisdom of Solomon did not prevent him from making a fool of himself, but it was by his own choice. I do not set up a justification of my misconduct here; I only vindicate, as I ever must, the dignity of rhyme. Blank verse of the highest order (I mean the *best* blank verse of every order) I read with true delight; but I cannot tolerate it when it is only tolerable. When I was fourteen years old, I wrote a long poem (about 150 lines), in blank verse, which I thought divine as I was composing it; when it was finished I thought better of it, for I burnt it as soon as I had read it! I may say I have never fairly attempted blank verse since. A hundred rude lines in various fragments, at different times, as far as I can recollect, would comprehend all my exploits in that stony ground of literature.

I have been exceedingly gratified with the few things concerning Southey that I find in your late letters. I wish you had seen more of him, for, as I could not see him with my own eyes, I should have been happy to have seen him with yours, and received the image of his mind reflected from a mirror worthy of it—from yours. This is not a compliment; if it looks like one, you must not believe its looks; when the truth comes, I will write it to my friend, though I know it will make him blush to read it. If Southey had chosen an antediluvian subject, he might have written it in blank verse; but it no more follows that I should do so, than that I should write a poem equal to him, because I have chosen the subject on which I understand his great mind once brooded. What a new creation rising from the old should we have witnessed, had he proceeded in his glorious work! He may yet resume it; I have not monopolized the theme. As you intimate, he would have given "a more antediluvian air to the drama." I have not thought it necessary, in my view of the subject, to exhibit a black-letter world, by building antiquarian stubble upon the magnificent foundation which I have chosen. I thought it sufficient that the manners, and persons, and scenes should be such as may, without violence of probability or any extraordinary effort of mind, be supposed to have existed before the flood; not displayed with minute and ostentatious

particularity, displaying at every step the learning and
labour of the author,`pressing into his service all that.
truth or tradition has told us concerning the infancy of.
Time. In all the poems of Walter Scott and Southey, I
find much of this extraneous learning and labour—descriptions for the sake of descriptions, that perpetually
remind me of deficiency by superfluity. It is not all that.
we know of an age and a people long past, that will present to our minds the most *natural*, or the most *perfect*
picture of the age and people ; for when all are exhibited.
together, however arranged by the hand of genius and
taste, there must be many heterogeneous materials that
prove how much is in reality wanting to complete
them. A selection of the principal characteristics of the
subject, brought home to our understandings and our
hearts by being blended with a great proportion of
those circumstances and sympathies which are common
in all periods and to all human beings, appears to me at
once the most rational and excellent way to treat of any
grand events remote from common life. I have twined a
Gordian knot about my pen, and I must cut it, or I shall
not unloose it to the end of my paper. I will only reply
to your remark that "Scott would have painted a better
forest," by saying that mine, I mean the wild part of it,
is a humble picture *of a primeval North American forest*,
growing up into a sylvan temple of stupendous height,
with columnar trunks, a roof of branches, and a floor of
massive roots. I am sorry that he paints "prettier cottages ;" but as for "more picturesque prophets," he is welcome to them. Without vanity, here I may borrow the
happy phrase of your friend, and say, Mr. Scott may
paint the "matter of which prophets are made ;" give me
to paint the "mind" that was in them. Thank you, my
dear friend, for all your animating commendations of

those features in my poem which pleased you, and your gentle, but deep-piercing strictures on those which did not satisfy you. The latter I am not disposed to defend now ; your opinion will have great weight with me when I reconsider the second canto.

You have very ably vindicated Mr. C. O'Reid, and you have convinced me that I ought meekly to submit to every consequence of my own imprudence, or the indiscreet kindness of those whom I love : as my friends must suffer at least as much from me as I can from them, the reciprocity is very fair. . . . . . Now, I'll tell you a secret— but not all of it neither. On the second day of last July, I think about five o'clock in the afternoon, your soul met mine in the second page of a certain sheet of paper, and told me (not in words, for souls do talk "with most miraculous organ") who Mr. O'Reid *is*. But I won't tell anybody. Now, my dear friend, if you can recollect that your soul was on travel that day, it will be proof positive of the truth of your speculation, that "spirit *can* with spirit blend, and that, in unseen communion, thought can hold the distant friend." Another proof of this ineffable intercourse is, that I was meditating on this very subject over your verses, at the time that you, in all probability, were forwarding your franked letter to the post-office; for it was in the evening of Tuesday, just as the shades were shutting in, and perhaps some of the obscurity which I then attributed to your poetry arose from the light in which I read it. . . . .

I shall be happy to hear that your honoured father has found the health, and quiet, and spirits, that you tell me he is gone from home to seek. May these, with a clear conscience, and a heart filled with the love of God and overflowing in love to man, be his portion and yours, and the portion of all whom you esteem upon earth. I have only this line to say, that your little address to Time pleases 'me very much, except the glance at "Feeling's inmost cell." Write freely and fully to me whenever you are disposed. I am sincerely your obliged friend,

J. MONTGOMERY.

P.S.—"It cannot rain but it pours."—*Old Proverb.* Here's a letter three leagues long; put on the giant's boots to get through it. I do not know who Z.Y.X. is. I have seen several pieces in the Christian Paper (?) so signed. They are close imitations of Wordsworth. *None but Southey could write* "Not to the grave," etc.

IX. . . . You will have seen, before you receive this letter, that I gratefully accepted your verses on the Comet, though the comet itself was but the nucleus of them, and the brilliant emanations of thought that arose from it gave a glory to the subject, more appropriate perhaps than even unity could have conferred. But this must not encourage you often to take such flights of unreturning fancy from the original theme. It is rarely in a poet's life, perhaps not oftener than the visitation of a comet, that he may indulge in such eccentricity. I have incurred much severe censure for giving-loose to imagination in this manner; in secret I love it, but I dare not now hazard it. The lady who dreamed of me in the shape of a comet, had an intuitive perception of my poetical character; neither the sun of a system, nor yet a primary or secondary planet, revolving round any superior luminary in a regular round, but cast off in an orbit so elliptical, that it is doubtful whether I belong to any certain centre, or, if I do, whether the age of man will allow me sufficient time to return to my *primum mobile.* I find the judgments of friends as well as my critics, concerning my productions, so exceedingly at variance with each other, and often so opposite to my own, that I begin to despair of ever accomplishing any work of imagination that will not lay me open to the pity of my well-wishers, and the contempt of my enemies. My repeated failures in the poem which has now been long under my hand, have taught me that I can seldom, almost never, rely upon my own feelings or taste; while the taste and feelings of my advisers being frequently irreconcileable, I am bewildered and disheartened to such a degree, that I have repeatedly thrown the work aside for months, and then resumed it with new spirit and hopes, to be broken and disappointed again, as soon as I put the decisions of my own mind to the test of those of another. If from him I appealed to a third or a fourth, I only plunged from one trouble into a greater, being differently condemned or praised for this passage or that throughout the whole piece; so that my poor poem is in the same predicament as the hog with the Mussulmen, each preferring a part, though he rejects the rest, " till quite from snout to tail 'tis eaten." . . .

Pray, where did Mr. Southey or yourself learn that rhyme, in the heroic measure, wearies more than blank verse? "Pope's ' Iliad ' wearies," you say; Milton's "Paradise Lost" does the same, Dr. Johnson will tell you. No long poem either in blank verse or rhyme will please idle readers, and the generality of readers are idle; therefore, no long poem, whatever be its form, will be read through by these; yet it may be popular on account of certain passages that seize every mind, and possess it with such fulness of delight, that the whole is admired and commended for their sake; though few read the whole, and none without that weariness which is consequent upon every exercise of the mind in following

the thoughts of another, especially if that other be superior.
I am perfectly convinced that a poem of any equal length
and equal merit, in rhyme, will be more successful than
another in blank verse; but were this not my persuasion,
I am such a stranger to the composition of the latter,
that it would be folly for me to attempt it at present.

Sheffield, Nov. 12, 1819.

X. MY DEAR FRIEND,—I have so long neglected
you, that I am ashamed, even on paper, to look you in
the face. An unanswered note of yours has lain, I believe,
two years in a drawer of my writing-desk, among many
others from east, west, north, and south, which I have
either not found time, or courage, or inclination, to
answer as they deserved. . . . This is the way that
I serve all my friends, and whether I can help it or not,
it *is* so, and *as* I am; thus you must either be content to
bear with me, or cast me off, for I fear I shall never
mend; and not one of them, nay, not all put together,
have so much reason to complain of this failing as I myself have. It is the misery of my life, for procrastina-
tion runs through all I do; and when or how I shall
overtake Time, I know not; I am always so far behind
him, that it is no very rash prophecy to say that I shall
live at least a month after the day of my death. But I
must not trifle any longer in preamble. Since I saw you
last (four years ago, I believe) I have had to pass through
many trials, and have suffered severely in mind, body,
and estate, from loss of peace, of health, and of property.
Into particulars I cannot go at present; suffice it to say,
that in the month of August last I was so far worn
down with sickness and exhaustion, that I seemed to
draw nigh to the gates of death. The mighty and the
merciful hand that led me thither did not leave me there,

but has preserved me to this hour, and strengthened me
so far, that I am nearly well, though yet a bruised reed,
and a reed shaken by every wind. I have been from
home nearly two months, for rest and refreshment. Your
letter met me on my return, and I take an early opportunity, *this time*, to answer it, and to assure you that I
have never forgotten you as a friend, nor remembered you
without self-reproach. If you knew how uncomfortably
I have been circumstanced for a long time past, and how
continually I have been harassed and overwhelmed with
necessary employments, both private and public, amidst
cares, anxieties, and sufferings, which have broken my
heart and borne down my spirit, you would not think
hardly of me, though, in the consciousness of superior
self-command, you might perceive that most of my mis-
fortunes were brought upon me by my own weakness,
and aggravated by my own perversity. I must not complain any more, or you will think me mad and going to
Bedlam, or bankrupt and going to prison. Neither of
these hideous alternatives is the case; I have still intellect enough to render all my follies inexcusable, and
property enough to make me the most ungrateful of
human beings if I repine at my lot. . . .

With respect to Campbell's Poets, it is true that I
long ago expressed a desire to have the work to review
when I was in the practice of writing occasionally for
the *E. R.* During the last six years, my mind has
been forced to bear the yoke, and exercise itself so
much on tasks, not of its own choosing, though tasks in
which it generally delighted, that all its superfluous
energy, if it had any such, has been expended in Bible,
Missionary, School, and other noble institutions, and
their concerns, as universal reporter and advocate in
every way that opened before me; I say, my mind (in

addition to poetry, to which I have paid little attention, and my business, to which I have perhaps paid less), has been so much engaged in these things, that I have found little time or interest for any other kind of literary exertions. This is the only reason why I declined to write for the *E. R.* If I had deserted it for any other work of the same kind, you might justly have condemned me. I am at present so crowded with duties, that I dare not undertake Campbell, . . . my time and talents (such as they are) being so little at my control, that I am uncertain when I could seriously sit down to the task. I must therefore forego it. . . . Remember me most gratefully and respectfully to Mrs. C., and believe me truly, your friend,

         ` J. MONTGOMERY.

FROM MR. ELLIOTT TO DR. J. PYE SMITH.*

         Sheffield, November 13, 1822.

REV. SIR,—I believe you will have no recollection of me, but in better days I have seen you at my cousin's, Dr. Robinson, of Masbro'. I, indeed, have not much recollection of you, but I remember I was always glad to find you at my cousin's, or to hear that you were expected; and it is this remembrance which emboldens me to violate my nature, by troubling you with a letter which concerns not you, and perhaps does not deserve to interest you at all. I have requested Mr. Warren, of Old Bond Street, to forward to the *Eclectic Review* Office, directed to you, a copy of my new publication, "Love, a poem; with The Giaour, a satire;" in the hope that you will read it and review it, if you find anything in it worthy of praise. The former poem was read in manuscript by Mr. Montgomery, two years ago, with considerable,

         * See *ante*, p. 128.

though qualified praise, and it owes him much. The satire I dared not to show him, and you will not like it, because it is one; but it is honestly, though warmly, written. Its object is to retort on Lord Byron the sarcasms with which he has assailed the Lake Poets. I am under great obligations to Mr. Southey, two of whose letters to me I annex. With a warm-hearted condescension, which I can never repay, he taught me all that I know of the art of poetry. Hitherto I have published without risk; but I am now risking what I cannot afford, if the book should not succeed. Perhaps it is not the least of my sins that, throughout all my troubles, I have retained an inextinguishable longing to leave behind me—a name. I compare my unsuccessful writings with the successful ones of others; and I cannot allow that their fate is deserved. Yet, as the Reviewers do not take up my books, I write in vain; and my first and last poor hope is withering amid the gloom that grows upon me. Since my removal to Sheffield I think I have had hints that my shattered frame will not last for ever; my constitution, at the early age of forty-two, is giving way; and I am not at this moment sure that my mind itself is in health. I seldom go to a place of worship without a dread approaching to horror; and I scarcely, of late, hear a sermon, but I return feverish, and pass a sleepless night, with a grating weight at my breast, as if I had swallowed a brick. While I retained in its integrity my belief in the doctrines of philosophical religion, I was at least calm; but what are now my bosom inmates? Not indifference—not, oh, not unbelief, but rebellious convicted reason's anxiety and terror; hopeless expectation, anticipated death. Yet, as Camoens, when shipwrecked, swam with the "Lusiad" in his hand, I, in the presence of despondency itself, still more and more earnestly yearn to leave behind me, in some faint shadow of my mind, a proof that "this intellectual being, these thoughts that wander through eternity," once existed; so indefatigable is the restless instinct that was born with me, whether it be of genius, of madness, or of folly. I am, reverend sir, most respectfully your servant,

E. ELLIOTT.

(*Copies.*)

Keswick, Jan. 30, 1819.

I received your little volume yesterday. There are abundant evidences of power in this poem.* Its merits are of the most striking kind; and its defects are not less striking, both in plan and execution. The stories had better have been separate than linked together without any natural or necessary connection. The first consists of such grossly improbable circumstances, that it is altogether as improbable as if it were a supernatural tale. It is also a hateful story, presenting nothing but what is painful. In the second, the machinery is preposterously disproportioned to the occasion. And in all the poems there is too much ornament, too much effort, too much labour. You think you can never embroider your drapery sufficiently, and that the more gold and jewels you fasten on it, the richer the effect must be. The consequence is, that there is a total want of what the painters call breadth and keeping; and therefore the effect is lost.

You will say that this opinion proceeds from the erroneous system which I have pursued in my own writings, and which has prevented my poems from obtaining the same popularity as those of Lord Byron and Walter Scott. But look at those poets whose rank is established beyond controversy. Look at the Homeric poems, at Virgil, Dante, Ariosto, Milton. Do not ask yourself

* "Night: a Descriptive Poem."

what are the causes of success or failure of your con-
temporaries; their failure or success is not determined
yet;—a generation—an age—a century will not suffice
to determine it: but see what it is by which those poets
have made themselves immortal, who, after the illapse of
centuries, are living and acting upon us still.

I should not speak to you thus plainly of your fault
—the sin by which the angels fell—if it were not for the
great powers which are impaired by misdirection. And
it is for the sake of bearing testimony to those powers
that I am now writing.

You may do great things, if you cease to attempt so
much; if you will learn to proportion your figures to
your canvas, cease to overlay your foreground with florid
ornaments, and be persuaded, that in a poem, as well as in
a picture, there must be lights and shades—that the general effect can never be good unless the subordinate parts
be kept down, and that the brilliancy of one part is
brought out and heightened by the repose of another.
One word more. With your powers of thought and
expression, you need not seek to produce effect by monstrous incidents and exaggerated characters. These drams
have been administered so often that they are beginning
to lose their effect. And it is to truth and nature that
we must come at last. Trust to them, and they will bear
you through. You must reverence your elders more.

Yours faithfully,
ROBERT SOUTHEY.

To Mr. Elliott,
    New Masbro', near Rotherham.

Keswick, June 29, 1821.

Your "Peter Faultless" has found his way to me, in
one of my slow parcels. Thank you for the book. The

charge of indecency ought not to have been made against it; but there are parts which are coarser than the age will bear. The surest criterion in such cases is a woman's feelings. Whatever Mrs. Elliott would not like to read aloud in company, you would do well to expunge.

There is great power both of conception and expression in even the most faulty of these poems. The stories are better imagined than they are made out. The serious poems have very great merit. Indeed, the graver your subject, and the higher you pitch your tone, the better you succeed. Thirty years ago, these pieces would have excited general attention. Thirty years hence, somebody will assume credit for finding out their merit. Present reputation depends far less upon real desert, than upon trick, tinsel, trashiness, mannerism, fashion, and accident. But merit outlives all these, and finds its place at last.

I am versifying a little, and prosing a great deal. My History of the Peninsular War keeps me closely employed.

It is, I hope, needless to say, that if any chance should bring you into these parts, I shall be heartily glad to shake you by the hand. Yours, very truly,

ROBT. SOUTHEY.

(FROM ROBERT SOUTHEY TO JOSIAH CONDER.)

Keswick, May 5, 1812.

MY DEAR SIR,—I received last night the communications with which you and your highly esteemed friends have favoured me. They are sent off this evening to Edinburgh, with my recommendation, little as they stand in need of it; and if the editor be not already overstocked, or if they should not arrive too late, I have no doubt but that he will be as happy to insert them as I shall be to see them there. The discretion which you gave me, I so far used as to affix your name to the stanzas with the Latin motto, knowing how naturally every reader into whose hands they may fall will inquire who is the author.

Upon the subject of the new system of education, two persons who desire the general good, and have neither party nor private interests to serve, can hardly fail of coming to the same conclusion, when they understand each other, and understand the system. My view of the subject is, that it is a thing of far too great importance to be trusted to so evanescent a source of support as contributions, of which nine-tenths are procured like votes at a county election, by dint of earnest solicitation and the activity of party spirit. It is the interest, the business, and the duty of the State to provide for the education of all those whose parents have not the means of providing it for them. Parochial schools ought to be established in every parish throughout the kingdom. If this were done, it is absurd to expect that the State should not provide that these children be educated according to the religion of the State; that is to say, that they should be instructed in the Church catechism. And it would naturally follow, that the parish priest should become the superintendent of the parish school. My own wish would be, that the parish clerk should always be the master; care being taken to train up a race for this purpose, for thus the character would be raised into respectability.

Thus much for the application of the system in England. In Scotland, of course, such alterations are to be made as would suit the catechism to the Kirk (though I believe little, if any, would be required); and in Ireland, when you give it to the Catholics, you must let them teach their monstrous idolatry. But you are not to expect that a scheme will succeed in that country, which

endeavours to embrace Papist and Protestant, by care-
fully excluding all points of difference. The Papists are
far too wise to suffer this; and I know that when it has
been tried, and a few parents have been found willing to
send their children to these schools, the priest has way-
laid them with a horsewhip, and horsewhipped them
back. I have not seen your friend's book, but Mr.
Wakefield and the Bishop of Meath have told me several
curious facts which tend to show that the horsewhip is
of almost as much use to the Irish priest as the crucifix!

With regard to the origin of the new system, it is
no more a matter of consequence than that it is always
of consequence that impostors should be exposed, and
honour awarded where it is due. Lancaster is not only,
by the admission of his own partisans, a worthless and an
impudent fellow, but he has materially injured the system
which he has stolen. The mode of teaching spelling and
writing at once, destroys entirely the two fundamental
laws of the Madras system—that whatever is learnt must
be learnt thoroughly, and that every boy must find his
level. And by his system of punishment he sows the
seeds of the vilest passions.

He derives his popularity from the worthlessness of
his most conspicuous opponents—John Bowles, Arch-
deacon Daubeny, the Rev. Dr. Hook, etc.—fellows with
whom it is mortifying to think alike upon any subject,
because you are sure they would not be right, if it were
not for some unworthy motive. The Dissenters are consistent in taking up his cause, but I do not think they
are wise in doing it. There is a monstrous coalition of
fanatics, infidels, and Roman Catholics against the Church
of England. I do not subscribe to the Church; if I could
do it, I should be in orders—an office to which my inclination would always strongly have led me. My mind has

undergone many changes, and is in many points nearer to the Church than when I forbore to enter it as a minister. Still, I am far from being in communion with it, or from ever expecting to be so. But I am perfectly sensible of the infinite good which we derive from such a Church, and of the dreadful consequences which would inevitably attend its overthrow. Your metaphor of the waste lands is a happy one ; what I contend against is that scheme of improvement which would throw down the inclosures. You will agree with me that the great object is to secure the benefit of national education ; this can only be done by a permanent parochial establishment. When next I write to Murray, I will desire him to give you my treatise upon Bell and the Dragon, which goes to this end. It is in a spirit of controversy, which is not ill directed when its aim is to expose the falsehoods of such writers as the Edinburgh Reviewers.

I hope your good father continues well. Believe me, yours very truly,

ROBERT SOUTHEY.

Keswick, May 15, 1813.

II. At length I have received your packet, with your letter of March 2nd. I thank you for its contents. Robert Hall's pamphlet has done its work. I trust also that the important object for which Claudius Buchanan has so long pleaded will now be effected, and that there will be a regular Church Establishment formed for India. It will greatly facilitate the progress of the missionaries, and give stability to all which they do. And the missionaries themselves, of whatever persuasion they may be, will feel as Britons of every reformed communion used to feel in Portugal, when Protestant and Papist were the only demarcations which were acknowledged.

The poem is spirited, and in a good strain. It happens that the first two lines rhyme, and this leading me to suppose that the poem was in couplets, I felt *balked* in the fourth verse, at coming to *nigh* instead of *near*.

The Hymns, like all the other productions from that quarter, succeed admirably in what they aim at. I shall rejoice to see your "Reverie" preserved in a proper place. If the editors of the *Ed. An. Register* had known what was good from what was good for nothing, they would have found no difficulty in making room for its insertion. My influence in that quarter is confined to my own department.

Thank you for your letter respecting our excellent friend Neville. I have been too much occupied to write to him, and of late my spirits have wanted their usual elasticity. A brother of my wife's, who came here hoping to enjoy a few weeks of relaxation, is lingering under a complication of obscure and incurable diseases ; and how long he may live, or rather how long he may continue dying, is what no medical skill can foresee. I know just enough of nosology to punish me for ever having looked into the science without making it my study. Not an ailment can occur among my children that I cannot in my own mind explain by some alarming cause ; and thus little illnesses, which men who lived less with their children would hardly hear of, and men in healthier feelings and happier ignorance would never think of, give me serious disquietude. It seems as if I had as many hopes and fears as the veriest worldling, and that having none with respect to common worldly objects, they had all taken this direction.

Montgomery has not written to me for many months, and I have long intended to tell him so. I see his " World before the Flood" advertised, and when next I write to Murray, will take a place in the *Quarterly* for it. Reviews, unluckily, are much more effectual instruments in the hands of an enemy than of a friend; but I will do what I can to procure justice for him, with as much sincerity as good will.

My own poem is but half written. My annual and quarterly avocations fill up a larger portion of my time than I would spare to them if I were but equally remunerated for better things. However, if no untoward events should impede me, I shall get on rapidly with the poem during the summer, and put the concluding volume of Brazil to the press in the course of six or eight weeks.

Why did not your cousin bring you an account of the *inside* of my house, as well as of the outside? A line from you would have procured him ready admittance, and such attentions as a stranger may find useful. Remember this in future.

Keswick, May 4, 1814.

III. Thank you for the Reviews. . . . They contain much to repay a perusal, and a man need not be as tolerant as I am to excuse a little that he may disapprove, for the sake of a great deal which deserves his approbation.

Like all other journals, it sins sometimes on the side of severity, and drags an unhappy author into notice for the mere purpose of disgracing him. If it professed to notice every work which comes out, it would, of course, be proper to condemn all that deserved condemnation; but even in that case, it is condemnation enough to be merely noticed without praise. Beyond this, severity is unnecessary (except where there be some especial demerit), and therefore, I think, not to be justified. . . .

Faults of this kind will never injure the sale of the

journal, for even in that portion of the public for whom it is more particularly designed, the more amusing it is the better it will be received. In this point of view I think there are *some* theological articles which would have been better adapted to the *Evangelical Magazine.* Professing to be eclectic, it is certainly not necessary to notice works which have no other merit than that of being orthodox according to the creed of the *Review.* Of divinity, I should think that one article for controversy and one for edification would be a sufficient proportion for each number—speaking entirely with reference to the interests of the publisher. The publisher also should write more in it himself.

In the October number, page 368, I was pleased to see that you had said of artists exactly what I had said of men—that, to judge their works fairly, we must look at them in the same light in which they were considered by the authors. You will find my sentence, with its wide application, in the reviewal of Bogue and Bennet, page 91. There is another remark of yours which shows that your thoughts and mine have been travelling in the same direction; it is when you ask whether the character of a poem determines its form, or the form determines its character. No man but a poet could have asked the question. I find the metre influences the style so materially, that nothing ever embarasses me so much as the choice of the mould in which a new poem shall be cast. The only thing of which experience has made me certain is, that blank verse, of all measures the easiest to a beginner, is the most difficult to a proficient in versification.

Montgomery (he is easily recognised) has given me the best kind of praise, though he has considered as an ode a poem to which I affixed a generic name purposely, that an ode might not be expected. The Greeks, on such an occasion, would have had an oration; our custom required something in verse. The circumstances and the subject therefore led me to compose an oration in verse, to which the running strain of thanksgiving gives the unity which is required in a poem. I am at work upon an epithalamium for the Princess's marriage, which in its moral tone may redeem that class of compositions from their merited contempt.

I see by the *Evangelical Magazine* that a Cornish minister is about to travel from Bayonne to Lisbon, distributing Bibles and Testaments and tracts as he goes. Indeed, this is very rash, and dreadfully ill timed. The partisans of the Inquisition in Spain have by no means given up the hope of recovering the ground which they have lost. In Portugal, on the other hand, those persons who know the evil which that devilish institution has brought upon their country, are endeavouring silently to destroy its power. I know of nothing which would tend so materially to defeat the efforts of the good in one country, and to assist the persecuting party in the other, as the appearance of this heretical missionary. He himself may be thrown into prison (which no doubt he would cheerfully encounter)—this is a light evil; but he may bring his own country into most unpleasant difficulties with the Spanish Government; and I am perfectly sure that he must impede the good work which he is desirous of accelerating. God knows, there never was a man who felt a more rooted abhorrence than I do for the abominations of Popery, or who longs more earnestly to see the Bible brought into action against them. But this mode of proceeding is madness. The only way to get the Bible into use there is through the agency of persons of their own religion and their own country. There are some priests who are really pious enough to do it. An Englishman settled in Spain might have an edition of the licensed Spanish Bible printed there, and distribute it through such persons. There is no other way in which we could interfere safely, and even this might involve him in some difficulties. If you should ever, as you talked of, embark in a Magazine, let it be a part of your plan to collect for the missionary societies as much previous information as can be found to direct their future or assist their present establishments. At this time, a paper upon the state of religion in the Peninsula, written with proper knowledge of the subject, might perhaps prevent this very injurious and mischievous experiment.

Keswick, January 28, 1815.

IV. MY DEAR SIR,—I have dealt very uncivilly by you, and am heartily ashamed of it. Let this suffice for apology—and forgive me.

I thought ere this to have offered you an article for your *Review*, taking for its text some pamphlets of Perring's upon the state of our ships in the navy, and from thence examining, with all freedom and in the real spirit of reform, the state of the men as well as of the timber. The delay has not been from idleness, but from over-occupation; and in some respects it has been fortunate, for I understand Perring's plans have now been so far adopted as to satisfy him, and a most essential step has been taken towards improving the condition of the men, by setting them free after twenty-one years of service, with a fair pension for life: a measure which I earnestly called for some years ago. What I have to say therefore may be said now with more grace, as there will be much to commend.

The moral defects of Lord Byron's poems are well pointed out in the *Eclectic*, and due justice is done to the vigour of his style. But there is a radical and characteristic fault in most of his tales, which has not been sufficiently exposed: the characters which he describes are impossible; no such ever have existed, or ever can exist. It is perfectly absurd to suppose that anything like the strong, abiding, soul-rooted feeling of love can be found in a buccaneer—setting all the other unaccountable parts of the story out of the question. His characters are made up of contradictions; and because the parts are all powerfully drawn, common readers never pause to ask themselves whether they could possibly cohere. Do not imagine that I blame him for portraying *mixed* characters—there is alloy enough in the best of us, God knows!—I condemn him for making an impossible mixture. The real cause of this monstrosity is sufficiently obvious. Like Montgomery, he has been painting from the looking-glass; but he had not so good an original, and, unlike Montgomery, his day-dreams have been of evil. His fancy has brooded upon his own heart, and, cameleon-like, taken its colour from thence: unhappily, the colour is a dark one. And being conscious that he is in many of his feelings, and most or all of his opinions (certainly in all that relates to the highest and holiest subjects), a sort of outlaw in the world, he makes his heroes bid defiance to all positive law, and transfers to them all his own unhappy principles. But men who act like his characters are men not of *bad* principles, but of *no* principles; not of *diseased* feelings, but of *callous* ones. Lord B. has just married a woman who is said to be one of the loveliest and most accomplished of her sex. When he finds himself a happier man, he may perhaps become a better one. But the experiment on her part is a perilous one; and I should tremble if she were my daughter.

You have not, in my judgment, given Bloomfield more praise than he deserves. The sort of popularity, indeed, which he obtained at one time could not, from its nature, be lasting; but he will hold his place. A very interesting man, and a thoroughly estimable one, who never over-valued himself, but poured forth a sweet strain of his own.

Of the many self-taught men who have appeared in this country, Hogg, the Ettrick Shepherd, is one of the most remarkable. He spent a couple of days with me last summer, and left me as much pleased with the un-affected plainness and simplicity of his conversation, as I was with the vigour and life that appear in his writings. He is the rising star of Scotland. The Scotch, you know, have a public of their own. Edinburgh is a Scotchman's London, and I might almost say his king-dom come—for most of them seem to think that nothing greater or better can be found anywhere else, here or hereafter.

I have heard of Jeffrey's reviewal of the "Excursion," not seen it. But it is my full intention to take this occasion of exposing Jeffrey's ignorance, malice, and self-contradictions. Most likely it will be through the medium of a newspaper, as giving it the widest circula-tion. I shall enter fully into the subject, and treat him with all the severity that he so amply has deserved. There can be no difficulty in showing that a man who does not admire the "Excursion" cannot possibly under-stand what he may pretend to admire in Milton.

. . . . I do not like the political aspects. The good which might have been done at the overthrow of Buona-parte has been left undone; and even if exhaustion should produce a peace for some time to come, there are abundant seeds of war left to germinate. Italy, ought to have been formed into one great state. I would rather have seen it a federal republic than a kingdom; for when we have to begin anew upon clear unencumbered ground, I cannot but believe a republic to be the best thing. But as kingdoms, naturally enough, are most in fashion, I would gladly have seen it a kingdom, and given to anybody—who had not actually deserved the gallows. Had Buonaparte been a wise man, he would, at the Peace of Amiens, have restored the Bourbons, and taken Italy for himself; but he had already given himself over to evil. I suppose you know that a Frenchman who, in 1802, published a "History of the Egyptian Expedition," has now published a second edition, and inserted a full account of the massacre at Jaffa, to which he was himself eye-witness!

Keswick, March 29, 1815.

V. MY DEAR SIR,—I thank you for your Reviews, and thank you for your letter, and I thank you for remembering me in the distribution of your wedding-cake. I wish you all the happiness which your new state of life can bestow, and which can not be experienced in any other. It has its anxieties, its trials, and its sufferings also: may few of these be dispensed to your lot! Present my congratulations to Mrs. Conder. We have long known each other in print; and one of the pleasures which I look forward to in my next visit to London, is that of becoming personally acquainted with one whom I so sincerely respect.

Had I known you were about to visit Bristol, I would have directed you to some of my favourite haunts in former times, and would have introduced you to my old friend Joseph Cottle, who, though he has mistaken the bent of his powers most deplorably, is nevertheless a

man of no common powers, and of most exemplary goodness in all relations of life that he has been called to fill.

I put the review of the "Excursion" into Wordsworth's
hands ; he was much pleased with it, and desired me to
convey to the author his sense of the very handsome
and very able manner in which his work was treated, and
especially of the spirit in which the criticism is written.
Your articles on the "Velvet Cushion" and on Allison
are both exceedingly well written : in great part of both
I agree with you, and where I do not, still I admire both
the manner and spirit. My attachment to the Established Church, in preference to any other existing form of
Christianity, is not founded in bigotry or in prejudice ;
for, though I conform to it, I do not subscribe to its
articles, and am thereby precluded from being (what
otherwise I should most ardently desire to be) one of its
ministers. You are wrong in thinking that our cathedral
service is inferior to that of the mass-book. The
cathedral service you feel to be solemn ; who indeed can
fail to feel it so ? But it would be impossible for you
not to see that the mass is a mummery, and not to feel,
if you reflected upon what was going on, that it is gross
and monstrous idolatry. I have seen it performed before
the Court of Portugal, and the only thing which I could
have borrowed from it was its incense. P. 345 : Sir
Henry Vane is classed by Towgood, upon Clarendon's
authority, as a member of the Church of England. It is
enough for me to remember Milton's sonnet to Vane,
and to know how he behaved upon his trial and at his
death, to hold him in high veneration. But he was
certainly a Puritan and a fanatic. I have one of his
books, which contains abundant proof that fanaticism
had deprived him of all judgment, and even of all genius,
when treating upon religious subjects. The account

which you have quoted of Mr. Sutcliffe's death is very fine; and your concluding passage perfectly expresses my feeling upon these subjects. Mr. Gilbert made a very just remark to me, when, agreeing with me that men might go to heaven by different paths, he observed that the path which might lead me there might not lead him. I entirely assent to this. Every man must walk according to his light.

I thought you a little too severe to Child Alarique. And with regard to Scott, though it is impossible that I should not perceive the faults of the story, and the extreme inaccuracy of the style, yet my opinion is much more favourable than yours. There is frequently a fine conception of the old chivalrous character, and almost always a strength and vividness in the outline which he offers you. Lord Byron's faults are to me far worse than Scott's, and they are likely to produce a much worse effect upon the herd of imitative writers. It is a clumsy mode of narration to give you the characters of men by describing them, instead of letting the character describe itself in the course of the story; but strip one of Lord Byron's poems of these descriptions, and what remains? The fable is a mere nothing; and the characters themselves are incongruous even to absurdity.

. . . . How dismally has the prospect changed! Buonaparte will have the Italians with him, and a powerful party in Switzerland, and the wishes of the Belgians. But I think the struggle will end in his destruction. I could almost persuade myself that he is the instrument of drawing upon France those evils which she has so long and so mercilessly inflicted upon other countries; that the generation which he has bred up in blood and blasphemy are to perish by the sword; and that Paris, which I verily believe to be a guiltier city than even Rome or

Constantinople, will be made a signal example of the vengeance of God and man. I wish I could feel the same confidence respecting the state of things at home; but the more I reflect upon the changes that have taken place within my own remembrance, and upon the principles which are at work, the more reason there appears to me for apprehending a dreadful overthrow of all established institutions.

Keswick, July 5, 1815.

VI. You ask me upon what grounds I apprehend that all established institutions are in danger. The stream of events seems to have set against them, and, in the depth and sincerity of my heart, I fear that, at no very distant time, they will all be swept away.

You are not old enough to remember the morning of the French Revolution, and the delirious effect it produced upon generous and inexperienced minds. Did you ever inhale the nitrous oxide? We seemed to be *living* in such an atmosphere. The republicans and levellers (or, in one word, the Jacobins) of that day consisted of the best and worst members of society. There were the daring and the desperate, the profligate and the atheist; but there were also those who would have offered up their lives like martyrs, and who gave proof of their sincerity by trampling all worldly interests under foot. The Government went mad in an opposite direction, and plunged the country into a war, of which the third act is only just begun! From that error (in my coolest and most unbiassed judgment) I believe the chief calamities of Europe are to be dated. They had the mob with them, who were then anti-Jacobins to a man; and what the spirit of anti-Jacobinism is was shown by the Emperor's treatment of Lafayette, and by the Birmingham rioters.

In those days I was a Jacobin, and so was almost every man whom I knew, who had any claims to my love or respect. But you would hardly believe how small a minority we were. I am old enough, and have been diligent enough, to have acquired the groundwork of historical knowledge, without which any political principles must be referred to inclination rather than judgment; and the last twenty-five years have added much to the great book of experience. The Jacobins now are so numerous, that in the lower classes I believe they are greatly the majority. Where there was one reader in those classes then, there are twenty now. There were not half a dozen opposition newspapers then; there are scarcely as many now that are not Jacobinical. And when the half-learned address themselves to the ignorant, their misrepresentations, their mistakes, their malice, and their blunders are all received as gospel. Upon this subject I said something in the *Quarterly*, which, mutilated as it was, will explain what I would now say more fully than I can express myself. The populace are at this time decidedly Jacobinical. Our friend Neville can tell you how perfectly well they understand the art of finance; and you have lately seen in London, as well as in the Luddite countries, that they are well skilled in the art of insurrection. The question is—is there time for the education which the populace at last are beginning to receive to produce its effect, before the prevailing levelling principles bring about a revolution in this country? I hope so, but verily I think there is not.

I am inclined to believe that no doctrines have ever obtained a wide and influential belief, without some foundation in truth. Most heresies, for instance, are founded upon a strong perception of some particular truth or tenet, which possesses the mind, to the exclusion of others not less important in themselves. The evils of the existing state of society are but too obvious—every man may perceive them; but every man does not know that, in the present condition of the human race, we have only a choice of evils, and that if reform be not gradual, it brings with it worse evils than those which it removes. Inequality, in the extent to which it prevails among us, is an evil; I know not how a man of cultivated intellect and feelings can contemplate the difference between himself and a hackney-coachman without shuddering. There are evils inseparable from a monarchical system; but, gracious God! what are the evils which would overwhelm us, if we were to attempt to change it! Our Church Establishment has its evils. You and I should not agree as to what those evils are; my conception of them is such as to exclude me from the clerical profession. But I am fully convinced of the utility of an Establishment; and though, if I were to form one for a colony, it would differ materially from our own, I dare not wish an alteration which would entail upon us ages of religious anarchy, and perhaps of civil war.

Let me save time by referring you, on this subject, to the *Ed. Ann. Register*, vol. iv. p. 138. There you may see what dangers (in my opinion) assail one part of our complicated system. The monarchy has to contend, not only with the spirit of the times, but with other causes which it is enough to hint at. The science of finance I do not pretend to understand; this, however, is apparent, that it rests upon public credit for its basis, and I *know* that if the bullionists in 1811 had carried the question in Parliament, it would have been utterly impossible to have carried on the war.

The world has its intellectual as well as its physical plagues. Religious intolerance has been the endemic in one age, the lust of conquest in another; in this it is the spirit of revolution. The mind of the populace *is* revolutionized in England. As soon as the army is so, all is over. A great statesman might fail in averting the danger; but where are we to look for a great one? This country never sustained a greater loss than in Percival, who had two of the great essentials—sound moral principles and undaunted courage. I have filled my sheet, and yet very imperfectly expressed what I would say. I have a book of Gregoire's to review ("Hist. des Sectes"), in which I will bring in your pamphlet; and I owe your Review a paper, which I will pay whenever I can command time. Accord with it I do not, neither do I with the *Quarterly* in many things; but it is enough if I be consistent with myself, and so I cast my bread upon the waters. The review of "Roderick" is from a friendly hand—indeed, I know it is Montgomery's; but it is singularly erroneous. How could he read so inattentively as to imagine that Siverian had married Roderick's mother? or complain that there was too much of costume in a poem, the subject of which laboured under the grievous defect of literally having none? And upon what Christian principles, except those of the Socinians, can he object to my addressing the mother of Christ, as "Holiest Mary, maid and mother?" There is something so divine in the belief, it is so exactly what one would wish it to be, that I confess this fitness inclines me to believe it more than any evidence for the authenticity of those parts in Matthew and Luke which the Socinians dispute. I would say more, and upon other topics, if there were room.

Keswick, March 18, 1816.

VII. Would that my poem were as free from other faults as it is from that which you have apprehended!

A Quaker would not subscribe to its feelings, but you, I think, might without scruple. Upon this subject I hold it equally a crime to foster the military spirit in time of peace, as it is to deaden and depress it in time of need. While Buonaparte reigned, the object to be kept in view was not the horrors of war, but the degradation of the human race, to which his system (exclusively military as it was) directly, and almost avowedly, tended. We may shudder at a field of battle with safety now, and instruct others to shudder at it.

. . . I must complain of an omission in your letter. You mention Mrs. Conder, but there is a third person in the family of whose well-doing I should be glad to hear. This person must now be growing fast in your favour; when they begin to know you, and you can handle their soft frames without fear, they very soon lay fast hold upon a father's heart, and he finds that there are deeper springs of affection in his nature than he had ever before discovered.

Another reading, and you and I shall not differ about the "White Doe." The faults are glaring and on the surface; admit them, and then read for the beauties. There is neither impiety nor nonsense there—there is much mysticism. This evening I came upon a text in the Wisdom implying pre-existence in the belief of its writer: "For I was a witty child, and had a good spirit. *Yea rather, being good, I came into a body undefiled.*" This notion will explain a good deal in Wordsworth.

Keswick, August 13, 1816.

VIII. The date which I have just written reminds me that yesterday completed my forty-second year. Few men have lived longer—if the expression may be allowed —in the same length of time. I have been married more than twenty years, and have experienced, in no common degree, both good and ill; wrongs and benefits, happiness and affliction, changes of opinion, loss of dear friends, of parents, and of children. I am younger, perhaps, in constitution than in years, but older in feelings than in either. Both my father and mother died at the age of fifty. Their deaths, in both instances, were accelerated, if not occasioned, by wasting anxieties; but the race is not long-lived, and I do not expect to prove an exception to it. I used to pray for continued life; without being weary of life, I have ceased to do this. No person *could* have supplied my place to Herbert; daughters neither require nor admit of the same tuition; and as they will be decently provided for after my departure, they can spare me, and I need not be solicitous concerning them.

Do not mistake me. I possess abundant blessings, and am capable of enjoying them. With what feelings I have long contemplated death many of my poems will indicate;—it may be seen in "Thalaba," in "Kehama," and in "Roderick,"—still more in the proem to an unfinished poem, written two years ago. The late loss which I have sustained has not created these feelings, but it has rendered them more vivid. The strongest root which fastened me to the world is broken, and I have now more ties in heaven than upon earth. I have borne the loss with much self-command, and perfect resignation. Common sense, common humanity, some little mixture of pride perhaps, and the stoicism which I laid to my heart in youth might have produced the first; and of all virtues there is surely none which deserves to be held so cheaply as that of resignation to what is inevitable and irremediable. But I hope I have persuaded myself feelingly that what has happened is best; that I acquiesce in the dispensation, and neither indulge nor acknowledge a wish that it should have been otherwise. My will is annihilated, and my heart is strong; but, in spite of that outward control which I am constantly able to maintain, recollections will come upon me by day and by night, and every hour, which make me feel the weakness of philosophy, and the inestimable value of the faith which looks beyond the grave. The best teachers are Love and Affliction. Enough, or too much of this. I thought to have sent you some remarks on some of your last numbers, but the time went by, and the feeling has evaporated. They related to some wrong-headed and mischievous politics (coming, I believe, from Foster), and to the unbecoming manner in which the Abbé Edgeworth's memoirs were mentioned. : . . . . When we see men doing their duty with heroic devotion, if a difference of opinion prevent us from feeling sympathy or expressing admiration, we have some reason to suspect that our own opinions are not what they ought to be. I can feel equal respect and equal compassion for Madame Roland and Madame Elizabeth, for the better part of the Girondists, and the better part of the Vendeans. My mind was not always capable of this equity. In the days of Jacobinism I did not like to contemplate the virtues of the Royalist party; and when the Queen of France suffered, I strove to qualify or quench the compassion and indignation which I could not help feeling at her murder, by dwelling upon her vices and her imputed crimes. In this, as in many other things, time has done me good, and taught me to do more justice to human nature.

In this new *Quarterly* I have written upon the Vendean war, and upon the Poor. For this latter article Murray pays me £100. Chance-hits in literature have sometimes produced even more disproportionate profit to the writer; but for a deliberate price this is very great, and much more than I should ever have thought of asking. . . . . I conclude this letter after and amid many interruptions. Yours, very truly,

ROBERT SOUTHEY.

FROM THE REV. ROBERT HALL.

8th May, 1814.

DEAR SIR,—I have made some beginning in the article of Belsham's "Memoirs of Lindsay," but have been much hindered by several unexpected engagements. I heartily repent having undertaken it, as there is nothing more irksome to me than reviewing. But having promised, I will (God willing) go through with it. I cannot set about it immediately; I am printing an address, delivered to Mr. Carey. When this is finished I have a circular letter to write for the Baptist Association, so that I cannot enter upon Belsham till the Whitsun week. I will then set upon it in earnest, and hope I shall complete it in a fortnight or three weeks. You may probably wonder I should want so long a period, but I am an *amazing* slow writer, and my interruptions and avocations, of one kind or another, are very numerous; so that it is but a small part of my time I can devote to writing. I am sorry to have occasioned you any uneasiness. When I have completed the two things I have mentioned, I will try immediately and finish as soon as I can. I am, dear sir, yours most respectfully,

R. HALL.

3d July, 1814.

II. I have read with much pleasure the last number

of the *Eclectic*, and thank you for the notes you enclosed, which is more than an adequate remuneration of my labour. The article respecting Burgess is written with much ability, and an excellent spirit. I have only to regret that the writer persists in giving the appellation of Unitarian to the Socinians. Much mischief, I know, is effected by the appellation, fraught with insolence and collusion. For my own part, I am determined never to bestow it upon them.

The third article I should say without hesitation, were I not writing to its author, is by far the most vigorous and eloquent in the number. I am persuaded you cannot consult the interest of the work better than by similar contributions to it. With Foster's I was not equally pleased. It appears to me to be written, certainly, with considerable originality, but in a very bad taste. What a pity it is Mr. Foster cannot be induced to pay more attention to the construction of his periods, and to many other of the subordinate graces of composition. As it is, he often instructs, sometimes astonishes, but seldom pleases me. If he would take pains to write . . . he might alone raise the *Eclectic* to a very considerable eminence. I am much charmed with the review of Collinson. It is altogether masterly—just what it ought to be. He is a writer you cannot employ too often. On the whole, I think the work is considerably improving, and I am delighted to hear you have no doubt of its permanence. With all its imperfections, it appears to be a most useful and important publication. I wish its Calvinism (?) were less prominent, its reviews more analytical, and its composition more simple, transparent, and Addisonian. Elegance, not an affected splendour, is the quality which always longest pleases. I am perfectly satisfied with the alterations; they are all improvements, except the change of " audacity" for "impudence."* For my own part, I like to call a spade a spade. Pardon my freedom, and believe me to be, with much respect, yours sincerely,

R. HALL.

20th September, 1815.

III. I owe you many apologies for not sooner noticing the letter you were so good as to address to me a considerable time since. The only reason I can plead for my silence is the pain it necessarily gives me to put a negative upon your wishes, warmly and, as I believe, sincerely expressed. After having so frequently stated my repugnance to writing reviews, I feel myself at an utter loss to express the same sentiment in terms more strong or efficacious. There is no kind of literary exertion to which [I feel] an equal aversion by many degrees; and were such things determined by choice, it is my deliberate opinion I should prefer going out of the world by any tolerable mode of death, than incur the necessity of writing three or four articles in a year. I must therefore beg and entreat I may not be urged again upon a subject so ineffably repugnant to all the sentiments of my heart. From what I have seen of the recent execution of the work especially, I am convinced my assistance is not in the least wanted. It is, I believe, growing daily in reputation, and I hope in circulation; and I have no doubt but that, under your skillful management and that of your coadjutors, its reputation will not only be sustained, but will be sufficient to engage far superior assistance to mine. I admire the Bible Society inexpressibly;

---

* This, as it happened, was the *only* alteration in Mr. Hall's article which the editorial pen had made.

but how is it possible to say anything in its praise or vindication which has not been said a thousand times? . . . . Besides, let me add, my dear sir, that my other engagements are such, that the business of reviewing is incompatible with them, unless I were to form the resolution of having nothing to do with the press in any other form. I feel myself much honoured by the expression of your kind regard, and beg leave to assure you that I am, with the truest esteem, your sincere friend and obedient servant,

ROBERT HALL.

FROM THE REV. JOHN FOSTER.

1814.

SIR,—It is not given me to attain anything like the power of despatch, and I am forced to look to to-morrow for the conclusion of this trifling article, which I am vexed to have been betrayed into the making all of introduction. This bulk of head will decline fast into a slight snipped tail, as in some fishes.

I have been looking at the article, "History of Dissenting Deputies." As to the first part of it, it is most unconscionable to eke, and fill, and lengthen by such monstrous quantities of extract, especially when the book itself costs but a few shillings. It looks a most palpable and evident shift of book-making art. And then, too, a slow toilsome journeyman like me, who takes very little advantage of this resource for getting up an article, begins to look about him, and say—If this sort of workmanship is to be paid just the same as my toiling method, I shall be a fool to go on in my present manner; I will earn my pence more easily, and will not, by the proportion, in *my* jobs, of continuous composition, just contribute to give other journeymen the fair occasion and plea for filling *their* spaces in this slight and easy way. It is against all equity that thus *work* and *no work* should, as to the doers, come to the same thing; and that even the *work* should absolutely be taken advantage of, in the way of securing a tolerance for the *no-work*. I have often enough grumbled within myself (for since Parken's time I have never said to an editor one word about it) at seeing articles made up in such a way as that I could not have thought myself fairly earning the pence, if I had worked so. . . . Reviews of poetry, especially, have been done in this· most inequitable manner. After two or three pages of observations, there would be page after page of mere dead transcription; indeed, less than that—mere *trans-printing,* interlined with just here and there a trifling sentence, as a link. I have, in now and then an instance, very seldom, made the experiment whether *I* could not thus earn a half-crown or two by transcribing a page of verse, as an *eker-out;* but I have generally found *there had not been room for its insertion!* And possibly there would be, in the very same number, an article absolutely made up of such *ekings.* The only thing that can prevent the honest genuine fags among your workpeople being indignant at such an article as this about the "*Dissenters*" is, that all articles made up in such a way be understood to be done by the *Proprietor* of the *Review. He* stands on quite a different ground, and it may be perfectly fair for *him* to take this advantage, as a trade expedient for lessening expense.

. . . Southey was very incompetently criticised, and unhandsomely treated in the first instance or two of notice in the *Eclectic.* But subsequently there has been enough of conscience done to placate him. In the review of "Kehama," he was, as to his talents, lauded and *incensed, speciali gratiâ,* with a designed effort to go the very utmost outside length of conscious truth, partly in consideration of former injustice. Since that time, our reviewers have several times gone directly out of their way to cajole him with laudations and reverences, which have appeared to me as little due as the occasions of offering them were forced and awkward. With great admiration of his genius, or at least some of its properties, I am quite of the opinion of the *Edinburgh Review*, that it is perverted and depraved abominably. I utterly nauseate and abhor a great part of his poetical productions. The substitution of an affected, quaint, false simplicity for a genuine and manly simplicity; the incurable passion for queer, grotesque, paltry, and even dirty superstitions—above all, his lending himself, with at least as much of his heart and soul as he gives to *any* of the subjects of his poetry, to the abominations, at once loathsome, inexpressibly puerile, and enormous, of the Mexican and Hindoo idolatries—expose to me a mind at once of the worst possible taste, destitute of all the high order of moral sentiments, and most wickedly trifling with respect to religion. He never seems to be truly and honestly serious about anything; there is nothing of the deep manly tone of firm conviction and earnest interest. In his prose, you find him perpetually paltering with conceits, and catches, and hits, and gibes, instead of intently pursuing an object with a sustained appearance of feeling its importance. He is the sneerer-general of our literature; and he has his appropriate reward—the butt of sack.

II. SIR,—It was about that Southey that we were talking;—and here is his *Carmen Triumphale* bepraised in our sapient *Review*, with some staring extravagance about one of the stanzas being enough to " create a soul beneath the ribs of death," and the like; as puerile rant as any enemy of the *Review* could desire to see in its pages. The poem itself appears to me in just the same light as it seems to do to the generality of its readers, to its newspaper critics, and to the Edinburgh reviewer. This very stanza, here selected for its poetic omni-potence, is among the *Edinburgh Review's* specimens of the imbecility of the production. . . . . It is one of the most prominent circumstances about Southey, that he seems to have no perception of what is profane—or worse, does not care about it. In his "Madoc" and "Kehama," he applies largely, without the smallest scruple, to the filthy infernalities of the two superstitions the terms peculiarly consecrated to the Almighty, even in the Bible. . . . . "Up, Germany!"—a very vulgar-sounding apos-trophe, to be sure. But it is the "land of the virtuous and the wise," and of "free mind:" perhaps he here means almost universal infidelity. I have heard as acute and vigilant and wide-viewing an observer as ever looked at Germany (Coleridge) describe the majority, if not the substantial body, of even the *Protestant preachers* there as real genuine Deists. . . . . I cannot help having a suspicious guess at this critic, and have had a number of occasions for repeating an opinion that there is something in his mind that will always keep him a very young man, in the less desirable sense of the word. But pray, in the name of seventeen years of age, let me conjure you not to let the *Review* be disgraced with such ostentatious schoolboy rants. . . . .

III. SIR,—In the last, in which I spoke of Southey, I meant fully and finally to dismiss the subject. My refer-ence to him had been chiefly with a view to try to do a little in the way of preventing, if it might be possible, the

Eclectic Review being made a vehicle of fulsome cajolery to him. Very probably it is not possible, and the effort may go to the large amount of labour lost. . . . . I have not the slightest personal acquaintance with Southey. The only time I was ever within the same walls with him was once, some seven or eight years since, in a news-room in Bristol, where, sitting in a corner, I most vigilantly listened to a conversation between him and another of the literati, and was a little surprised (for I had not read his poetry with much attention) at the heedless and careless manner in which he made use of the name of the Almighty. And truly, it appears to me that profaneness—virtual irreligion—is one of the most prominent features of his authorship. He has trifled with epithets, appellations, attributes of Divinity— bandied about expressions of solemnity and phrases of worship among the idols and phantasms of Paganism— *accepted* all sorts of superstitions for the sake of poetical effect—till I believe he has really lost all steady perception of that awful interdictive boundary which guards, if I may so express it, the Holy Mount of the Divine Presence . . . .

One is less aggrieved, and indeed perhaps less than one ought, with his *Mahommedanism.* His *Allah* has, at any rate, nothing to do with polytheism ; modern philosophic liberality may be pleased to take it as another, only a heretical, name of the true God.* But I am afraid some part of one's comparative tolerance arises from its being so immensely more *dignified* in poetry than the silly and filthy abominables of Mexico and India. I am greatly more pleased with "Thalaba" than the other performances.

---

* How can it be called "*another* name" when it is one of the names constantly employed in the Hebrew Scriptures ?

But, setting aside the Allah, etc., etc., of the piece, there are some parts which, by their infinite silliness, make one shrink with irksomeness and shame. Think, for instance, of the *Simorg*, the *bird* that knows all things! . . . . The man seems to have no perception of the difference between a *dignified* boldness, and even extravagance, of fiction, and a *childish*, *silly* extravagance—between *epic giantism*, if I may so express it, and a futile, phantastic monstrosity. He has been so much and fondly conversant with the insipid ravings and dreams of so many drivelling superstitions, that he has spoiled, most likely irrecoverably, his own great genius. His pride of independence would not let him stay in the school of Milton, and here are the consequences. With all his pride, he was not strong enough to venture into vastness without a guide or attendant. He could not tread the crude consistence of Chaos with an angel's port, step, and stride. But he will certainly go floundering on—I mean, unless you, recollecting that "friendship" should be a compact of mutual utility, shall set yourself earnestly to recall him, instead of shouting honour and glory, as you do, without exception or limit, when he sends you a canto of his MSS. As to our "*differing in toto*" about the merits of his poetry, that can hardly be, unless even my praises are in the wrong place—unless it is *not* for the vividness of his conception, the perfection of his painting, the richness and diversity and accuracy of whatever he writes in the way of description, the tenderness sometimes of his sentiments, and the vast scope of his observation and knowledge, that he is to be admired. . . . I have now positively and finally done with Southey. I will not say one word more about him, though you should in the impending article about his "Nelson," extol him to the very heavens, to which he has so profanely extolled so many idols before.

IV. The sequel of the article on Dr. William's books I have read but a few pages of, though I mean immediately to read the whole of it, and even, I think, the book itself. I have read enough of this second part to see that it is marked with the same matchless insensibility to the real views and difficulty of the speculation. I do marvel, with the most unfeigned emotion, to see with what perfect self-complacency (in this respect, I should hope, not resembling his author) the theological critic goes on, settling every question with perfect ease, and avoiding just those very aspects of the subject which render it desirable that that subject should be elucidated. The stupendous fact is, that an Almighty Being *could* have made all his intelligent creatures such, and placed them in such circumstances, that they would infallibly be good and happy; but that, on the contrary, He has, of choice infinitely sovereign and free, made and placed them so that many of them would infallibly, from their nature and situation, be bad and miserable.* The fact is be-

---

* The master-difficulty of theology and of religion could hardly be more pointedly stated; yet the statement rests on two assumptions, of which one is not evidently true, and the other is evidently false. The first is, that there are *no conditions of creation*, because the Creator is almighty. But Omnipotence itself cannot accomplish a contradiction. And to create a moral nature that *cannot* be made good by compulsion, but only by love, wisdom, habit, and spiritual influence, and then to *compel* it to be good, would be a contradiction. God's power, *per se*, is illimitable; but by the very fact of creation, He *limits* Himself; *e. g.*, if He decides to create according to fixed laws, He limits Himself to observe these laws. *If* God has made creatures who *cannot* be good and happy by necessity or circumstance, He has limited his own power in one direction, that He might exercise it in another. The other assumption is in the word "*good;*" as if there could be moral goodness with no power or temptation to go wrong. "Infallible goodness" in a creature, means *power to choose only one way*.

yond all question, and it appears to me that all attempts to explain it, and, as they somewhat profanely say, "justify" it, are wretched and fruitless trifling. In a perfect Calvinist they are so to a desperate excess. The only kind of philosopher or divine that would, with any -glimmer of reasonable hope, pretend to touch or come near the subject would be a believer in final restitution. As to this critic, a man, I dare say, of learning, and obviously, to a certain extent, of sense, he is about as ignorant, whoever he be, of himself as he is of the subject.

FROM MR. CONDER TO MR. FOSTER.

XXXIV. REV. SIR,—Whatever circumlocution I might think it politic or necessary to employ, were I writing to some persons, I am sure you would wish me to come, in honest terms, at once to the point of the unpleasant business I have now to write about. I cannot *print this article on Franklin. Literally,* I DARE NOT.* It would certainly expose me to prosecution, and prosecution for what, I must frankly confess, I do not coincide in as to the reasonings, or quite approve of as to the expressions. You will be just to my motives, and I do not fear therefore, whatever vexation this may give you, that I run any risk of offending you; but I wish you to believe that I have looked at the papers again and again, since the editor returned them, to see what could be done. The retrenchments absolutely necesssary would be so considerable, that I must have your distinct permission to cut it up as I like, before I venture upon the experiment. The simple fact is, as I have stated in a few

* The relations of the Government and the press were very different forty years ago from what they now are.

words, that *I am afraid* to use it, and this argument is an absolute one. But if you will bear with me—what is the bearing of the whole article? Is it not an appeal to "the people," to take into their own hands the remodelling of the constitution upon republican principles, *à l'Amérique?* In other words, an exhortation to revolt. Of course an armed revolt, for any other would be perilously ineffective. Now, admitting that this is good advice, ought the *Eclectic* to be committed as the adviser? Is no risk run (and if it be, a most thankless and useless one) in taking this means and this moment of offering it? Whom would you wish our readers to understand by the people? Does not the term refer us at once to *the mob?* If so, bad as the nobility is, it is better than the *mobility;* and I am of old Landaff's opinion, better one tyrant than a hundred. As to the extracts from Franklin, they strike me as very weak and flippant. I may labour under prejudices against the American patriarch, but I confess I think you vastly over-appreciate him. His hatred of English institutions was indeed natural, and his misrepresentations pardonable, considering the pains which the ministry of the day took to make England despicable in the eyes of the Americans; but I do not see why we should at this time of day adopt his opinions as fair and profound, and so forth, any more than those of that shrewd fellow-infidel, Thomas Paine. Your own comment on one of his remarks (as to the venality of the nation) exposes the witlessness of his sarcasm. And after all, is this a subject—I know we are at issue here—is this, I must still say, a subject for sarcasm? You will cite the instance of • Pascal and Voltaire as proofs of the effectiveness of such weapons, but Pascal and Voltaire attacked what they each deemed *intellectual errors* with intellectual weapons. In writing against corruption,

o

despotism, etc. etc., such a style can have only the effect to inflame; it can be of no use but as the pen should be the means of calling up the sword. From such a contest may the Divine mercy deliver us. The corruption of the state, with all the attendant moral and political evils, awakens in my mind feelings of a very different character. I could devote—I will not boast of being ready to sacrifice—my life 'to any rational and lawful means of combating the hydra, but I am too much of an enthusiast, too honest a fanatic, to go otherwise than quite gravely, calmly, and religiously about it. Something is due, if the N. T. be an authority for our conduct, to rulers as such; what that something is I should be glad to have defined without sophistry, but how indefinite soever may be my ideas on the subject, I cannot give up the notion that that something ought to be recognised. As an Englishman, I have some old-fashioned constitutional prejudices too, which refuse to submit to the American politico-philosophy. The destruction of the strength of our old aristocracy has, as it appears to me, removed a constitutional barrier to the influence of the Crown. I feel with unfeigned depth of concern the resurrection of Toryism; but the way of resisting the tide you have taken I am sure is personally unsafe, and I do not think it would have any good effect, even could I resolve to ensure for the *Eclectic* the honour of martyrdom.

But to business. I have paid you double for the whole review of Chalmers, and wish I could afford to do more; and, in a pecuniary way, I will make you any reasonable compensation for this destruction of your labour. If you will have the kindness to return the article with a *carte blanche*, I will put in what I can, provided you have no objection to carry on the delineation of Franklin's character so as to do justice to his brutal ignorance of religion. For this purpose I enclose you the volume just published.

(FROM MR. FOSTER.)

Downend, Wednesday.

V. MY DEAR SIR,—I do not know whether this will go to-morrow or not, nor is it of any consequence. This morning I shut up the last sheet of "Ayton and Daniell" in such precipitation, as not to have time for a word. A nine o'clock post is a very inconvenient thing. This morning it had the effect of being considerably earlier, for I saw, through the window, at a distance, the postman going, and had a run for it along the king's highroad to overtake him—when it proved he was not going, just then, *for good*. But the half-hour was lost. . . .

FRANKLIN. Untaught by all previous lessons, I really had not conscience or sense enough awake to make, previous to looking into your letter, the slightest suggestion to me *why* the *whole* of the article should be sent back. Amazing simplicity, you will think, but literally so it was. . . . . As to the general estimate of Franklin, whom you pronounce that I "vastly over-appreciate," I might fairly ask—*How* are you entitled to say this? Have you attentively read this "Correspondence," or any other work adapted to unfold him fully to view? It was on the "Correspondence," indeed, more than on any other works or documents (though aided by the recollection of a few of his practical essays), that the estimate made out in the article was formed; and it was formed with the greatest possible deliberation, with a special attention to every line and phrase, and a protracted balancing of expressions, in many of the sentences, in order to bring them as nearly as I could to the right mark; and I think it probable that EVERY expression is just, both in matter and degree. As you say you read the thing, you might have perceived that I was very careful to avoid any dashing extravagance. I did not talk of his intellectual character as including anything sublime, nor, though you write the word as if I had used it, "profound." (I am persuaded I did not use it—I have not looked at the article.) I used no terms to imply *any kind of intellectual loftiness or magnificence;* but, on the contrary, at considerable length described it as a deficiency, and even inferiority, that his unvaried *good-sense mode* of intellectual action had the effect of reducing all subjects to one level; reducing great ones, therefore, from their grandeur. In this *good-sense mode* I did, certainly, represent him as superlative, and with perfect truth. Excepting perhaps Dean Swift, I should doubt if we can name an equal, for the direct simplifying mode of penetrating a subject, and disposing of it. He is most admirable, too, in the power of applying principles, or general facts, to a specific practical purpose. Let any one but have occasion to read, as I had just been doing, his essay *On Chimneys,* for instance. I probably said, too, that he was sagacious of the characters and purposes of men, of the probable consequences of measures, of the operation of laws and institutions, all which is abundantly proved in the " Correspondence ;" and so forth.

As to the *moral* portion of the man, the estimate, I believe, is equally clear of any ethereal element. Not a word about elevated sentiment, heroic ardour, noble enthusiasm, romantic generosity, martyr's or confessor's devotement ; but a constant aim at tangible, plain utility. Now, I was conscientiously anxious to do full justice to this sort of mental and moral human composition, *for the very reason that it is far from being that*

which I am most prone to admire. It *is* the daring elation
of thought, the splendid imagination, the poetical and
eloquent strain—it *is* the glowing sentiment, the lofty
enthusiasm, the energetic passion, the adventurous virtue, and everything of this moral order, that enchants
me, even to the extent of disparaging in the estimate of
feeling, even below the pitch of its just claims, the
homely sort of plain sense-and-utility character. Aware
of this, *I took pains to be just* to this signal sample of that
character—yet delineating the character by no means in
a way to carry any implication of valuing it more highly
than, or so highly as, the loftier style of intellectual and
moral being. There are, indeed, some expressions descriptive of his abhorrence of the war-and-ambition
" heroics ;" and *there*, certainly, I was in full sympathy
with him, feeling an infinite detestation and contempt
of that execrable delusion of *this* sort of grandeur, for
which at this hour, all around me, the community is
paying the price in beggary, debasement, and wretchedness.

As to the *safety*, or rather *hazard*, of publishing the
political passages, you are necessarily to be the judge,
without appeal. To me they appear but to approach, in
a tame and restricted manner, the line to which the
Edinburgh Review advances boldly any day. As to
their being *an appeal to the people*, what *but* such appeal are all public representations of the corruptions of
the government, by which it is necessarily shown that
the people are oppressed with taxation, are deluded and
stimulated to wars, and, on the whole, have their affairs
managed with very little regard to their interests, and
often to their collective opinion and wishes ? What are
all representations of the necessity of political reform
but such an appeal ? How, as to any intelligible *human*

means, are corrupt governments to be practically checked, or institutionally reformed, *but* by a vigilant, examining, and suspicious superintendence by the national mind? How is this vigilant suspicion to be fully excited but by representations such as that supplied by the obstinate perseverance in the American war, of the miserable and dreadful consequences of national credulity, and confidence in the wisdom and virtue of a profligate government. . . . . .

"Cobbett's Address to the Mob," or some such thing, is written in pencil, against one of the to-be erased paragraphs, I see. It is a delightful thing to a profligate government, when good sort of people, pretending to more independence than their direct partisans can do, —when such, for instance, as write in the *Eclectic Review*, and a large proportion of the Dissenters—are scared into silence about corruption, a mock-representation in Parliament, pensions, and Court splendour amidst national poverty, etc., etc., etc., by such words as *Cobbett* and *Jacobinism*. These governors see very well that so long as these good people dare not reprobate anything that Cobbett has reprobated, all will be smooth and quiet, it happening so luckily that if there *be* any political corruptions, they are just those things which said Cobbett dwells upon.

I have alluded already to an apparent mark of erasure across one paragraph. It is one that you make some reference to; a representation, in the simplest, plainest terms I could find to put it in, of the palpable good that would arise from a wider scale of election, and a shorter duration of parliament, which would render venality and corruption much less practicable, even though there were not a particle more virtue in the community; with an enforcement of the extreme desirable-

ness of forming and correcting institutions in such a
way that by their very structure they should counteract corruption, instead of being so framed as to be
adapted to avail themselves of it, and indefinitely aug-
ment it. Now, if a representation like this may not
comport with the loyalty of the *Eclectic Review*, that
humble production would do well, methinks, to apply,
without delay and in a direct manner, for the countenance and patronage of Mr. Vansittart and Co. And on
this proceeding, it will be extremely proper, I allow, to
erase also a passage to the effect of warning some of
the good sort of men, co-operators and abettors of war-
and-corruption statesmen, lest they should one day
have the strange surprise (as I have no doubt they will)
of finding themselves in hell with those statesmen. On
any other plan I should have thought it not at all amiss
for a religious Review to give some hint of such a warning—some hint of admonition that the superstitious or
the servile principle of acquiescing in and advocating the
actual system of the government, out of deference to the
government *as such*, will do nothing to save, in the last
audit, men who have had influence in society from
*standing directly accountable for the nature of the things
which they abetted.*

You cannot away with half a page of extract, descriptive of the corrupt political state of England, as to
its representation especially. It is true that, from
wretchedness of memory, and some defect of the due
particularity of noting, as I read, the precise *habitat* of the
most applicable passages, one or two of the paragraphs
in that cluster are not the very best in the volume for
the purpose ; but one or two are excellent, as that which
describes the difficulty the Honourable House had to
avoid bursting into a horse-laugh at the grave farce of

punishing the Oxford people for some matter of election-bribery; and also a retort of Alderman Beckford's. But the innocents of the *Eclectic* are to be too religiously reverent of that Honourable House to have the slightest perception, sweet babies, of any farce or corruption there.

You revert to the topic which (I ought certainly to tremble at my own temerity while I say it) always sounds to me with a grievous resemblance to *cant*—the impropriety and mischief of anything like *sarcasm* in exposing follies and corruptions. It is not clear whether in the present instance the inculpation is meant against *me* as well as Dr. Franklin: if it be, its introduction here would only show (what one has observed in scores of instances) that when persons get some favourite and *singular* notion, it must and will be coming out, whether the occasion be one to which it is applicable or not; for, as far as I recollect, there is a prevailing gravity, and very little attempt at any sort of biting, in the passages excepted against in the article. As to the notion or principle itself, I am quite of the old and orthodox faith, that satire and sarcasm are legitimate, and may be valuable expedients in aid of truth, justice, and reformation. I see that inspired Prophets thought so; that Luther and many of his co-operators thought so; that some of the zealous Puritans thought so, Alsop, and several others; I may include Milton under the denomination; that Cervantes restored all Europe to its senses by this very expedient; that, in short, it has been a powerful co-agent in almost all grand improvements in society; while of course it is capable (as argument and eloquence also are) of being made the instrument of great mischief.

You seem half aware that you are unlucky in naming *Pascal*, an attempt being made to neutralize the effect of that name by an observation which I am not certain I understand :—" he attacked what he deemed *intellectual errors* with intellectual weapons." The essence of sarcasm (of such as is of any force) *is intellectual*—it is a mode of showing the absurdity or incongruity of things in a pointed, sudden, concentrated manner ; which same absurdity *reasoning* might equally show by a laborious process, and often [with] a less convincing effect. But as to Pascal, he showered his *aqua fortis* indiscriminately on *everything he wrote against* in the " Provincial Letters,"—the intellectual errors, the pride, the hypocrisy, the wicked policy, and the altogether, of Jesuitism.

I cannot mean that this should be the *chief* expedient for promoting a good cause, but that it is proved to have great sanction and great effect as *one* of the means. For brief and transitory works like reviews, it has this circumstance of fitness, that it can be employed within *a very short space*, where there is absolutely no room for formal statements and regular dissertations. As to its effect (in politics) being " *to inflame*," verily, the people of England have vastly needed something to inflame them, I think, or in any way to stimulate their attention to the detestable system under which they have reverently suffered themselves to be exhausted and corrupted during the greater part of this vile reign. They have shown themselves *un*combustible enough with a vengeance. And in addition to all the other considerations, all the world knows how dull is *mere preaching* on any subject. You may fag at a mere cold discussion as long as you please, and with as much of ponderous moralization as you please, and have your labour for your reward, unless you have a miraculous talent of throwing into the composition, *without* the aid of satire, a good portion of something much more inspiriting and stimulant than a grave prosing about right and wrong.

But I will rather throw this sheet in the fire than spend any more minutes on any of these matters. . . . . .

[1817.]

VI. . . . . Nothing was further from my intentions than this prolixity on the first part of the subject, the immensity of creation;* but now that I have been doomed and betrayed to this prolixity, I am willing to find out that there is hardly a more glaring defect in the religion of many good people, than the atomic narrowness of its field of view, and the almost total exclusion of those amazing scenes and sublimities which might all be available to religion, and which it becomes even a duty to take into that connection. Think how poor, how wretchedly mean and contracted, is the idea of the *Divinity* in far the greatest number of minds!—and let it be acknowledged that, do what we will about the ideas of Spirit, we do, after all, depend on some ideas of material magnitude for a really enlarged conception of the Divine Being Himself. We cannot help ourselves. So if Dr. C., and, at humble distance, his reviewers, shall contribute to assist their readers, by splendid and vast ideas of the scene of the Creator's presence and agency, to magnify those more abstracted forms of thought in which they apprehend that great Being Himself, it will have been a very direct service to religion, however indirectly, at first view, the stars may seem to belong to religion.

. . . . I am more than apprehensive that in the article about it that has gone from this den, it will appear that the commentator got colder, just progressively and proportionably as his author got warmer. The kind of

* In the review of Dr. Chalmers's "Astronomical Discourses."

thinking required and the very strong sense of the Dr.'s extravagance of theory, and the badness, in some respects, of his eloquence, were of most frigorific influence on my imagination.

I wonder much what *will* be about the level to which the fame of this performance will subside in a few years. I cannot even conjecture. There can, however, be no doubt that it will have had a very considerable permanent effect. It will have infused into the habits of thought of many minds, not at all acquainted with what had before been written on the subject, a notion, a haunting idea of greatness, and a sentiment of which they can never be quite exorcised. More than was previously felt, the universe will be recognised as claiming to be *something* in the means of forming an idea of the Almighty Creator—will be something therefore in the general theory of religion.

Thursday [July, 1817].

VII. MY DEAR SIR,—As I can avail myself of *privilege* so far forth as the twopenny post, I may as well despatch a line or two, and congratulate you on the consent of Mrs. C. to plunge again, for your sake, into the smoke and the mephitics of St. Paul's Churchyard. I am not, however, without some apprehensions that this long rural absentation may prove to have been a disastrous thing. My surmise is founded simply on your own acknowledgment, that the lady's consent to return imposes on you a distinct super-additional obligation to be an EXTRA good husband. Whereas, in fact, you will be just the same sort of husband that you were before, and not an atom better, excepting for a very short time; and so you will not have paid the fair compensation for this sacrifice of "sylvan" luxury; and so you will incur—either reproaches, or a great weight of unrepaid obligation for their being forborne. But let me see : this was really my impression of what you had said in your letter; but on turning to it, I find I am quite out, for that you are asserting yourself to be, *bona fide*, such a super-excellent husband that there is no merit or generosity in this sacrifice. I am very glad if this be true. I hope it is, but I have not heard the *right deponent*.

As to the young fellow, as he is to be one of the things for the rough wear and tear service of the world, the sooner in life *his* likings and preferences are accustomed to be crossed the better. . . .

Downend, November 18 [1819].

VIII. MY DEAR SIR,—The very paper may suffice to indicate my being in the midst of *neater* adjustments than the accustomed. But I am not yet on my own premises in any sense of the word. A number more days at Dr. Cox's must precede the appointed occupancy, where matters are making ready with what expedition they can. The fine books, however, have, as yet, no more business to venture out of their wooden cases than the scarlet butterflies have to come out with their opened beauties at this dreary season. Indeed, for *any* sort of books there is not yet a single shelf put in place. As in the former place, though not quite in the same degree, the quarters for their reception and array are greatly too much of the nature of *make-shift*, in point of dimensions. I *should* have been glad of a good roomy apartment for them, and for space and licence for studious or musing *trampling* backward and forward—a habit in which I am inveterate, and which is not the worst of habits, though a somewhat tiresome one. But whatever other deficiency there may be about the destined house, there is nothing approaching to deficiency in the articles of rent and taxes, which will triple or quadruple the rate of the Cotswold mansion.

Every new residence to which I have ever yet góne (with perhaps one exception, in Somersetshire) I have *hated*, in the most literal sense of the word, and that not from any partiality acquired for the previous residence, locally considered. Such could not fail to be the case now, the more so from the more advanced period of life, and the consequent diminution of anything like accommodating flexibility and sanguine expectation. I take the position with a concentration of dislikes—a dislike of making a local transit at all, a dislike of this district, a dislike of the house, a dislike, especially, of the part of it which I am more immediately to occupy, a dislike of the imposed necessity of meeting the recurring public services as regular and unavoidable ; and how many more of them come into this convergence there would be no end of telling.

The belief on which I have acted in the concern (without, however, anything in the least degree sanguine in *that* either) still continues, that the position may have somewhat more excitement, and somewhat more utility. I do not think that on the whole I shall repent the change, at the same time that there is gratification in the idea that I am not precluded from changing again. Whether the vicinity of a city (at the distance of four miles only) *will* bring much of that sort of advantage which in a very vague way I was willing to anticipate, is yet to be seen ; at the same time, I cannot help being well aware that I shall have extremely little disposition to frequent city society ; that, consequently, in whatever degree I do go into such society, it will be in the way of self-denial ; that the distance of even four miles forms a very advantageous protection against the *compulsory* necessity of such self-denial ; that, therefore, the strong probability is, that such self-denial will be very little exercised, and that I shall have infinitely slight benefit of the vicinity of a great town, beyond an occasional walk or ride about its environs, and perhaps a look now and then into its cathedral, or its principal library, of which, however, I have several times, of late years, a little inspected the finest articles (not so fine, by the way, as my own plunder), and can have no interest about the great mass of inferior ones. As to exhibitions of wonders of nature or art, there is nothing in the grand metropolitan style. I am little likely to fall into much intercourse with *professional* brethren, if Non-con. preaching may be called a profession. They are chiefly the same persons, several of them much respected ones, especially Dr. Ryland, that were in their present situations when *I*, so many years since, was also several years in *this* situation, and when I had very little more acquaintance with them than I have had during the subsequent total disconnection and insuperable distance. The one of them with whom I *should* have been most likely to be on social terms (Page) is gone, or as good as gone.

An inexpressible coldness and unexcitability of nature, accompanied by a certain *pessimism* of opinions and estimates, have placed me in such a *moral* situation, that I fear I have little to hope, after all, from anything in a *local* one. Nothing but an augmentation of *religion* in the mind can counterwork this fatal repression; and, certainly, I cannot have dreamed that that augmentation should accrue from any change of external situation; nor can it be from any such cause that I earnestly hope that grand advantage and felicity will be realized.

Downend, Monday Morning.
[December, 1819.]

IX. MY DEAR SIR,—I recollect you have once or

.wice, on very fierce and furious occasions, professed to congratulate yourself on being beyond arm's reach, in the physical sense. I was going to take to myself this same felicitation, but recollect to have heard that you are not so strong in the arm as in the head. By to-morrow's post I shall send what may add a couple of printed pages to the trivial scrap contained in this half-sheet. But how come all my good intentions and pledges to this? Not for want of their sincerity, but this miserable "Substance of a Discourse" job, again. The *Eclectic* obligation has haunted me every day like an evil spirit. I have felt it would be a much easier task than the one I was about; but when on each, and still the next, and the next, of these dark days, I seemed getting into a decent sentence or two of the more responsible thing, it seemed to me *such* a point gained, that those sentences *should not be to be made to-morrow.*

CHAPTER V.

THE commencement of the present chapter, in which our narrative turns "to fresh woods and pastures new," seems the appropriate place for introducing the following sketch, from the pen of one of Mr. Conder's earliest friends and fellow-labourers in the domain of theological literature,*. which possesses the value and interest of a contemporary portrait, by a hand of acknowledged power :—

'It was at a very early age that Josiah Conder, by the tacit but undisputed suffrages of the circle in which he moved, was allowed to occupy the place of a sort of presidentship among them. It was he who gave decisions in matters of taste and criticism ; it was he who suggested and carried forward any literary project ; he was looked to also as the source of the most authentic information, and the latest intelligence concerning books and authors; and he became a centre of the animated correspondence which gave life to the friendships that flourished around him.

'The qualifications which fitted him for holding such a position among those who, most of them, were his seniors, were—the graceful vivacity and attractiveness of his manners, his intellectual tastes, his literary proficiency, and acquaintedness with books, the beauty and

* Isaac Taylor, Esq.

feeling of his poetical compositions, and the acknowledged correctness of his judgment in questions of taste. Beside these intrinsic merits, Josiah Conder's position—so near to the heart of the book-selling, book-buying, and publishing world—gave him, in relation to his friends, and especially to his provincial friends, a very great advantage. He, among them, was the first to learn whatever was known, or whispered, or surmised, in the great literary commonwealth. It was to him that the inquiry was directed as to any rumoured novelty in the literary heavens, and from his eagerly-perused letters were gathered those crumbs of intellectual sustenance upon which the more remote of his correspondents were to live on from month to month. As bookseller, publisher, poet, man of taste, and as a hearer of learned and unlearned gossip, his correspondents thought themselves always the favoured parties in receiving his well-filled sheets.

'The fruit of the friendships of which Josiah Conder was the centre, appeared in a volume comprising the poetic contributions of the more literary or gifted members of this circle of friends. This book, entitled "The Associate Minstrels," appeared in 1810, and was reprinted in 1812. Conder's pieces in this collection may be taken as a fair sample of the range and of the characteristics of his poetic vein; they exhibit an elegant vivacity, and correctness of feeling, the most appropriate sphere of which is presented by the incidents and the attachments of intellectual friendship. It was at a later period of his course, and after that time when the trying experiences of real life had given greater depth to his religious sentiments, that his hymns, many of which have taken a permanent place in our devotional literature, appeared, and which may be held to entitle him to an honourable

P

place in the company which is graced by the names of C. Wesley, Cowper, Montgomery, and others not less esteemed by the devout.

'But to revert for a moment to an earlier time: that sort of readily admitted superiority, as the centre of a circle of intellectual friends, male and female, which continued to be conceded to him during a course of years, seemed to be a good preparation for the position he afterwards occupied as editor of a review. Some of those who had long been his correspondents on terms of a willing deference to his critical judgment, thenceforward became his coadjutors as stated writers in the *Eclectic Review*. Toward these his control had become the usage of years; and it was nearly in the same mood of graceful authority, wholly exempt from arrogance or dogmatism on the one side, and from assentation on the other, that he entered upon his editorial functions, when his contributing friends were, some of them, writers possessed of an established literary repute. It is believed that men and writers such as Robert Hall and John Foster, Olinthus Gregory, and others, found their relationships with the youthful editor to be agreeable and easy, although a proper and needful tone of final determination, as master of the company, was maintained by him.

'As is the usual, or perhaps the universal, custom in such cases, the new editor of the Review himself wrote largely for it; and he took under his care those peculiar subjects, upon a discreet handling of which the wellbeing and security of the work depended. The *Eclectic Review*, commenced on a supposition which speedily proved itself to be unreal and impracticable, still made profession, and it did so sincerely, of a substantial neutrality on subjects controverted among (to take up the undesirable phrase) the several "Evangelical communions."

To this extent the impartial bearing of the editor was, in the main, well sustained through a course of years ; and it was so in fact until the eve of that stormy era during the passage of which, organic changes in the political system spread a sympathetic violence, or an extreme vehemence, through the fields of religious and ecclesiastical controversy. From that time forward, or, let us say, from about the year '29, and until the time of his relinquishment of his office as editor, Josiah Conder moved into the place which he thenceforward occupied as champion of Dissenting interests and principles in the columns of the *Patriot*.

'Throughout the earlier and more tranquil period already specified, Mr. Conder's *own mind*, his proper intellectual endowments, were fairly developed, as well in the general management of the Review, as in various articles of which he was the writer. It was the symmetry and equipoise of the faculties which distinguished him, rather than the depth or power of any one of them. He wrote competently and well upon philosophical questions—moral, intellectual, or political ; but he neither professed to be the philosopher, nor did he win a reputation as such. He wrote ably as *layman* upon professional subjects—biblical, theological, metaphysical, ecclesiastical—and displayed the freedom, and the facility, and the irresponsibility which usually characterise *lay* interferences with matters that are jealously guarded by authorised functionaries. It was thus that he gave a popular and lucid aspect to what is often made to be abstruse or shrouded in the fog of conventional grandiloquence.

'As to most men of marked intelligence, that which in moments of depression they are prone to say or think concerning themselves, may be assumed as substantially true, namely, that under conditions of less urgency and difficulty, they might, and probably would, have taken a higher place than in fact they have been able to win for themselves in the temple of fame. Whether it would actually have been so, no one can affirm with certainty, either as to himself or his friend. In the instance now in view, it is, however, quite safe to affirm that, whatever it may be which favourable and auspicious circumstances have done for some men, any such golden advantage would have found in Josiah Conder the pre-requisites of a vigorous understanding, a bright imaginative sensibility, a depth and tenderness of feeling; and these gifts, combined with great assiduity and a constitutional love of method and order, apart from which the most brilliant endowments so often fail of their purpose.'

The relinquishment of business, the retreat into the pure air and quiet of the country, and the adoption of literature as a profession, constituted that turn in the high-road of life which opened the very career for which Mr. Conder's tastes, talents, education, and previous experience appear most to have fitted him. Probably, amidst all the cares, vexations, and disappointments, neither few nor small, which the pursuit of literature brought with it in after years, he never repented the course he had adopted. Nowhere could his mind have been more in its element, except in the work of the Christian ministry, for which he had special endowments, and for which that regretful consciousness which he expressed of a deficiency in high-wrought spiritual feeling is no proof of his unfitness, but the contrary. But the Master had different work for his servant to do; and the path was so plainly marked out by God's providence, that he could never reproach himself with not having consecrated his talents and life to the sacred calling. He commenced, however, at St. Alban's the practice of preaching in the villages, which he continued, with more or less frequency, during his residence in the country; occasionally preaching also (in after years) in larger places of worship. He stedfastly observed two rules; one of which was, not to go unsent, but to labour in union with the church of which for the time being, he was a member, and under the sanction of the pastor; the other, to make his services strictly gratuitous. In the villages they were necessarily so; but when invited to occupy the pulpits of stated ministers, he invariably refused any recompense, considering that by taking it he would have been doing injustice to those who have devoted themselves to the ministry as their calling. His preaching was characterized by great clearness, method, fulness of Scriptural illustration, and a simple, practical, common-sense exposition of doctrines. It was rather exegetical than rhetorical. His views of doctrine, it is almost superfluous to say, harmonized with what is generally understood by "moderate Calvanism;" but he avoided much use of technical language; he valued Calvin more as an expositor than as a systematic theologian; and both his preaching and his theology bore the strong impress of independent, familiar, and searching study of the Bible.

The new home was as complete a contrast to St. Paul's Churchyard as could be desired. It was not in the town of St. Alban's, but in the little village of St. Michael's; a pretty cottage residence, the garden front of which looks across a lawn and shrubbery into the open country, while but a few steps lead from the garden gate into the quiet churchyard of the rustic little old church, in which is the monument of Lord Bacon. Close at hand is Gorhambury, the family seat of the Earls of Verulam. Over the peaceful landscape the genius of antiquity seems to

look down from the stately tower of that proud old
abbey, whose first stones were laid when the seven Saxon
kingdoms of Britain had not yet been brought under one
sceptre, and when the retirement of the Romans was an
event not more remote than the accession of the house
of Tudor is from our own times.

A fragment found among Mr. Conder's papers deli-
neates, in its opening pages, with an energy evidently
borrowed from personal experience, the intense desire
which he had long felt to make his escape from London.
The MS. is an unfinished tale, entitled "*Hints on the
Choice of a Residence : addressed to those who may live
where they choose, and who have to choose where to live ;
showing that the country is the worst place in the world
to live in, except London.*" Chapter the first commences
as follows :—

' When first I turned my back on the metropolis, and
set off on my exploratory excursions in search of a residence, I felt the happiest man in the world. Like Adam,

> " The world was all before me where to choose
> My place of rest."

But, unlike Adam, I left not paradise behind. Reader,
gentle reader, did you ever pass the dog-days in London ?
Were you ever doomed to exist in that vast brick labyrinth through the long, dull, suffocating days of August,
when

> " Nature proclaims one common lot
> For all conditions—*Be ye hot ?*"

Have you ever posted your way through its streets
at eventide, amid the crowd of gasping citizens pressing
towards the suburban outlets, just as you may have seen
turtles clambering over each other in a tub, to catch a
gulp of air ? And have you seen, with a throb of envy, the

loaded stages bearing away their evening freights ? At such a moment, the oblique rays of the western sun flaring full in your face, has the din of a postman's bell, a procession of drays, or a cart laden with bars of iron, conspired, with the general whirl and hum of men, to work you up well-nigh to frenzy ? Making your escape from the rapids of the main street into some tranquil back-water, have you found yourself checked by clouds of black dust, upborne on eddies of hot vapour, or the attar of gas, or the steam of some subterranean refectory ? You have at length gained, perhaps, the blissful expanse of a square, and have perused, in vapid mood, one by one, the deserted mansions from which peered forth the vacant faces of imprisoned servants, while here and there a gayer group afforded you a peep of low life above stairs ; and you have wandered on till you found yourself an object of attraction to some daughter of Hecate, or of suspicion to the patrole, and have been glad to plunge again into the privacy of the ever-flowing crowd. If, then, jaded, disgusted, fevered, you have looked up at the blue sky, through which a few pale stars were making an effort to shine down on the strange scene below, has not your heart ached to think on what breezy fields and quiet streams, and cheerful village landscapes, the soft light of evening was sleeping ? Then, then you have felt all the emphasis of the poet's sentiment—

"God made the country, and man made the town."

'O London ! thou immense catacomb of the living, thou spacious press-yard of incarcerated thousands, thou overgrown abomination, thou hideous wen upon the face of society, greedy all-absorbing excrescence—thou vast gasometer, thou atmosphere of pollution, feculent hot-bed of vice, still of iniquities, thou Babel, thou

Charybdis, thou *Limbus patrum* of the moral world,. sarcophagous, anthropophagous monster—leviathan of , cities!—by what adequate symbol shall I designate thee, or into what terms compress the energy of my hatred? Oh that to-morrow I might leave thee for ever! Away, away—east, west, north, or south, anywhere—so that I might but get loose from thy voluminous coils, thy deadly embrace; and leave far behind thy horrid din and palpable atmosphere, thy filmy sunbeams and coal-gas odours, thy towering parallels of brick and strips and sections of sky, thy infinite variety of nuisances, moral and physical, thy gin-shops innumerable, thy swarming sharpers, beggars, black-legs, courtesans, dandies, radicals—all Colquhoun's thirty thousand children of necessity and birds of prey—and hide me in the green lap of Nature from such a world!

'Oft and again have I thus vented the bitterness of my feelings, beating myself against the wires of my cage in the vain attempt to spread my wings. But when morning has returned, with its calm and commonplace look of business, and brought back the cheerful bustle of daylight, and restored the salutary equilibrium of the physical and moral being, taming down the imagination into due subordination to the animal system, London has again—especially if it rained—been endurable. Yet still I nursed and cherished a settled feeling of sullen enmity against my Titanic oppressor, and waited but for the first favourable moment to break my yoke. The auspicious moment at length arrived. My prison doors were thrown open, and I found myself, with a moderate independency, at large and at liberty to choose my own longitude and latitude. To leave London was a settled. point; the "whither" was a question which I had anticipated no possible difficulty in determining. I had an indefinite, intense longing after scenes that could not be localized, the essential charm of which consisted in the negation of all that breathed of the town. A congeries of poetical abstractions, indistinct recollections, sentimental projects, and romantic calculations, occupied my fancy; and I had nothing to do but to realize them. My will, released from the tyranny of over-ruling motives, was precisely in that delightful condition of equilibrium which some metaphysicians will have to be the perfection of moral freedom. I not only might, in this respect, do what I chose, but I had to choose what to do. This is a most important psychological distinction, upon which I at present forbear to enlarge, as it will receive illustration from the sequel. Like other envied prerogatives, it sometimes proves a splendid inconvenience; and it might perhaps be made to appear that an alternative is quite as much liberty as the mind can safely be trusted with; that even to be beguiled of one's choice by a mild necessity, is preferable to a state of sovereign indetermination; and that by much the easiest and pleasantest mode of willing is—to consent.'

The foregoing paragraphs were not written until two or three years afterwards, when enlarged experience had illustrated the pleasures and disappointments of house-hunting in the country; the opening scenes of the tale being laid in the locality of a subsequent sojourn. Mr. Conder's residence at St. Alban's lasted only two years. The first year was shadowed by two heavy trials. One of these was the death of Mr. Conder's brother-in-law (a man distinguished equally for talent in his profession, and for eminent piety), which took place in July. The other was a fall from his horse in the autumn, which laid him aside for some time. It was when suffering from this accident that he composed the hymn numbered 590 in the Congregational Hymn-book, and commencing—

'O Thou God, who hearest prayer
Every hour and everywhere!
Listen to my feeble breath
Now I touch the gates of death.
For his sake whose blood I plead,
Hear me in the hour of need.'

To the Rev. H. March.

St. Alban's, February 15, 1820.

XXXV. . . . . I am very sorry we could not meet when you passed through town. Whenever we do meet, however, whatever lapse of time may have intervened, we shall find that we can take up the thread just where it was broken off. Friendship is endangered only by a' change of character in one of the parties. Our friendship is exposed to no hazard, I believe, from this quarter; and though I wish not to repeat the experiment, how long it can endure a suspension of intercourse without suffering any 'degree of diminished action, I have no doubt that its resuscitation would at any time be effected with ease, within half an hour of our meeting, even if it should have exhibited all the signs of suspended animation. . . . . You and Isaac Taylor are two individuals whom we have particularly pleased ourselves with introducing here by anticipation.' . . . . What with the winding up of my affairs, journeyings, MOVING, the *Eclectic monthly*, and some literary jobs of the nature of taskwork, I have been as incessantly busy since Midsummer as at any period before; and this is the reason why you and other friends have had to reproach me for my seeming neglect. All the autumn we were at Hastings, for

the benefit of the sea-air and bathing, which were prescribed for Mrs. Conder. I say *we*, though I had one
foot in London all the time, and generally passed a third
of every month in town. When we broke up our establishment at St. Paul's, we had not the slightest idea in
what locality we should ultimately set up our tabernacle;
but my sister's marriage to one of the best of men—my
good brother Rogers, as I love to call him—decided us
to fix upon St. Alban's as our residence. Mr. Brown,
our pastor, is everything we could wish, both as a
preacher and as a man. Need I say how material a
circumstance it always was esteemed by us, in planning
a future settlement, to have the benefit of a faithful and
efficient ministry? But we could scarcely anticipate
being so completely satisfied. . . . . This has been a
seasoning winter, and we have planted ourselves, as if in
defiance, in the very teeth of the north-east. But we
have now the pleasure of watching the first approach of
spring. Oh how much, my dear friend, have I to be
thankful for! A great load, which was pressing me down
to the dust, has been removed. I have only anxieties
enough left to form a needful alloy. My health is greatly
improved, and by the help of God I hope to maintain the
advantage. But the great thing is, a closer walk with
God. Think of me and mine, dear March, in your best
and happiest moments. Of none of my friends do I
think with so much pleasure as of those who are engaged
in the work to which you have devoted yourself.

Among a few private memoranda of this year occur
the following:—

Oh to be emptied of self, the source of all evil; to
be more careless of happiness, bent on glorifying God,
and leaving Him to provide; desiring more to serve Him

than to enjoy Him; more solicitous to do his will than to be saved! Oh, how many fears would this love cast out, since there is no fear but his will shall be done, and those who are found desiring this shall never be frustrated in their aim.

March 5.—Cause me to know that Thou art the God that heareth prayer with regard to my spiritual wants, as Thou hast with regard to my temporal wants. Oh that I might but seek the infinitely higher blessings with the same faith, earnestness, importunity that I have prayed for providential mercies, and then it would be so. When shall I realize all I know, and taste and feel all I believe?

June 25.—Returned in peace and safety to my dear home. Two things have been forcibly impressed upon me by what has passed at Leamington: the high importance of *strict consistency*, the all-desirableness of *high spirituality;* these together make living Christianity. As to the first, Mr. Bromilly's sermon, "*Be not partaker of other men's sins; keep thyself pure*," was most applicable as a reproof of the false shame, which is a virtual participation in the guilt we suffer to pass uncensured. Strictness may make you disagreeable; inconsistency, contemptible. And the worldly are hawk-eyed to detect it. . . . As to the last, my good brother's heavenly frame of mind was a lesson, the benefit of which I trust not to lose. This *is* the secret of happiness.

August, 1820.

XXXVI. . . . The greater part of June I spent with my invaluable brother at Leamington—an excursion I now look back upon with peculiar pleasure, as it afforded me an opportunity of observing more closely than I could have done under any other circumstances, during the three weeks we were constantly together there, the fervent piety, the spirituality, the *entire* consistency, of one of the best of men. I consider it a high privilege to have known him, and I hope that I have not known him altogether in vain. . . . His sufferings were extreme, so as not to allow of that intercourse in his last moments which is most delightful in the restrospect. But his faith was firm. "I have not a gleam of hope," he said to me, "but what comes from the blood of Christ." His letters to my sister during the six weeks he was absent from home, are written in the very spirit of a Christian just about to be made perfect, ripe for immortality.

At the close of October occurs the following entry:—This has been a month of trials and temptations, bodily illness, disappointments, and vexations; anxieties about our house, and much dejection, impatience, and distrust. God blot out in mercy the sinful infirmities his eye alone has witnessed! At times, the idea that I had done wrong to trust Him presented itself. Never has my mind seemed to lose so much of its anchor. And this is chiefly distressing, to find how such things affect my mind, instead of softening it, and driving me nearer to God. Oh save me from being the worse for my sufferings and cares! Save me from this unchildlike sullenness, in which my sins and my mercies are alike forgotten in anxiety about the future! Oh for *patience* and strength to wait!

January 1, 1821.

XXXVII. This is the first time my pen has traced the mystic signs of a new year—1821! How strange they look till the eye has become familiarized to the change, and how full of latent meaning! How the mind runs out into speculation on the possibilities to which these figures will be an historic date! St. Michael's bells are very busy, giving the new year joy, I suppose, on its accession; but bells can never be so merry but that an under-tone of pathos is still heard amid the peal. Now they have just left off, and the Abbey bells at a distance are taking up the strain. I could listen to them till they made me sad. They are Time's psalmody. What words shall we set to them? The best I can think of is that sentiment of Dr. Watts's—

> "Yet would I not be much concerned,
> Nor vainly long to see
> The volume of his deep decrees,
> What lines are writ for me."

You know what follows.

Among the prominent mercies of the past year, my fall claims certainly to be recorded as a kind interposition of Divine Providence. I had been passing the night at Mr. Easthope's, at Finchley, and was returning on horseback, in company with him and the Rev. Mr. Foster in a chaise. The horse ran away with me, more out of spirit than mischief, and I either fell or was thrown, but the fall was not severe. I soon recovered my recollection, and was brought back to Finchley, where I remained for three weeks. There was neither fracture nor contusion, but the wounds were ragged, and would not heal with the first intention; and the irritability of the stomach which the shake produced, kept them open for a long time. Had there been more serious local injury, it is very questionable how far my constitution would have rallied, as I was evidently not in health when it happened. But I have quite got over it now.

I wish I could retain more impressively the lesson which it read me on the mercy of God in sparing my *life*. It is a great mercy to be alive, when there is so much that it behoves us to be and do before the summons comes. I know that if I live until I am seventy I shall have no other ground for trust, no other plea than that upon which now all my hope is built—the blood of the Great Sacrifice. But there are many, many things which the husband and the father may, I hope, lawfully wish to live for, besides what ought to be the supreme reason—to do something for the glory of God before he goes home.

I am truly rejoiced to hear of your comfortable situation and animating prospects. Your brother must indeed be a staff to you. Do you employ him as your *curate* in the villages, or do you not encourage lay brethren in speaking to the people? Lay preaching is a subject which demands to be placed in a proper light. I go once a month (in turn with some other friends) to a village three miles off, where about forty or fifty poor people come together in the evening from the farm houses round. They seem to hear with great attention. This is, on my part, rather an experiment; but I act under a very strong feeling that it is a *general* duty.

I shall be very glad to be introduced to Mr. P——. A pious clergyman in this part of the country is indeed a *rara avis*. We have seven clergymen in St. Alban's, and several more in the neighbourhood, not one of whom approaches to evangelical. Did you mention my name to Mr. P——? If not, the author of "Protestant Non-conformity" will require some introduction to bespeak his friendly regard. I have more than once encountered a very visible shyness on the part of clergymen, although I have been so fortunate as to overcome it.

You ask about the *Eclectic*. The sale does not increase. The times are against it, and its enemies are very numerous, among those who ought to be its friends.

It is thrown away upon the Dissenters. They prefer the *Evangelical Magazine* and the *Congregational*. I am very glad to hear any remarks which may occur to you. You allude, I suppose, to the review of Cornwall's poems, when you speak of objectionable extracts. It did not strike me in the same light, but I dare say you are right. I am, however, almost sick of the work; it is an ungracious, and laborious, and not very profitable task to conduct it; and had I a few additional hundreds (*inter nos*) I should have great pleasure in publishing a farewell number. And yet there have been some very valuable articles. That on Southey's "Wesley" in this Number is an admirable one. Tell me anything you hear about the *E. R.* that can be a help or encouragement to me.

. . . I was very much pleased with my Leicester visit. I spent the whole of one day, and the greater part of two others, in Mr. Hall's company. He was quite himself—exceedingly affable and conversational, but quiet and regulated, nothing eccentric, perfectly simple; in the pulpit very serious.

Sept. 19, 1821.—In how much mercy does this day return! All my comforts spared—and such comforts— my health regained, and, may I hope, some growth.

I am more and more willing to be in God's hands. I *must* walk by faith.

Here seems the prospect of usefulness, the sphere of duty. I shall either be kept here, or see why I am not to stay. God can do without me anywhere; I without Him nowhere. If He has given me a desire to serve

Him, He will either employ me, or, if not, He will accept the desire.

It is a great lesson to be content to be nothing, and to do nothing, but at his bidding; to be satisfied just with the station, the boundary, and the work He has assigned; not to 'suffer even the wish to be useful to seduce my desires out of the allotted sphere of present duty; to act just the part allotted me. The Lord grant me wisdom to know what this is; to make it my choice, and humbly to confine myself to it with cheerful diligence, as the best and fittest for me.

> "They also serve who only stand and wait."

I have been several times striking myself against the wires of my cage. God is teaching me thus to be quiet under his wise restraints, to wait till his hand opens the door. I do not know myself, but God does. But for these wires that restrain, mortify, hurt me, I might have fled into the world. Politics, literature, the polite world, the pride of life; how I could yet enjoy them, vanity and vexation as they are! Blessed be God for salutary mortifications.

Nov. 1821.—Dreamed that I was in great trouble and perplexity with my father, and had been weeping, when the words suddenly occurred, " I will bless the Lord at *all* times;" that it suggested itself that times of sorrow and distress must be included in the words "*all times;*" that blessing God was never out of season; and that I began singing, which gave an immediate turn to my feelings. My mind was relieved, and I woke in a serene state of mind, under the strong impression of the sentiment.

At the close of 1821, Mr. Conder left St. Alban's, though with the full intention of returning (having engaged another house there), and spent some time with

Q

Mrs. Conder's family at Chelsea. For the nine or ten Sabbaths previous to quitting St. Alban's, he was constantly engaged in village preaching—"whether to any effectual purpose is known only to the Searcher of hearts. The people generally were extremely attentive, and in two instances transitory conversions were the result." At all events, he felt that he "got good," and was "willing to work for those wages." Circumstances prevented the fulfilment of his plans and expectations in reference to returning into Hertfordshire, and that year was passed at Brompton. Here he attended the ministry of the Rev. John Morison, whose preaching and friendship he highly valued; for whom, during three-and-forty years, he maintained an unbroken regard and esteem; and who, on his part, gave the strongest expression of the value which he set on that long-continued friendship, by undertaking, at great risk to his own health and even life, the melancholy and solemn office—which no one else could so fittingly have discharged—of conducting the funeral service, when the mortal remains of his old friend and fellow-labourer were laid to rest.

In the spring of the following year, 1823, Mr. Conder again removed into the country, and took up a temporary residence at Chenies, in Buckinghamshire, in a pleasant cottage belonging to some friends. This quiet retreat, further distant from smoky, toilsome London than could be measured by miles, afforded a sojourn fit for a poet. Untouched almost by the hand of modern improvement, with its unenclosed common and single row of thatched cottages, on one side only of the road, parted from each other by trim gardens; with its great house, and its great oak, its pump, sheltered by aged elms; its simple, homely, kindly population of peasants and lace-makers; its "white house" and its paper-mill; its venerable church, proud of its old hatchments and monuments, and its modest Baptist meeting; with its neighbouring park and mansion of Lattimers; and its corn-fields, beech-woods, and meadow-bordered trout stream—its likeness might have been painted for the ideal of an English village. The very existence of London was attested only by the post walking in at noon, or by the arrival of the leisurely stage-coach in the evening, bringing the newest news, and sometimes a passenger; which, after exciting due attention among the urchins, curs, and idlers of the little village, rolled down the steep chalky road cut through the common, and away further yet into the deep country. In this rural retirement, literary toil was pleasantly relieved by out-door exercise, and converse with simple nature in those homely and thoroughly English scenes; poetry continued to be an occasional recreation; and those Sabbath labours which had commenced at St. Alban's, and were not altogether discontinued at Brompton, found scope sometimes in the village chapel, sometimes in the neighbouring hamlets. The stage-coach usually stopped several times in the week at the garden gate, to receive or deliver precious little packets of printer's " copy," for the days of penny stamps and book postage were not yet dreamed of; and once a month the editor was wont to mount the roof or shut himself inside, as the weather might dictate, and rush up to London, at the giddy rate, of eight miles per hour, to superintend the " getting out" of the *Eclectic.*

Welcome as the fresh escape to the country was, the year spent in London had been one of great mercy, and had passed happily and profitably. A retrospective memorandum of its circumstances concludes thus :—
" I could not probably have spent it so usefully at St. Alban's, nor, with all the drawbacks, so happily. Were

not those reasons for our going there?" A journey into Suffolk, Norfolk, and Essex had formed a pleasant interlude; and when railways were not, and the separation of friends by a hundred or two hundred miles interposed a barrier which it is difficult now to realize, such a journey was anticipated and remembered with a degree of interest in which it requires some little stretch of imagination—or of memory—to sympathize. Family mercies occupied a large space in the retrospect. A fourth son, born at St. Michael's, and a fifth at Brompton, filled the place of the two lost ones; and effectually guarded against the danger of dulness in the new country home.

The following brief extracts touch upon some of the literary and ecclesiastical occupations of this interval. Mr. Conder's village labours had led to the publications here referred to—"The Village Lecturer," a 12mo volume of sermons for rustic congregations; and "Thomas Johnson's Reasons for Dissent," a plain discussion of Noncomformist principles, in two tracts, in dialogue form, of which several thousands were sold, and which is still suited for distribution among cottage readers.

To JOHN RYLEY, ESQ.

November 7, 1822.

XXXVIII. . . . . You will be surprised to receive a communication from me for the *Congregational Magazine*. I wrote it off to-day on the spur of the moment; and as Philippensis ought not to go unanswered, I hope it will please you. My sermon was not wholly suggested by Joyce, though I got some valuable ideas from him. But I have been lately paying particular attention to the 1st Epistle of John, which has obtained far less attention than it merits. I preached again for M. last night, on Justification, from Rom. v. 9. It was an old village sermon—at least, I had preached it once in the village of Park Street. It is a most comprehensive text. Your high pulpits, however, make one feel very differently from the plain deal desk just overlooking the forms of a rustic tenement, half-lighted up with thin candles. But M.'s Wednesday evening congregation are simple-minded pious people.

To REV. H. MARCH.

December, 1822.

XXXIX. Art thou in health, my brother? I have no sword in my hand to accompany the question with a thrust under the fifth rib, but such castigation as my pen may administer were most worthily bestowed on you, could I be sure that you would answer in the affirmative. I have written to you twice, at distant intervals—have sent you the "Village Lecturer" at one time, and "Thomas Johnson," Part II., at another—have been waiting, with all the vain solicitude of an author, superinduced on all the honest anxiety of a friend, for a notice in reply; but all in vain. The year has almost run out, and we parted at Midsummer, since which your existence in this world has been a mere presumption with me, an hypothesis which is fast losing its probability. Have you been ill? Have you got married? Are you compiling a folio? Or what has so strangely absorbed you? I shall expect no ordinary matter-of-course explanation of so pertinacious and unreasonable a silence. Overwhelmed as I am with demands on my pen just now, you must consider it as an unaffected proof of my thinking more of you than you appear to do of us, that I sit up an extra half-hour to send this scrawl of inquiry to find you out, or your executors.

. . . . Have you ever seen Calvin's sermons on Jacob and Esau, from the passage in Genesis ? There is some naughty theology in them. I wish you could learn from Creak whether they are in his works: They were preached in French. I want chiefly to know at what time of his life they were preached, whether in the days of raw zeal, or of mellow orthodoxy.

XL. Thank you for your remarks on the "Village Lecturer." The work has been abundantly lauded in the *Christian Monitor*, a Scotch periodical, in the *Congregational Magazine, Guardian,* etc. But you have found the most fault, and given the most emphatic praise ; for I value more the praise of having urged truth home on the conscience, than any other encomium that could be passed on it. As to your objection to the want of a formal division in some (for to some only it applies— *plan* there is, strictly and steadily adhered to, in all), Morison says you are right ; and I am therefore bound to defer to your concurrent decision. I am not indeed inclined to dispute that your plan is *generally* preferable; but I am disposed to advocate a *variety* of method, and cannot quite think that every subject must needs be treated in the same method. I have no objection to exposition, sermon, and homily, in turn. And if the heads and outline of the less formal discourse may not stick in the memory quite so well, the end may be answered if but a general impression is left. But, as I said before, I do not mean to dispute the general correctness of your remark. I think I may venture to say that those sermons, as delivered, were understood. Whether any lasting good was the result, will probably not be known in this world. I am quite uncertain whether a second volume will be called for. I have more than a sufficient number of sketches, some that I have preached from, and others drawn up as the subject occurred.

A catechism on Nonconformity—is it really wanted? I should like to draw up one, if I thought it was, but should like to talk it over with you. You have seen Miller's "Catechism on a Christian Church," of course. I think I should prefer giving lectures on Nonconformity to teaching its principles in a catechism. Would you in a catechism go into history, as Palmer has done? If not, the whole will go into a nutshell. Let me have your matured ideas. My abridgment* you will find improved and simplified, if I do not deceive myself. . . . . I can beat your Roman Catholic story. Morison's father was explicitly told by a Scotch Catholic, that if the priest told him that a crow which appeared to him black, was white, he should believe it, for that the priest must be infallible.

Chenies, April, 1823.

XLI. What do you use as a *doctrinal* catechism? Do you use any? I have been lately looking at the Assembly's Catechism, but cannot bring myself to approve of it. This would have been a confession of heresy a century ago; but do we not really want a *doctrinal catechism*, with Scripture proofs, suited to the present state of theological knowledge? I have sometimes thought of attempting such a thing. My whole spare time has lately been occupied with revising the "Memoirs of Pious Women," by Gibbons and Burder, and writing several new lives for the new edition, in the place of a good deal of religious trash which I have cast out. I hope I shall have done a service to the cause, as the work is a popular one, and some of the lives are very interesting.

* Second Edition of "Protestant Nonconformity."

My next job must be a second volume of "The Village Lecturer," which is called for. It is a mercy that I can stand writing better than you, or I should long since have been knocked up. But He who has given us our respective tasks, "knoweth our frame."

Chénies, July 5, 1823.—Three months have elapsed since we came into this sweet retreat. He maketh us lie down in green and flowery pastures. Lord, show me what I can do for Thee here; and teach me to learn of Thee, the *meek and lowly* Teacher, who didst not think it beneath Thee to attend to infant disciples. That is not a sincere, simple desire to be useful, which disdains the narrowest sphere—which is not faithful in a little, or content to toil much for a little success—which cannot at times *stand by*, and when little is to be done with man, occupy itself in "besieging" heaven.

September 21, 1823.—This day three years I was lying great part of the day on my bed, after my fall. Blessed be my God for life prolonged. Lord bless me, and make me a blessing. . . . . God is condescending to employ me here. How unexpectedly can he open a door of usefulness! But "*thou that teachest another*"—needful is the caution. How much easier and pleasanter it is to serve God in some ways, than to trust in Him, submit to Him, wait for Him. Yet may I not hope my life has been spared in mercy for God's service? "Truly I am thy servant; Thou hast loosed my bonds." If I have been useful, it has been *since then*.

While residing at Chenies, Mr. Conder published a volume of poems, "the casual production of leisure hours, during the last twelve years;" and commenced what

proved the most laborious work of his life, and made a
heavy demand on his active brain and pen during seven
years, the "Modern Traveller." The former work came
out under the title of "The Star in the East, with other
Poems; by Josiah Conder." It included, as the preface
intimates, some compositions from Mrs. Conder's pen.
The principal poem was in part a republication ("to the
extent of about ninety lines") of a poem published in 1812,
under the title "Gloria in Excelsis Deo," of which the
greater part of the impression was given away. The other
poems are arranged under the three heads of "Sacred,"
"Domestic," and "Miscellaneous," including several
descriptive sketches from nature. Of the sacred pieces,
several have established themselves in our psalmody; and
those which come under the denomination of hymns or
psalms have been recently reprinted in the little volume
which their author was engaged in carrying through the
press, when he was unexpectedly called to close his earthly
course, and learn the "new song" of the Church above.

The "Modern Traveller" was designed to supply for
general readers a popular, correct, and comprehensive
survey of the principal countries of the world, and a
convenient *vade-mecum* for travellers, the description of
each country forming a complete work in a very portable
form. It was published in monthly parts, two of which
formed a volume. The series, extending to thirty volumes,
was completed in the year 1830. "Italy," in three
volumes, was subsequently added. It is curious that the
most laborious and complete account as yet existing in
the language of the various countries of the globe, should
have been the production of a writer who never crossed
either of the channels in his life, nor, until he had passed his
sixtieth year, ever travelled as far from London as even to
the English lakes. Mr. Conder at first undertook to edit

the whole work, and to execute a portion of it himself. Writing (in March) to his friend Mr. Ryley, who had engaged to write the volume on Greece, he says:—" The work is meant to be strictly popular—as light and *anecdotistical* as you please. I have undertaken to edit the whole work; but as to writing it all it is quite impossible, and I should be glad to have yet further assistance than you can give. You will see that I have taken no small pains with Palestine, and it pleases, I am told, very much. I am pledged to get out Syria, Part I., for May 1st, and must work very hard." Eventually he received assistance in but one or two volumes, and even those involved considerable labour in editing. The work, with these exceptions, was the product of his single pen, and forms a monument of literary industry not often surpassed. Every work of importance or value was consulted, extended accounts were laboriously digested, and conflicting statements scrutinized and reconciled. Great pains were bestowed, in several instances, on the history of the country under consideration, as in the case of the four volumes on India. Several of the volumes still remain the best guide-books to the traveller in the respective countries. It is simple fact to say, that the thirty-three volumes constitute one of the most accurate, faithful, and laborious compilations in the compass of literature.

Chenics, May, 1824.

XLII. . . . . I have been compelled to suspend all correspondence, and have hardly been able to take time sufficient for needful exercise. I have unwittingly involved myself in more task-work than I can well accomplish. For the past three months I have produced a part per month (180 pages) of a certain work called the " Modern Traveller," and must still do so until relieved

by my coadjutors in the work. Before that commenced
I had to get out my poems. I have had half a volume
of sermons transcribed for some months, but have been
wholly unable to proceed with them. All this, in addition to what comes upon me monthly—the *Eclectic!*
And in the midst of this, my poor friend R—— has been
of little service to me for some months, owing to the
anxiety connected with the illness and death of his son.
. . . . I am now writing while you are slumbering, not
because I am more at leisure, but because I am too tired
to prosecute my literary toils to-night. I have reason
to be thankful that, notwithstanding late hours and hard
work, my health has been very good, as well as that of
my dear wife and our triumpuerate.

    . . . . The *Eclectic* has contained some articles I
should like to chat about, but I will not fill up my paper
with them. Some of our wiseacres are finding out that
the *Eclectic* is *rising*—that is, they *read* it. You will
find an article of Robert Hall's in the last number.

    . . . . We leave Chenies, that is to say, our term
expires, at Midsummer, but our future *locale* is undeter-
mined. We are anxious to fix in the neighbourhood of
Uxbridge, for the sake of being near my sister, but no
house has as yet turned up. This is a delightful retreat,
and we are attached to the place and the people; but
here is strict communion, no doctor, and—*no house:*
three sufficient reasons for not staying you will say.
But it has been a pleasant inn by the way; and I have
found abundant village-work. Whether any good has
been done, another day will reveal. I have occasionally
supplied my excellent neighbour's pulpit (though de-
barred from the table), and have found myself none the
worse for three services on the Sunday. My *first* Sabbaths are spent in London.

The hoped-for house made its appearance just in time, not in the neighbourhood of Uxbridge, but in the outskirts of the quiet little town of Watford. Thither Mr. Conder and his family removed at Midsummer, 1824, when the pleasant sojourn at Chenies terminated, and there the following fifteen years of his life were spent.

, As the volume of poems above referred to has for many years been out of print, and it is doubtful if they will ever be reprinted, the reader may not be displeased by the insertion of the following two sketches of Buck-·· inghamshire scenery, which will answer for any other autumn, as well as for one thirty years ago. The village clocks have ticked out the last moments of a whole gene-ration since then, and a second generation reaps the harvest; but the same beech woods slope down to the meadowy valley, and the trout stream murmurs among the rushes and under the drooping boughs the same song as of old :—

> " For men may come, and men may go,
> But I go on for ever."

The first of these sonnets is from Mrs. Conder's pen ; the second from Mr. Conder's own hand. In the original volume they form half of a series of four sonnets on " Autumn."

I.

> A glorious day ! The village is a-field :
> Her pillow'd lace no thrifty housewife weaves,
> Nor platters sit beneath the flowery eaves.
> The golden slopes an ample harvest yield ;
> And every hand that can a sickle wield
> Is busy now. Some stoop to bind the sheaves,
> While to the o'erburden'd waggon one upheaves
> The load, among its streamers half conceal'd.

* " Star in the East," etc., pages 173, 174.

We heard the ticking of the lonely clock
  Plain thro' each open door, all was so still.
For, busily dispersed, near every shock
  Their hands with trailing ears the urchins fill.
Where all is clear'd, small birds securely flock,
  While full on lingering day the moon shines from the hill.

II.

Now that the flowers have faded, 'tis the turn
  Of leaves to flaunt in all their gayest dyes.
  'Tis Autumn's gala: every dryad vies
In decking out her bower. How richly burn
  The gorgeous masses in the amber skies,
Where to the west, the valley, with its stream,
Is shut with woods that drink the setting beam
  There by its crimson foliage one descries
The cherry, thrown out by the auburn shades
  Of beech, with russet oak, and hoary sallow,
And greenest ash, bearing its golden keys,
  With here and there wych-elm of paler yellow.
How gracefully the waning season fades !
So Nature's every dress and every look can please.

CHAPTER VI.

WATFORD.

EVERYBODY knows where Watford is; for it is a station on the North-Western Railway, and everybody has travelled by the North-Western Railway. Everybody knows how the railway sweeps in a quarter-circle round the quiet little town, as if it liked to look at it, but thought it a pity to touch it; and how, rushing over the viaduct, which seems, by its length and loftiness, a standing mockery of the quiet little river that wanders beneath it amongst water-meadows and rows of pollard willows, the "down express" sweeps past a pleasant picture of houses girdled with hedge-rows and corn-fields; the old church, picturesquely odd and charmingly ugly, keeping guard over the other buildings, like an old sentinel asleep at his post, and the modest Baptist chapel in ambush, as it were, among the trees; how it flashes past the station, and between the steep chalk banks of the deep cutting, and plunges into the darkness of a mile-long tunnel.

But thirty years ago, everybody did not know where Watford was. Railways and locomotives were among the undeveloped possibilities of the future. Any one who had talked of travelling from London to Birmingham in four hours, and of crossing the Atlantic in a week, would have been laughed to scorn as a hair-brained enthusiast; and any one who had foretold, that within forty years, we should talk round our dinner-tables in London of what has been done and said the same morning in New York, or, in a few years more, in Pekin and Australia, would have run great risk of being shut up as a madman. It would have been as ridiculous and absurd as to have asserted that spoons and forks would be plated or gilded by electricity, and portraits painted by sunbeams; or that Papists and Dissenters might be admitted to Parliament, and the corn-laws abolished, and yet the British Constitution survive the shock.

In those quiet old days—only a generation ago, yet separated by what a wide intellectual interval from this sixth decade of the century!—Watford was a most quiet little country town, exceedingly well-known by the four thousand people who dwelt there, but not very widely known to the rest of the world. It possessed the usual features and social elements of a small market-town in an agricultural district, with no staple trade or manufacture. There were the neighbouring nobility and gentry, who made their appearance on great occasions, as at public meetings, concerts, or county elections. There were triumphant Tories, and wistful Whigs. There was the vicar, an earl's nephew, generally to be seen on a fine day, with his portly figure, white trousers, and jovial face, chatting with his parishioners; or not seldom, in the hunting season, riding through the street (there was but one street), in his scarlet jacket and white cords. There was the dissenting minister who preached at the quaint little old Baptist chapel (since superseded by a modern structure), the secluded position of which, entrenched among crooked back-lanes, told of the times in which Nonconformity had been fain to seek safety in obscurity. There were two or three rival lawyers, and two or three rival doctors, and two rival principal inns, one with a gentlemanly landlord, the other with an unparalleled waiter. There was the retired great book-seller, and the great brewer preparing to retire, and the great nobody, at the great white house, and the great man, who drove about in a little chaise, because he was too bulky to walk, never went to church because he could not get into his pew, and was credibly reported always to eat a leg of mutton as a precaution before he went out to dine. There were rich millers and farmers, and well-to-do shopkeepers, and hard-working cottagers, too many publicans, and a full average of beggars and scamps. There were electioneering squabbles (for the county), and great savings' bank questions, and great right-of-way questions; and, in later years, a great Reform banquet and illumination; and, as in most small country towns, where everybody knows everybody, a great deal of gossip. As the town lay several miles off the Great North Road, there was no great amount of traffic passing through. Two or three London coaches, on their way to Chesham, Hempstead, or some other town further down in the country, were the modest substitute for long railway trains, with their two or three hundred passengers. A few lumbering carriers' vans represented the "goods trains" of later and more impatient times. Every night, the mail-coach, with its flaring eyes and red-coated guard, made the quiet streets echo to its horn, picked up, perhaps, its one passenger, and excited mysterious feelings of respect and wonder in the minds of little boys. All around the dear, dull, quiet little town lay the still more quiet country. Two minutes would bring you into it; on the one side across the little river Colne, into green low-lying meadows, which the artificially-raised banks do not keep the stream from overflowing for miles after very heavy rains; on the other, through the lime-shaded churchyard, out among corn-fields and homesteads, and shady lanes; or over stiles and through footpaths, to where the deer browse among the spreading limes and beeches, or hide in the thickets of tall fern, in Cassiobury Park.

On the outskirts of the town, surrounded by a pleasant garden, orchard, and meadows, stood (and still stands) a white, slate-roofed house, yclept "Watford Field House." It was so named from a large open piece of ground known as Watford Field, which was what is termed "Lammas land," being under cultivation during summer, and common after the harvest has been got in. The writer can scarcely persuade himself to describe the house as small, so lofty and capacious did it seem in childish eyes; but it was not particularly commodious, having been altered from an inferior building. It afforded but two sitting-rooms, one of which was necessarily occupied as library and literary workshop; so the other had to do double duty as dining-room and drawing-room. But in summer-time, the garden made a delightful withdrawing-room, where the tea-table was not seldom set in front of the house, on what the children called "mamma's lawn," in distinction from "papa's lawn," on which the study looked out. The charm of the residence lay outside the house; in the garden, where walks were turned, and new portions enclosed, and fences set up, and flower-beds designed, and hedges and shrubberies planted, and which, as years rolled by, amply repaid with its growing beauty the labour bestowed on it; in the orchard and meadows, where violets grew in spring, and hay was cut in summer, and fruit ripened in autumn, demanding, on the part of the juvenile scions of the house, rigorous watch and ward against stealthy invasions of greedy swine or lawless urchins from the hostile border terri-

R

tory of the Lammas land; in a word, in the pure, healthful, cheerful atmosphere of the country which breathed around.

Amidst these quiet country scenes fifteen years of Mr. Conder's life were passed; years of intense and almost unremitting labour, chequered with some corroding cares and trials, and now and then shadowed with heavy sorrows; yet years of great and manifold mercy, during which, though death entered once under his roof, the fireside circle of wife and children was not only preserved unbroken, but augmented by the birth of a daughter and a sixth son. In addition to his literary toils, Mr. Conder found time to take part in various benevolent and religious movements and institutions, not only in the town, but in a somewhat extended district. He was very frequently engaged in preaching, sometimes at the Baptist Chapel in the town, or the Independent Chapel at the neighbouring village of Bushey, but more often at some humble place of worship in the surrounding country. Sometimes, after a week of hard work, and in prospect of another, his Sabbath rest consisted in taking three full services. His catholic spirit led him frankly to co-operate with Christians of all denominations. His house was always open to ministers; he never grudged his labour in a good cause; and as the standing rule, with the Church as well as with the world, is that those who are willing to work shall do not only their own share, but the share of those who are not willing, the time spent in attending meetings of various religious societies, and in other gratuitous labours, must have amounted to something very considerable. Curiously enough (as the writer learned accidentally from a gentleman who knew Mr. Conder only from meeting him on these occasions, in a town at some distance), these disinterested and, to him, costly labours led many to imagine that he was a wealthy man; perhaps the only instance in which he was estimated above his merit.

While residing at Watford, Mr. Conder completed the "Modern Traveller" and "Italy;" continued to edit the *Eclectic*, until he parted with it at the close of 1836 to Dr. Thomas Price; compiled and edited the "Congregational Hymn Book;" published a "Dictionary of Geography," a second volume of Poems, a new translation of the "Epistle to the Hebrews," an "Analytical View of all Religions," and several smaller works; and commenced the editorship of the *Patriot* newspaper, which he continued until his decease.

Some of the following extracts from his correspondence will indicate at what pressure his mental powers were worked. He wrote a good deal standing, at a desk made for the purpose, which no doubt contributed to his health. Often his pen was at work far into the night, not from preference, but from necessity. Had not his constitution been naturally very sound and strong, it could not have stood the strain often put upon it. But his capacity for intellectual labour, and delight in it, were great; he wrote with amazing facility and rapidity, and if only his mind could have been kept free from care and anxiety, it seemed as if he could execute any amount of work without distress. Almost his only recreations were walking, working in his garden, and music, with occasional relaxation in the society of a pleasant circle of friends. Change of occupation seemed to serve him for rest. If not engaged in preaching on the Sabbath, his recreation was found in translating an epistle of the New Testament, or in studying various biblical and theological subjects; and more than one of his published works were the result of these Sabbath studies.

He had a great power of abstraction; and although he usually worked alone in his study, he could also carry on his labour in the midst of the fireside circle, undistracted by what was going on around, though not always inattentive to it. One of his sisters writes:—"While I was astonished at the versatility of his mind and his industry, I often feared his brain would give way under the pressure. His mind was, however, remarkably buoyant; he could cast off care for a time, and dismiss subjects from his mind as often as he laid down the pen; and this saved him." He had in a remarkable measure the "power of giving attention to two totally different subjects at the same time. I have often known him busily engaged writing a review, while a party were reading aloud an interesting book; when he would make intelligent remarks upon it, proving that he thoroughly entered into what was being read." This habitually strong mastery over his own thoughts, combined with his calm and elastic temperament, no doubt enabled him to carry cheerfully a load under which most men would have staggered. But his natural gifts would not have stood him in such stead as they did, had he not possessed the secret of that strength which prayer lays hold of, and that antidote to anxious fear which is found in "casting all our care upon God." His faith in the overruling and fatherly providence of God in all things, small as well as great, was remarkably simple and intense; and it was signally honoured by Him who loves to be trusted as well as obeyed implicitly, in many instances which it does not fall within the plan of this memoir to relate. Few Christians have believed with more entire confidence, or proved more fully and evidently in their personal experience, the truth of the promise, "The steps of a good man are ordered by the Lord, and He delighteth in his way. Though he

fall, he shall not be utterly cast down, for the Lord up-
holdeth him with his hand." The cheering light of such
promises was none the less welcome and precious in his
eyes, because it shone from "those old Hebrew stars;" for
he was not one of those who imagine that the New Testament—itself the fulfilment of an Old Testament promise—
contradicts or supersedes the elder Scriptures, or that in
a world like this we can afford to fling away any of God's
promises, or repose our faith upon a mutilated Bible.

Watford, Aug. 1824.—How little, three months ago,
did we think of residing here. Not more shut up did
our way seem before removing to St. Albans and to
Chenies, than it did before this turning opened. . . . . .
No sooner have we taken this, than houses are offered
where we had been seeking them, at Missenden, etc. But
I feel in a strange land, among strangers—the church of
a strange communion. ["Strict communion" here, too,
in those days; the preacher, after instructing his worthy
Baptist brethren from the Word of God and leading their
devotions, having to go and sit in the vestry, while they
celebrated around "*their* table" the communion of saints!]
For the poor people of Chenies I had formed an affectionate interest. But these are the conditions of a
journey. This is but another inn on the road.

Lord, fit me by the grace of humility for thy work
here. Give *Thou* me my directions and my message.
Lead me by thy Spirit in a *plain path*. Purify my zeal
from ambition. Let me not forget that important part
of likeness to Christ, self-denial. "For even Christ
pleased not Himself."

O God, I adore Thee that Thou canst make me holy
and meet to dwell with Thee, through the might of thy
transforming grace.

Lord, grant me grace to humble myself under the hand of thy mercy, that I may not need to be humbled by the hand of thy chastisement.

I trust I am pardoned by my Judge and Governor: I daily need the forgiveness of my heavenly Father.

May I feel more of the power of religion on my soul, connecting me with Thee as my Author, Preserver, and Happiness! That power, what is it but love, the only reality in knowledge?

To the Rev. H. March.

London, July 2, 1824.

XLIII. My dear Friend,—I am sitting down at Homerton to answer your letter of May 31, that I may put a letter for you into the post-office before I leave town to recommence the toils of the month. I was very sorry to hear of your having sustained the loss of your brother's society and effective services. It must have left you very lonely, and it is not ,good to be alone. How do you manage? Even a monastery is better than a hermitage. I do not advise you to marry; you would think it, perhaps, much like my saying, "Be rich, be in good health, be ye warmed and filled." But I should be glad to hear that you had so found favour of the Lord, as the wise man speaks, as to be directed to a help-meet. . .

You asked me some time ago to explain my objections to the Assembly's Catechism. I will detail a few; and if you can obviate them, I shall be glad to be set right. I object, then, in the first place, to Questions 7 and 8. Where did the venerable compilers get the phrase, *Decrees of God?* Why adopt an unscriptural, or at least non-scriptural word, on purpose to give an explanation of it, which explanation is little better than verbiage, and can, at all events, convey no rational idea to a child?

This is surely "vain philosophy." (2.) Q. 11. "Works of providence"—"preserving of actions"—what strangely incorrect expressions! And the providence of God is improperly identified with his moral government. (3.) Q. 12. "A covenant of life"—unintelligible, at least to me. I know, indeed, what must be meant, but the phrase is alike obscure and ambiguous—an affected wrapping-up of the fact in the technicalities of theology. (4.) Q. 13. "The freedom of their own will"—an idle attempt at explanation. "Why *left?*" says a child. "Why did God go away? Had they sinned before, and did God leave them to punish them?" . . . . (6.) Q. 18. Here is a strange confusion of sinfulness and guilt— hereditary taint and personal transgression. (7.) Q. 20. I object strongly to the phraseology ; and without holding anything in direct contradiction to what is here affirmed, I could neither teach nor subscribe such crude and un- scripture-like statements. I am not sure, however, that, taken in connection with what follows, the words do not imply what is incorrect in sentiment. (8.) Q. 21. He is the Redeemer *of the world.* (9.) Q. 29. The redemp- tion purchased is the purchase purchased. The language of Scripture is, that Christ has purchased the Church, not the salvation of the Church. The "purchased pos- session" is not heaven, or the blessings of salvation, but the Church itself, which He has ransomed. (10.) "Effec- tual calling," in Q. 30, is a technicality far from felicit- ous. (11.) Q. 67. "Kill" is a blunder. The magistrate may *kill.* War was at least lawful when the command- ments were given. The sixth commandment is, "Thou shalt *do no murder.*" . . . . (14.) Q. 94. I should say that it does *not* signify our ingrafting into Christ, etc.

Here is a formidable array of objections. I hope that you will not deem me captious or heretical. But I should doubtless have been considered as both in the "good old days" of King Noll. The Presbyterians would have been ready to grill me. But now for other matters. R. Hall's article was the review of Biet's lectures in the May number. It followed a very masterly one on the criminal jurisprudence of France. In the present number is an admirable article by our friend I. T., on the state of religion in France. If anything would make a Dissenting work sell, such articles would ; and if the Dissenters were worthy of the *Eclectic*, would make them at least prize it. Thank you for withstanding the flippant and indolent depreciation of it. I have not written much in the late numbers ; and nothing but my being a writer in the *Review* prevents my taking a much higher tone. I am continually receiving testimonies to its character from those who are *without*. . . . Thank you for your kind invitation, in my own name, and that of my wife; but it is impossible to accept of it, as we have more live stock than we could either bring or leave; and my books, which must follow me, would be a cartload. My health has been mercifully good in the midst of all my labours.

To Mr. Ryley.

London, July 31, 1824.

XLIV. . . . . I have never been so near being knocked up by hard work and anxiety combined, and had almost despaired of getting out this *Eclectic*. Your assistance has saved me. Indisposition in the early part of the month, and *removing into another house*, together with the quantity of work involved in this last part of the "Traveller," drove me at last into extremities. I worked on Monday from half-past five, a.m., to near twelve at night, with little intermission, and by this sort of exertion only I have been brought through. Next month I have the prospect of a respite, but I am almost afraid to reckon upon anything.

You express a wish to have had Asia Minor committed to you. You have, I am persuaded, no idea of the labour it has cost me, and the great perplexity in which great part of its geography is involved—far more than either Syria or Palestine. Greece cannot be more complicated. However, I have a proposal to make, which will, I hope, be agreeable to you. I will undertake Greece, if you will give it up and take *Spain*, which I had undertaken to do next. On account of the connection between Greece and Asia Minor, I should like to do it; and have, besides, materials by me for its modern history. Spain, I imagine, would bother you much less, and interest you almost as much. If you have no objection to this arrangement, have the goodness to send back all the books you have of Mr. Duncan's to him; and those which we have collected for Spain shall be forwarded to you, together with any which may occur to you.

XLV.—(TO THE REV. H. M.)

Watford Field House, November 9, 1824.

Let Mother Rome the banns forbid,
    When priests in wedlock join;
Sure Paul might do as Peter did,
    And Luther's right is thine;
And we will keep, in spite of Rome,
Our wives, our Bibles, and our home.

Such was the thought on hearing first,
    My friend, that you were mated,
For which most Christian act you'd erst
    Been excommunicated,—
In spite of what, as runs the Vulgate,
St. Paul did specially promulgate;—

"*Honorabile in omnibus*
  Conjugium," and so forth.
They honour it, they tell you, thus :
  (The strangest gloss to go forth !)
Marriage a sacrament they make,
Yet will not let the priest partake !

Far worse this barbarous interdict,
  Than Baptist strict communion !
But you are now a Benedict,
  And blessed be your union.
What joy to find a faithful wife
A fellow-heir of endless life !

That hermitage of yours, how changed
  Will now its aspect seem !
The walks where once you lonely ranged
  In meditative dream ;
Or, when without 'twas dark or muddy,
The once dull parlour, lonely study !

That *sanctum !* May a wife intrude,
  Unauthorized, so far ?
And what if little Harry should,
  Or Miss, besiege Papa ?
O March ! wilt thou become like me,—
Not even have your study free ?

Like me ?—I need not wish my friend
  A more indulgent lot.
May Health and Peace and Love attend
  (Whether boys come or not)
Your wedded life, and may your way
Be ever *bon*, and ever *gai !*

                              JOSIAH CONDER.

                              March 1, 1826.
XLVI. . . . . I have before protested against the
inequitable rule of letter for letter. I cannot correspond
with an old friend on such formal terms, nor can I write
to any friend I value so often as I like to hear from him.

After you had *seen* how I am circumstanced, I should have thought my longest silence might be accounted for. I have just got through a month of literary labour that I dreaded to look forward to, and almost shudder to look back upon—12 sheets to compose and print in 24 days—*i. e.*, 96 octavo pages, and 216 in 18mo. Through the goodness of God, my health has lasted me through it all; and this month I shall have a short interval to recover my breath, as the next part of the "Modern Traveller" is not to appear till the 1st of May, I am thus taking literally the first moment I could conscientiously spare to reply to your letter.

. . . . In your previous letter you ask me whether my literary cares and employments deaden the spirit towards things divine. I think I may say, as *interests*, certainly not. I think I found myself in quite as much danger when employed on my Commentary,* as when engaged upon works less connected with religion. I think it is more difficult to be spiritual, when occupied with religion as it were professionally or critically, than when studying Horace, or compiling the "Traveller." Literature is not my pursuit, but my business; and to succeed in it—to get through the mere quantity of work per month which I must do, I feel the necessity of Divine help and direction. The review of Milton was a serious effort, and was not, as you will perceive, drawn up in a hurry. I had taken months to think over the chief points, and, distrusting the effect of plunging into such controversies on my mind, had endeavoured to arm myself with prayer against the encounter with scepticism under so specious a form. I have found the result beneficial to my own mind, and believe that the view I have

---

* A brief but careful commentary on St. Matthew's Gospel, never published.

taken is the only satisfactory one. I am glad that *you* approve of it.

XLVII. Did you and our friend —— have any talk about Mother Church and Dissenterism ? I find from a recent letter, that, though a practical Dissenter, he has some *penchant* towards conformity. I find *I* am considered by some persons as not decided enough, having been two or three times seen at Bushey Church, and being on terms of friendship with the excellent rector and curate. The subject of Dissent wants to be thoroughly revised in a philosophic spirit. I value our *privileges* as Dissenters more and more. I admire our practice, in some respects, less. The pious clergyman is "an ambassador in bonds;" and I am sometimes ready to wish to be "altogether such except these bonds." We, as Dissenters, have the best of the *argument;* but there is "something against us." Tell me what you say to these things.

A few brief extracts from Mr. Conder's correspondence during these years, with his youngest sister, will serve to show how thoroughly the real work of life, and the deep, solemn realities which underlie all the changes, storms, and shadows of its surface, were present to his mind amidst all his daily toils ; and how ready his busy pen was to turn, when needful, to the difficult yet grateful task of Christian exhortation and consolation.

XLVIII. I feel disposed to say to you in the words of St. James, "Let patience have its perfect work." "Ye have heard," he says, " of the patience of Job, and have seen the *end of the Lord;* that the Lord is very pitiful and of tender mercy." That is, what the Lord did in the end. As if he had said, the beginning of Job's history seemed to make this almost questionable. It must have been a long two years that Joseph passed in the prison, after the chief butler was restored to favour, under the sickening feeling of hope deferred. But though the chief butler had forgotten him, his heavenly Father had not. There is nothing more hard than to wait for the Lord, to "rest in the Lord, and wait patiently for Him," when answers to prayers seem so long delayed as almost to amount to denial; when you have been watching events and changes as they came on, in hope that each would prove the friend you were looking for, but when it drew near, the countenance was different, and you kept looking out still.

The time has been that I have been led to say with Job, "Show me wherefore thou contendest with me?" But were the gold to say this to the refiner, it would get for answer, Silly metal, I am not angry with you, I should not take such pains with baser minerals. To interpret trying dispensations as marks of displeasure is the sure way to "faint when rebuked," which we are forbidden to do, because He loveth whom He chasteneth.

(On occasion of the dangerous illness of two nephews.) —Let me say to you, my dear sister, what I was enabled to say to my dear wife, at the *most trying* moment. Now is the time to show your principles. Place your dear boys, for life or death, in the hands of Him who has the keys of the grave and of death, your Saviour and theirs. Commit these lambs to the Good Shepherd, who laid down his life for them. Repose on his wisdom and his love. He knows the issue, and it will be well. I pray that they may both be spared to you for good, if it be his will. If not, He can and will support you, and heaven will be the dearer to you.

The love of Him who gave his life for us ought to be a compensation for the unkindness of the whole world.

It is a world of changes; but there is One who changes not, and if the right sort of change is going on within us, we need not much care what changes are going on without us, for the last change to us will then be the best, "Who shall change this vile body," etc.

As to feeling thankful—thankful to God, it is a great luxury, and, sad to say, a great attainment, but one that we ought daily to be striving after, by calling up to remembrance past benefits, and dwelling upon all the realities of the believer's portion in both worlds. Being thankful is a different thing from feeling thankful, which is delighting in thankfulness; but the former will lead to the latter. Let us cherish the conviction, and give expression to it in acknowledging God's mercies, and this will give birth to the feeling and emotion so beautifully expressed by the Psalmist, "I love the Lord, because He hath heard my voice and my supplications."

The one occasion, already alluded to, when death entered under a roof at other times signally defended from his attacks, was in the first week of the year 1828. Mrs. Conder's favourite niece, a singularly lovely girl, had been staying with them for three months, with a rapidly diminishing hope of her restoration to health. For some weeks that faint hope had been almost entirely extinguished, but the summons came at last, as it so often does, with a stunning suddenness. She was conversing as usual, when in an instant she became insensible, and "in an hour all was over." The circumstances of the event combined with the loss itself to make the trial a very severe one. It was among those things which cannot be spoken of, after many years have rolled by, without a saddened look and a subdued tone; while to those on whom the bereavement fell most heavily, it was one of those chasms which no lapse of years can fill; they open an abyss into the very centre of our being, and nothing but eternity can repair them.

In the summer of the same year, the busy pen thus records its incessant labours :—

XLIX. I would have replied to your letter of June 11 immediately, had I not been so hard pressed, having to get out *six* sheets of the "Traveller," beside the usual quantum for the *Eclectic.* . . . As to Vaughan's " Wiclif,"* if it is not everything that it might have been, it will perform a great service, by placing the great reformer's character in a more prominent light. How has Sharon Turner treated him ? As to the alterations he has made in the language, my advice would have been to modernize the *citations,* so far as to make them intelligible to general readers, but *in every case* to give the original in notes or an appendix. No fault could then, I think, have been found, . Wiclif requires translating almost as much as a foreign writer. Vaughan felt his difficulty, although he has not taken, perhaps, the best method of surmounting it. But he had to think of the usefulness and the sale of his book.

. . . I have finished my history of India. Blacker I found, as you said, a mere military commentary, but very sensible; and I have made use of him, together with Prinsep, Malcolm, and Grant Duff. Certainly, Lord Hastings was a fine fellow, notwithstanding all the mean-

---

* First edition.

ness of his private character. I have turned to all your
Indian articles in the E. R., as well as Marsh's, and have
derived some assistance from them. It is singular that
in our little work should appear the first complete history
of India that was ever written. Mill is acting very un-
wisely in leaving his work unfinished; but I have found
him very tedious in his long lawyer dissertations. His six
volumes might have been easily compressed into four,
without lessening their value; and in fact I have endeavoured to give the *results* of all his "*argufying*," with all
his facts, corrected by other authorities. It has been a
work of immense toil.

Watford, Dec. 2, 1830.

L. . . . . I had entirely given up the idea of receiving any assistance from you this month, beyond the
articles received too late for the November number; but
I have been glad to use the small articles you sent. I
must, however, turn over a new leaf, and, if I am obliged
to write the whole *Review* myself,* not expose myself to
the ruinous and exhausting effects of disappointment.
If you can oblige me with any articles by the 15th of
this month, I shall be *very much obliged.* If not, I must
try what I can do, as both the sale of the work and my
own health suffer by the driving-off system. . . .

I should have sent you the "Landscape Annual," but
as it related to Venice, the subject I had in hand, I was
obliged to detain it. I had finished my article upon it
when your remarks upon the plates reached me, and I
cancelled all that I had said upon them that was not
actually in print. I never like to give an opinion on
these matters, not that ninety-nine readers out of a
hundred would detect me in a blunder if I were to make
one, but because I have no confidence in my own judg-

* A feat which he actually performed once, if not more than once.

ment. It is not often, however, that I find my opinions clashing with yours, which ought to make me think more highly of my own penetration. I am sometimes at a loss for technical expressions, which you bring in with an air of authority. . . . . Prout's "Falls of Terni" I think superior to Turner's in Hakewill. His view of Bologna, which you praise, is, I am assured by *two artists* who have been there, extremely faulty—indeed, a failure, being out of drawing and out of nature. This plate has cost me some trouble; for as it happens, in the first place, to contradict the letterpress, and as, in the next place, almost every account of the dimensions of these towers differs—some making the higher tower 350, others 320, others 250 high—some asserting that it is three feet out of the perpendicular, others that it does not lean at all, with endless other variations—it was of the more consequence to me to have a correct representation, and it is one of the few instances in which Prout has erred. Brockedon, with whom I dined at Duncan's and spent some hours next day, told me that he had pointed out to Prout the blunder. B. is reading my first volume of " Italy," to make corrections, which, if important, I shall notice in a list of *errata*. He is an exceedingly well-informed man, and has taken infinite pains with the whole subject of the Alps. He has been over the Viso, and taken drawings of it.

LII. . . . . There would be no difficulty in your earning money enough to make you easy, provided your health serves you, and that you were among us in London. I know it is of little use saying this—perhaps it is only annoying. Your daughter and your library bind you to Newark, and, when it came to the point, you would not like to leave that old house. Near London too, you will say, your expenses will be greater. On the other hand, at Leicester you are buried; you are too far off to run up to town often enough to rub off the rust; you want the stimulus of good and varied society, and your health suffers from insufficient mental excitement. Am I right? I have my *impossible* moods, believe it, as well as you; but I can still less than you afford to be the gentleman, and I have been ridden with the spur. You are living below your capabilities in more respects than one. But perhaps you are not the less happy. I do not pretend that it is simply for your own sake that I wish circumstances allowed of your being a resident within the compass of the *Court Guide*. I expect to meet Croly (who wants to know you), Allan Cunningham, Macculloch, Pringle, and "two or three more," on Tuesday, at Duncan's. I will promise you a knife and fork if you can be there.

LIII. . . . What is the "Enthusiasm Controversy?" You are not, I hope, a worldling—I mean, a reader of, and contributor to "*The World.*" I will be bound to say that had you reviewed the "Natural History of Enthusiasm" in the *E. R.*, you would have praised it as highly as I did. . . . . I am quite serious when I say that there are few reviewers, I believe, who display more conscientious candour and kindness than you do in your written articles, although you may be cynical or satirical enough in the critical humour of your unbending moods. What you say of *Sartorius* is surely applicable, *a fortiori*, to Foster, so far as it is just. But you know the Sartorian style is *really* unaffected—I mean as natural to the writer as the plainest English; and his thoughts, even when not new, are original in the sense of being elaborated by his own brain, not copied or stolen. I do not

know how you have arrived at the secret of the authorship of the N. H. Holdsworth and Ball, as well as the
author, will feel *much obliged* by your not disclosing your
suspicions. S., of Camberwell, who thought for some
time the author was I. T., has now *satisfied himself* that
he was quite wrong. The only reason for secresy on the
part of the author was the knowledge that his name
would operate to the prejudice of the work, especially
among his own people; just as my own name would
operate among the same excellent body. The Dissenters
have always had the reputation of never thinking too
highly of any one of their own body, unless he be a
popular declaimer; and I have no reason for feeling gratitude to them. My anonymous works have sold best.
The wise folks stare a little, I believe, at my name on the
title-page of the " Modern Traveller ;" and as that work
does not solicit their patronage, they may condescend to
think somewhat more highly of the author than they have
done of the editor of the poor *E. R.*, or the author of
" Nonconformity." Excuse all this egotism.

LIV. . . . . I am not going to plague you with re-
joinder, fully acquiescing in your conclusion, that you
and I are " clever fellows." I admit that the style of the
" Natural History" would identify its author *if* there
were half a dozen persons besides *ourselves* capable of
appreciating that sort of evidence. But there are not.
Mrs. Conder, indeed, found out the author entirely from
the style of the passages extracted, without a hint from
me. But it was chiefly from the style of *thought*, not of
expression. On the other hand, almost every one
ascribes it to Douglas. Then again, as to being identified by style, the review of " Acaster" in the *E. R.* is by
almost every one given to *me*, whereas I should imagine

nothing could be less like my style, if I have any. Of this I might doubt, as all sorts of articles by different contributors have been supposed to be mine, and mine have been ascribed to various writers. I do not believe you could hang any one by his style, if you must find a jury of twelve competent men to agree in the verdict. As to your remarks on the Sartorian style, there is a friend of mine who occasionally meets a question or position with the oracular response,' "yes and no." Such is my reply, to save you the annoyance of argumentation. I think you in many respects a cleverer fellow than Sartorius. I think myself (to be honest) as clever as he on some points; but I know no one who, in my judgment, has a more truly philosophic cast of mind or reach of thought. His brain is (pardon the word) *costive*, but he is as original a thinker as you will find in these times, and in my earlier days I was much indebted to intercourse with him for intellectual improvement and stimulus.

P. N. Row, April 9, 1831.

. LV. . . . By a very desperate effort I finished the MS. of "Italy," between twelve and one on the 29th, midnight; and then had two days to get out more than half the *Eclectic*. The last proofs of "Italy" occupied me the whole of Good Friday. It is now out, and herewith you receive a copy. . . . . Such a job I do not wish to have again. It has not only fagged me, but half ruined me, and I must work very hard upon the jobs I have been obliged to postpone, in order to bring myself round. . . . . I have no fault to find with Mr. D. He must sell 2500 copies, he says, before he pockets anything. If I could possibly have knocked up the thing, as I hoped, in six or eight months, instead of its occupying

the incessant labour of thirteen, I should have been sufficiently paid.

To the Rev. H. M.

LVI. . . . The " Law of the Sabbath" was an episode.
It cost me considerable pains, and has, I hope, done
some service, although it has been very coldly and sus-
piciously received by the Dissenters. The *Baptist Magazine* has *abused* and misrepresented it. The *Evangelical
Magazine* has praised it very cautiously. The *Congregational Magazine* has hitherto said nothing about it. The
World and the *Record* have pointedly refrained from
noticing it. On the other hand, I have had some private
expressions of satisfaction of a gratifying nature, of which
yours is not the least valuable. . . . I want to see
you, and to have a long chat with you about your
bishopric and other matters. Are you in possession of
any facts and documents which would be available towards
deciding the knotty point, at what precise point a church
in the progress of decline loses its collective capacity,
and becomes *de facto* extinct—so as, for instance, to cease
to be entitled to an endowment? If you can help me at
all towards solving this enigma, pray write *immediately.*
If not, let me hear at your convenience—the sooner the
more welcome.

The case referred to in the preceding extract was a
curious one; and, if it be regarded as affording a precedent in reference to the usages and principles of Protestant Dissenters, an important one. It was one referred
to the general body of Protestant Dissenting ministers
of the three denominations by the trustees of the estates
of the Sabbatarian Protestant Dissenters, in the year
1831. The case submitted to the body states, that "the-

Sabbatarian churches hitherto existing in London were, first, that assembling in Mill Yard, Goodman's Fields, formerly under the pastorship of the Rev. William Slater, who died in 1819, and since then without a pastor; and, secondly, that assembling in Still's Alley, Devonshire Square, under the pastorship of the Rev. Robert Burnside, and afterwards removed to the Welsh Chapel in Eldon Street, Finsbury, under the pastorship of the Rev. J. B. Shenstone, the present minister. During the later period of the ministry of the Rev. W. Slater, the church in Mill Yard, which had, together with the Sabbatarian interest generally, been long experiencing great decay, consisted of three male members (nephews of the minister) and seven female members, five of whom were also of the family of Slater. For some years previous to the death of the Rev. W. Slater, the three male members discontinued the observance of the seventh day Sabbath, and were in attendance on the worship of the Church of England; but one or two of them still continued to attend on the days of communion, in order to act as deacons in the office of the ordinance, down to the period of Mr. Slater's death."

It is further stated, that on Mr. Slater's death the chapel was shut up, and fell into gradual decay, no attempt having been made to secure a successor. The property was at that time in Chancery, and the suit did not terminate till 1826. New trustees were appointed by the Court to act with the surviving trustee; and though not themselves Dissenters, they endeavoured to carry out the trust. They repaired the chapel, advertised for a minister holding Sabbatarian, Baptist, and Armenian sentiments; and appointed, *ad interim*, the Rev. Thomas Russell, A.M., to officiate. This state of things continued until the year 1830, during which time one member had withdrawn, and two died; and of the remaining four, one had become confined to her bed by infirmity; but, it is added, " three others (daughters of Mrs. W. Slater) were, on the 5th August, 1826, admitted as members by the unanimous suffrages of the five other members then assembled, and in the presence of Mr. Russell. The existing number therefore, assuming the three last-mentioned to have been duly admitted, is seven females, of whom, from three to six have uniformly assembled at worship."

Under these circumstances, the trustees considered " that, in the absence of any indications of revival, it was impossible to consider the remaining members of Mill Yard as constituting a church, or even the *nucleus* of a church." They therefore decided that the *ad interim* arrangement could no longer be continued, and resolved to offer the place of worship to the Rev. Mr. Shenstone, " the only acting minister of the Sabbatarian persuasion in London," and to his congregation. The seven ladies, however, asserted that they *were* a church, and that no one had a right to obtrude a minister on them contrary to their choice. They refused to elect Mr. Shenstone, and protested against the decision of the trustees. After considerable discussion, all parties united in the following agreement :—" We agree to give jurisdiction to the general body of Dissenting ministers, meeting at Dr. Williams's Library in Red-cross Street, to determine the question, *Whether the existing members of Mill Yard Sabbatarian Meeting are or are not a church, with the power of choosing a pastor ?* and to join in all such arrangements as shall be expedient for the purpose of procuring that question to be properly submitted to the body, and obtaining their decision upon it, which decision is to be final."

Mr. Conder was requested by the trustees to act as

their advocate, the case having been previously submitted to him for his private opinion. He at first refused, not from the slightest hesitation as to what appeared to him the only common-sense view of the question, but from the fear that he might be regarded as stepping out of his line, and that some personal feeling against himself might prejudice the cause of his clients. Finding, however, that he was more likely to damage them by declining, he consented. The case was heard in May, 1831, at three several sittings, the Rev. Dr. Pye Smith occupying the chair. The Rev. Mr. Russell appeared to maintain the existence and rights of the "church." The case was argued on the grounds of abstract principle, authority, and precedent. Mr. Russell, on behalf of the protesters, spoke first. Mr. Conder's argument, in reply, occupied several hours, and the report of that part of it delivered on the second day of hearing fills 128 folios. He completed his argument at the third day's sitting, and Mr. Russell rejoined. The question involved was a knotty one. At what period in the downward progress of decay does an Independent Church cease to exist? Obviously, the question is one of no practical importance, except where endowments are concerned; for where there is no endowment, as soon as the congregation sinks to that ebb at which they can no longer sustain public worship, the society naturally dissolves itself. An endowment, however, causes the life to linger in the body ecclesiastical with an amazing tenacity. Some curious illustrative facts were quoted on this occasion. "I know," said Mr. Conder, "a number of churches, so called, of the real validity of which I should entertain doubts. I heard the other day of a church, so called, of *three women*, existing, and an endowed church also. I happened to fall in with a reverend gentleman of the Baptist denomination, to whom I put the question, 'How many sisters make a brotherhood?' and he immediately told me of this church; and I said, 'Do you call it a church?' (for, observe, this very minister was in the habit of going over to preach to them.) He shook his head. 'No,' said he; 'a very odd sort of church: certainly I could not.' Now this is a fact. I could mention the place. They keep themselves together for the sake of the endowment, and he goes over to them and preaches; but he himself doubted whether they were a church in any proper sense of the word. . . . . I knew another church consisting of one man, his wife, and his maid, who were in possession of a considerable endowment. Now, will you in the face of the world say that these are precedents establishing the nature of a Christian church, and that these abuses, which, if they were known, would excite general indignation, are the constituent principles of Independency?"

The verdict of the assembled ministers, after hearing the arguments on both sides, was, that "the existing members of Mill Yard Meeting" did constitute "a church, with the power of choosing a pastor." The copy of their resolution, signed by Dr. Pye Smith, is dated June 2, 1831.

During the same month, Mr. Conder was called to part with his venerable father, whose singularly peaceful, though almost sudden removal, at the ripe old age of fourscore, has already been chronicled in the introductory chapter of this memoir. It was, in every sense of the word, a *euthanasia*, grief for which was swallowed up in thankfulness for so happy an ending of a prolonged life and Christian course, and in the sure and certain hope of a blessed meeting in the world of life. The event (with some other family bereavements) is referred to in some lines published in the " Choir and Oratory," under the title " Sacred to Memory."

The following letter belongs to the beginning of the same year. It was addressed to a friend suffering under a complication of most distressing sorrows and anxieties; and it is inserted, not without hope that it may be the means of consolation to some of the children of God in trouble, who may recognise here the language of one who had learned to " comfort others with the comfort wherewith he himself was comforted of God;" and may be reminded that no new thing has befallen them, but that they are treading the same path which so many have trodden before them to the land of promise and of peace.

Watford, Jan. 23, 1831.

LVII. I need not say how incessantly you have been in my thoughts ever since we parted. The difficulties and uncertainties of your situation and prospects are a subject of painful and perplexing consideration. But on *this* day I have been endeavouring to view them chiefly in reference to spiritual things; and I will set down what has occurred to me, praying that the Holy Spirit will vouchsafe to render these considerations useful and consolatory to your heart.

What a striking declaration is that of our Lord— " If thy hand offend thee (or rather cause thee to offend), cut it off: it is better for thee to enter into life maimed, than, having two hands, to be cast into hell," Mark ix. 43. Some are called to bear literal maiming of the body by disease; some to part with what seems as dear and necessary as an eye or as a right hand; some to bear the spoiling of their goods. This is no new thing in the history of God's children. But what then ? " Think it not strange," says St. Peter, " concerning the fiery trial which is to try you, as though some strange thing happened unto you." But think of those words, "better to enter into life maimed"—life everlasting, which will make infinite amends for all.

All, and more than all, that you have been called to put up with and to suffer, you might have been called to endure with hundreds of Christ's people in times of war, or times of religious persecution. Those of whom the world was not worthy have wandered in deserts and mountains, in dens and caves, clothed with goat-skins and the meanest apparel, destitute, afflicted, tormented. Do not imagine that because they suffered for the sake of religion or in the cause of Christ, their sufferings were less hard to be borne. The same grace is needful and sufficient for you that upheld them.

I have, no doubt, my dear ——, that you are one of the sheep of Christ, whom He will never suffer to perish; one of God's children, whom He will chasten for your profit, that you may be partakers of his holiness, and when patience has had its *perfect* work, take to his own bosom. But you must allow Him to judge of the proper heat of the fire that is to burn up the dross and refine the gold, and of the length the process requires. You have prayed, I know, sincerely for submission to his will; but remember Newton's beautiful hymn, "I asked the Lord," etc.

> " 'Twas He who taught me thus to pray,
>   And He, I trust, has answered prayer;
> But it has been in such a way
>   As almost drove me to despair.
>
> " Lord, why is this? I trembling cried;
>   Wilt Thou pursue thy worm to death?
> 'Tis in this way, the Lord replied,
>   I answer prayer for grace and faith.

"These various trials I employ
From self and pride to set thee free;
And break thy schemes of earthly joy,
That thou may'st seek *thine all in Me!*"

To this you will be conscious that you are not yet brought. Your schemes of *earthly joy* are indeed broken; broken, I fear, for ever. But will you then say, Am I to look for nothing but misery here? Far from it; you may be happier yet than you have ever been, but it must be in God's way, not in your own. Those who were called to hate—that is, to forsake or give up—for conscience sake, husband, or wife, or children, or parents, or house, or lands, were yet promised a hundredfold in this world. Do you doubt God's power to make you happy? You do so, if you think you can be happy only by having the things on which your heart is fixed—your home comforts. God must be and will be your all, and He is worth the sacrifice of all. If it be his will that you should be meanly clad, that your love of neatness and your constitutional particularities, however innocent they may seem, should all be rooted out and cut off, this will be no proof that God does not love you. Sometimes giving up *little* things is as painful a sacrifice, or more painful, than giving up great ones. But true love and true resignation are shown by parting with what we love most, great or small. Perhaps it is harder to seem poor than to be poor. We are not laid low till the world knows it. We may feel a change of dress more than a change of circumstances. But the Great Physician, in order to heal, must probe the sore places of the mind. The child says, Touch me anywhere else; but the surgeon knows that the tender part is the diseased part. So it is, Self, when driven out of some parts, may yet lurk in these unsuspected corners.

That your mind and character have already been greatly strengthened and matured by what you have suffered, is apparent to your friends; but I entertain the consoling assurance that you will come out brighter yet. In order to this, you must fix your mind on *great things*, and learn to overlook and despise subordinate ones. Live in and for your children. Be willing to live for them, not as idols, but as Christ's charge committed to you. They may yet repay you with happiness. But, above all, let this be your first desire (Phil. i. 2, 3), that Christ may be magnified in your body, whether it be by life or by death.

. . . Only believe that God loves you, that Christ and heaven are yours, and give up everything, without reserve, to his disposal, and He will do for you exceedingly abundantly above all you can ask or think. You know not what you are capable of, God assisting and strengthening you; and even should health or flesh, as well as heart, fail in the attempt to glorify Him, by acting the difficult part to which you are called, He will be the strength of your heart and your portion for ever. To Him unite with me in ascribing glory and praise for ever and ever.

CHAPTER VII.

POLITICS AND THEOLOGY.

The reform agitation, which swept like a tempest over this country, about the end of the third decade of the present century, lashed into fury by the stubborn opposition of the Tory peers, until the very foundations of society trembled, compelled religious and thoughtful men earnestly to turn their thoughts to politics. While Churchmen foreboded with dismay an invasion of schism and infidelity, and the downfall of their Establishment, Dissenters saw a new future opening before them. The repeal of the Corporation Test Act in 1828, and the emancipation of the Roman Catholics in 1829, had broken down the two strongest bulwarks of the political supremacy of the Church of England. The aim of the reform movement was to destroy that aristocratic monopoly of the representation which virtually constituted a third. That agitation had not ostensibly any religious character or object. But, as it aimed to give political power to the unrepresented mass of the middle classes, in which the strength of Nonconformity has always lain, it was obvious that Dissenters, already relieved from their heaviest disabilities, and now invested with a greatly increased share of political influence, might hope to make their great principles felt in the country in a degree previously impossible. The great body of Protestant Nonconformists had especial reason to join heartily in that peal of triumphant joy which rung through England when Lord Gréy's Reform Bill became law. Perhaps, indeed, there were but few who had sagacity to perceive how great was the gain. The fundamental principle was conceded—impossible to be thenceforth withdrawn from the British constitution—that the House of Commons is intended to represent the people, ought to represent the people, and, if necessary, must be altered, so that it shall represent the people. It follows, that whatever principles and opinions take wide and firm hold of the nation, ought to have place and voice in the legislature. This principle, once irrevocably conceded, lays the axe to the root of Church control over the State, or Church tyranny *through* the State,—that is to say, in the present condition of the English mind; and plants the germs, which must sooner or later bear fruit, of perfect religious liberty. Progress, it is true, has been slow, since, after five-and-twenty years, the question of church-rates has yet to be discussed in a new Parliament, and the Voluntary party in the House of Commons is but in process of formation. But it is a progress which permits *nulla vestigia retrorsum.* Nonconformity has become a power, a growing power, in the State, in the elections, in the legislature, in ministerial policy, in the formation of colonial constitutions, and the government of vast foreign provinces; it can never be put back again into the position which it occupied previous to the year '32.

A profound conviction of the inseparable connection between politics and religion was the governing idea in Mr. Conder's mind, in all his labours of a political character. He accepted and continued the editorship of a newspaper, and engaged in various political schemes, labours, and agitations, in exactly the spirit in which, had the path been open, he would have engaged in the

Christian ministry, and in which, indeed, his occasional pulpit labours were carried on._ He believed that it was the work to which he was called by God. Few things surprised or grieved him more than the frequent blind inattention of religious men to the dealings of God's providence in the government of nations, and the world. Politics was not the field in which his tastes could be most fully gratified, or in which his talents most fitted him to excel. Probably there were times in which he longed to escape from that turbid and unwholesome atmosphere to some more pure and calm region of intellectual activity; and sighed to think how the labour of toilsome hours was scanned by careless eyes, in scarcely as many minutes, and then flung aside and forgotten. Nor had he the consolation of feeling that he was enriching himself, in a pecuniary sense, by the labours in which the pith and strength of the last three-and-twenty years of his life were consumed. But he had the satisfaction of knowing that, however much of his labour might be waste, he was exerting an influence on many minds, not otherwise within his reach, in favour of principles of whose truth and value, and ultimate triumph, he never had the shadow of a doubt. So he worked on, according to the ability which God gave him, and in the post to which he believed that God had called him, serving his generation and the church of Christ, hopefully assured that the cause of truth and freedom must advance, whether his own share in advancing it were great or small, and not greatly surprised, though sometimes a little disheartened and saddened, by finding that gratitude to public servants is not the most distinguishing feature of public bodies (ecclesiastical any more than civil), and that they who work for God's wages must not expect them to be paid in the world's coin.

The *Patriot* newspaper was started as a weekly journal in the year in which the Reform Bill passed into law (1832). The prospectus stated that it would be "devoted to the maintenance of the great principles cherished by Evangelical Nonconformists," and that its tone and spirit would be "constitutional but independent, candid but decided, and liberal though firm." The profits were to be applied, under the direction of twelve trustees of different denominations, "to literary and benevolent objects connected with Dissenters in Great Britain and Ireland." A large number of leading ministers and laymen, of the two Congregational denominations, appended their names to a recommendation, calling on "the friends of sound political knowledge, of evangelical sentiments, and religious liberty," to support the new enterprise. The publication commenced in February. The gentleman who edited it for some months having resigned, Mr. Conder was requested to undertake the editorship, which, after anxious and serious deliberation, he did, beginning his labours with the new year. The circulation at that time was 1587. By the end of the second year of his editorship, the circulation had risen to 2400, to which point, after having receded about 300, it was again raised in the year 1839, when the *Christian Advocate* was incorporated with it, and the paper enlarged. Subsequent enlargements took place, and the publication was changed from once to twice a week. Mr. Conder retained the editorship until the close of his life. Upon the alteration of the stamp duties, when newspaper proprietors were seized with a panic fear of the anticipated invasion of innumerable penny journals, it was deemed politic to publish the paper thrice a week. There can be little doubt that the increased fatigue and anxiety thus incurred, coming at a time when habits are not easily

T

broken, and when his health had been somewhat impaired by other causes, and his once indefatigable powers of literary toil were beginning to feel the touch of time, contributed effectively to shorten his life.

Mr. Conder's acceptance of the editorship, though it necessitated a weekly, and afterwards a bi-weekly visit to London, did not prevent his continuing to reside at Watford for between six and seven years longer. In the year 1837, Watford was brought practically much nearer London, and his journeys rendered much less inconvenient, by the opening of the Birmingham railway as far as Boxmoor. Still, the ties which bound him to London were gradually strengthening. The constant journeys involved both expense and discomfort. The loss of several valued and intimate friends, whose society formed a strong tie to the neighbourhood, loosened the attachment of Mr. and Mrs. Conder to Watford ; and as the children began to grow up, and one by one were quitting home, one of the strongest reasons for preferring a country residence passed away. In fine, in the summer of 1839, Mr. Conder once more returned to the metropolis, and resided in one or other of its suburbs until the close of his life.

Watford, November 3, 1832.

LVIII. . . . Apropos of the *Patriot*, what do *you* think of it ? You in the singular, yourself, and you in the plural, the Dissenting clergy of Essex. I have my reasons for making the inquiry. . . . And touching the *Eclectic*, how is it that the Essex ministers, if I am correctly informed, are for the most part so (willingly?) ignorant of the principles of the *Review*, as to avow their persuasion that it is the advocate of an altered system of Episcopacy in the Church of England, rather than of the broad principles of religious liberty, and that thereby the interests of Dissent are compromised ? How is it that the review of "Acaster," three years ago, should have produced so general an impression, not, as I imagine, upon the readers of the *Eclectic*, but upon the larger number, who I find are *not* readers, and who are therefore credulous to receive, and not over-scrupulous to propagate the false impression ? I am advised to take some strong steps to combat this persuasion; and the only effectual way is, by getting people to *read* the *Review*. . . . I should wish the subject of the *Review* —I mean its general merit and importance—to be fairly brought before your county association, and canvassed, that I may know who are its friends and who its enemies, who are moderates among you, and who ultras. My own creed, touching Dissent, or rather the duties of Dissenters, will be found at large in the number for February last; to which I have little to add. I do not conceal, that as I detested the *World* newspaper, so I eschew the Ecclesiastical Society and all its works, and glory in having induced Vaughan and some others to retire from it. If this is to be vile in the eyes of Essex Dissenters, I will be yet more vile.

LIX. . . . You speak of " certain articles " in the plural. I am not aware of what you allude to. It was the review of " Acaster" that is said to have done the mischief, and that made your." plain honest " gospel men quarrel with a Review of thirty years' standing for a single article, which they happened to be displeased with, chiefly because the *World* newspaper told them they ought to be. This is the simple fact. That article *now* would be seen in another light, as was admitted to me by an eminent minister who took up the common prejudice at the time. The Dissenters *winced*, and it showed that they were unsound. They were neither upbraided nor betrayed in that article; but they showed the intolerance of Papists at being told a little plain truth. Could I have foreseen the strong effect, *policy*, but policy only, might have led me to suppress the article.

February 6, 1835.

LX. . . . . It was not without great reluctance that I consented to undertake the editorship [of the *Patriot*], upon representations and promises which proved deceptive. I will not fill my sheet with telling you the vexation and disappointments which, during eighteen months, I was made to suffer in connection with my office. *You* would not have held it six months; and I was restrained from throwing it up, several times, only by urgent advice, and by knowing that the paper would fall into bad hands. Things are now going on better, the paper having risen 900 in the last twelve months; but the whole labour rests upon me, with a most inadequate remuneration. . . . . Had it not been for *extra* earnings, independent both of the *Review* and the paper, I should have been in *great difficulties*. My "Dictionary of Geography" proved a ruinous job. At the rate of labour and time which it cost me, it should have brought me £750. Tegg paid me £250 (£50 over the stipulated sum), all the work would well bear. As I had undertaken it simply as a paste-and-scissors job, hoping to earn my money easily, this was a serious and indeed distressing disappointment, and I have not got over it. It was tantamount to a loss of £400 or £500. Last year my earnings doubled those of the preceding year, but still they have not brought me quite round. Excuse my entering into these egotistic details. I have such infinite cause for *thankfulness*, that I am ashamed to seem to use the language of murmuring. How hard I have worked I leave you to judge. Besides a weekly newspaper and a monthly journal resting chiefly on my shoulders, I have, in the last two years, finished and printed my " Geographical Dictionary," and put forth " Wages or the Whip," " Letter to the King," " Introduction to Dwight's Armenia," " New Translation of the Epistle to the Hebrews,"* new edition of " Thomas Johnson's Reasons for Dissent," with new dialogue, Itinerary to second edition of " Italy," and " Evangelical Almanack." Some of these are trifling jobs, but all have taken time. Besides these, my "Analytical View of all Religions" has advanced to the end of the fourth chapter; and I have some other irons in the fire. It is not *from choice* that I have engaged in these multifarious labours, but, with one exception, " to order," and for pay.

* The only work in which I plead guilty to supererogatory labour, for my own satisfaction, at a certain pecuniary loss.

Watford, June 4, 1835.

LXI. MY DEAR FRIEND,—It was in my heart to reply, without delay, to your affectionate and gratifying letter; but, lo! two months have elapsed without my being able to secure a half hour in which I could seize one of those breathing intervals you speak of. . . . . Last autumn, Mrs. Conder and two of our boys spent some months in Yorkshire and Derbyshire, and I joined them for a week or two. We had not left home together, with the exception of short visits to London and Homerton, for seven years! Mrs. Conder is bound to home by responsibilities and duties which you can well appreciate; and I live here at the end of a chain fifteen miles long, which ever and anon

is pulled in, and drags me to London, and prevents my
escaping to a further distance, unless by special management I obtain, as last year, a brief holiday; and even
then I carry my yoke with me in the necessity of going
on with my literary and political tasks. But of this,
when I can view my bounds, my times, and my tasks, as
fixed by the Great Master, and reflect upon the many
mercies which distinguish my lot, and cheer my labours,
and consider how my health has been sustained under
them, I dare not complain. Indeed, but for anxieties
which have formed the *needs be* discipline of my life, the
salutary alloy of *great blessings*, I should be well reconciled to any toils, in the hope that they were not altogether unavailing and fruitless; though sometimes, to a
great extent, thankless and distasteful.

Watford, January 7, 1837.

LXII. MY DEAR SIR,—Had not my abdication been
at last so suddenly determined, you should not have received the intelligence from any one but myself. I have,
as you are aware, long groaned under the burden of my
editorial honours and responsibilities, not feeling able to
manage the *Eclectic* and the *Patriot*, without being on the
constant stretch of anxiety and exertion, and yet being
alike unable and unwilling to throw up either. Different
plans and projects have been, from time to time, suggested
and canvassed; but this is the first offer that I could listen
to. Mr. Price being laid aside from the ministry, wishes
to employ himself at once usefully and beneficially; and
he has embarked his property in the adventure of raising the sale of the *Eclectic*, so as to make it, what it
has long ceased to be, a source of profit to the proprietor.
. . . You will easily suppose that, on closing the
labours of twenty-three years as editor, I have had feel-

ings in which some regret is mingled. . . . But I feel quite satisfied that I have consulted my health and my interests in this step; and as the *Review* will undergo no change of character or principle, I shall have much satisfaction in seeing it prosper, as I trust, for Price's sake, it will do.   He has no easy task before him.

. . . I have preached of late, once or more almost every Sunday, owing to Mr. Hall's indisposition and other calls, and have much pleasure in the work, although I have not lost the power of *hearing* with pleasure.   But I should shrink from any *charge*.

Watford, February 13, 1837.

LXIII. MY DEAR FRIEND,—I was beginning to wonder that we did not hear from you; and *you* may have expected to receive your copy of the "Congregational Hymn Book," and been waiting to acknowledge it.   Have patience.   The Committee have ordered, some months since, that each of the contributors named in the preface should have a copy of the large edition, handsomely bound; and, in a few months more, the copies will be ready, and you shall have one.   But you have seen it, and I am glad to infer from your kind expressions that it commends itself to you on examination.   About 20,000 are sold, and they have hitherto not been able to print the editions fast enough.   I am well persuaded that the longer it is used, the more it will be valued.   I am now, at intervals, revising Dr. Watts', with a view to the preparation of an arranged edition of all that is *usable.* . . .

My disposing of the *Eclectic* to Dr. Price was a very sudden thing; but you are aware that I had long groaned under my plural editorship, and the matter seemed altogether providential, both in itself and in the time.   I have engaged to be a regular contributor, and the article on the Congregational and Baptist Unions, in the February number, you have perhaps detected to be mine. I took great pains with it. You can appreciate my *Patriotic* toils. They are more distasteful and uncongenial to me than theological and literary labours, but they are at this juncture more important, and *less* thanklessly received by the public. I regard myself as *called* to the post, and your words are very cheering to me. It *is* " a sad strife, and yet a noble cause." And I only wish that Dissenters would not mistake selfish supineness for spirituality, and worldliness for catholic liberality. But the meetings of the week before last were really grand and imposing assemblies;* and they will tell powerfully upon the country. What we want, next to more of the vital spirit from the Head, is *organization*, ecclesiastical and political. I look to the Union to promote the former, and to the *Patriot*, and this Church-rate abolition agitation, to create the latter.

. . . I have thought much of the words, 2 Chron. xxix. 36, as applicable both to public changes and to one's private affairs, " the thing was done suddenly," for "God had prepared the people." I preached on New Year's Day evening from verse 17. Next Lord's Day I am to preach (D.V.) for Mr. Hall, and I intend to take 1 Cor. ix. 14. As Mr. W. Clayton is to preach for the Essex Benevolent Society in the evening, I shall have a fair occasion for speaking my mind; and I should have no objection to address a few words on the same subject to

---

* A great meeting of delegates, from all parts of England, Wales, and Scotland, which at the time it was thought would "give the death-blow to Church-rates." Mr. Conder regarded it as "the most effective public meeting he ever attended, and unalloyed by a single *faux pas*."

certain other congregations. If the author of " Spiritual
Despotism," instead of attacking and inveighing against
the Voluntary principle, had directed his efforts to exposing the causes of its comparative inefficiency, where
Scriptural motives are overlaid by the mercantile spirit
of English society, he would have rendered good service
to the churches of Christ.

To his Son, at College.

W. F. H., Sunday, September 9, 1838.

LXIV. Our dear E——,—You will have felt
assured that you could not be absent from our thoughts,
for many moments together of this day. We have
missed you, I need not say, at every meal and at every
service. We have conjectured that you would be perhaps dining at Mr. James's, and shall be anxious to hear
how your first Sunday at Birmingham has passed. I
trust that it has passed not unpleasantly nor unpro-
fitably! But upon these days, I doubt not, you will more
especially feel being separated from us, as we do from
you. We now seem to be a very little family; but
C—— is already beginning to talk about Christmas,
with pleased anticipation. I have been preaching for
Mr. Ferney to-day (in the morning), from the Apostle's
sublime and comprehensive prayer, Eph. iii. This is
what we are to ask for ourselves, and for those we love.
How little is it understood that love is the true wisdom,
for it is only by love that we can know what is the
highest object of knowledge, the perfection that God is.
I remarked on verse 19, that as a parent only can know
or understand the love of a parent, although a child who
loves his parents may, in some measure, understand their
love to him, so Christ only can fully know the love of

Deity—his own love, which is that of Deity; and to say that it transcends knowledge, that it is infinite, implies that He is God. I have since recollected that Charles Wesley has strikingly expressed this idea in one of his hymns, beginning, "O Love Divine, how sweet thou art!"—

"God only knows the love of God."

I did not insert the hymn in our collection, because it is unsuitable for congregational use; and like many other beautiful hymns of almost impassioned devotion, by the same author, it savours too much of the mystic school of piety, which is not the *Pauline*. There is nothing monastic, feminine, or mawkish, in the fervent devotion of the Apostle to his Master and Lord. The atmosphere he lived in was not that of a cave or a cell, but of the open air. There was no false excitement about it, and yet it was intense, and carried him through martyrdom Now the devotion of the Romish mystic, from which that of Wesley and Zinzendorf was borrowed as regards its style, is not of this masculine fibre, of this daylight character. In turning from the inspired writings of Paul and John to such hymns and devotional writings, you feel that you are passing into another region and temperature. At the same time, when one is cold, and cannot have sunshine, artificial warmth may be both pleasant and salutary; and a devout person may envy the feelings which inspired many of these compositions, with all their defects, and catch from them a genial glow.

LXV. . . . . You will find it advantageous to have at least two English works in reading at one time; first, because you will find yourself more disposed to pursue one course of reading at one time, and another at another, and by having a choice provided, you may escape the temptation to desultory reading, and yet have the benefit of humouring your mind; and, secondly, it is best not to pursue any subject so long at a time as to weary the attention, and you will find a change serve as rest, like shifting a posture. When the mind has stood upon one leg too long, change it for the other. Besides, the power of transferring attention, and returning to the point at which you left off, is a valuable acquisition. By this means, Southey has been enabled to carry on writing several works at once, never tiring himself, and improving fragments of time, which many throw away. You will find it useful to register your reading, and on completing a work, make a brief note of the impression it has left.

Watford, April 20 [1839].

LXVI. I met Mr. Kirk at dinner yesterday afternoon, and had the pleasure . . . of hearing a little about the meetings, which Mr. Kirk speaks of as some of the most interesting he ever attended.* I bless God for them, and that you had the opportunity of attending them. . . We want to hear all possible particulars about F—, and whether we are to hope to see him *here* for a peep, before we quit this most gay, hospitable, sociable, refined, enlightened Watford; from which, nevertheless, as the scene of your happy childhood, and of so much out-door and in-door happiness, it has taken a good deal of vexation to unloose and wean us. But now F— and you are away, it is no longer the same Watford; and my being of necessity so much in town makes it to dear mamma a

---

* Some special religious services held at Birmingham, when the Rev. E. N. Kirk was in this country; which were characterised by an unusual earnestness of devout feeling, and followed by striking results.

dreary seclusion. Else, as a place, one could be content with it. I had hoped before this to be able to tell you where we next look to pitch our tent, but it is not yet decided—that is, the decision of Him who fixes the bounds of our habitation is not yet known to us, but we are looking at every turn for the finger-post. Perhaps my next letter will inform you; but we are here, at all events, till the half-quarter, and probably till Midsummer.

This is mere chit-chat, but I find myself scarcely equal to-day, after the fatigues of the week, to anything else. You will see that I assisted, on Wednesday, in forming a new Anti-Slavery Society, for promoting the abolition of the slave trade and slavery throughout the world, in which the older societies will merge. The R. F. S. continues to *progress;* of course, it takes up a great deal of my time. Our general meeting is fixed for the 15th of May, and we are to have a public dinner of its friends. You will have noticed the unexpected death of good Mr. Hall, of Chesham, after a short but severe illness. He died as he lived, a consistent, faithful, simple-hearted, exemplary servant of Christ, and has left at Chesham a good name behind.

The initials in the last paragraph refer to the " Religious Freedom Society," the plan of which originated with Mr. Conder, and upon the establishment and working of which he bestowed a very large amount of labour and time. The idea was, the formation of "a general union for the promotion of religious equality." The object designed was to remedy what Mr. Conder deemed one of the greatest deficiencies and sources of weakness in the Dissenting body—the lack of organization for the maintenance and advancement of their distinctive principles. The "fundamental resolutions" were the three following:—" 1. That it is the paramount duty, and therefore the unalienable right, of every man to worship his Creator and Redeemer according to his religious convictions of the Divine will, as expressed in the Holy Scriptures, the only authoritative rule of faith.—2. That to compel any one to contribute to the support of religious rites of which he disapproves, or of the ministers of a church from which he dissents, is manifestly unjust, and at variance with the spirit and principles of Christianity.—3. That State Establishments, by which' any particular church or sect is selected as the object of political favour and patronage, and its clergy are invested with exclusive rights and secular pre-eminence, involve a violation of equity towards other denominations, create serious impediments to the propagation of the Gospel, render the religious union of Protestants impracticable, and are the occasion of inevitable social discord."

Based on these general principles, the Society was intended to furnish, by means of a Central Committee, Local Committees, and a Yearly Meeting of Deputies, a medium of communication and co-operation for the friends of religious liberty throughout the empire; and by watching the progress of legislation in reference to the rights of conscience, and procuring the introduction of requisite parliamentary measures, by collecting, recording, and diffusing information, by affording legal aid and advice, and by promoting the return of suitable representatives to the House of Commons, to advance the cause of freedom of conscience, both at home and abroad. It was not an exclusively Dissenting organization, but was designed to unite the friends of religious liberty in all Protestant communions; and a liberal Churchman was elected chairman. On this ground, the new Society sustained some coarse abuse from parties who were unable to separate the cause of religious freedom from their own peculiar views, and who mistook sectarian bitterness for fidelity to truth.   In other quarters it was welcomed with considerable cordiality, and several important provincial branches were formed.   But in the end the history of the Religious Freedom Society furnished a fresh proof that schemes of organization, however well planned and appropriate, cannot produce organic action.   The very defect which it was hoped to remedy had its causes too deep—causes which it would be out of place to discuss here—to be reached by such means. . The tendency to organize, when once it is called into energetic existence by common passions and objects, will create its own forms; but the forms will not create the tendency.   The Religious Freedom Society was dissolved in the year 1843.

 · In the year 1836 the " Congregational Hymn Book " was published.   It originated in a resolution of the Congregational Union, passed in May, 1833, and was prepared under the authority and supervision of a committee; but the main labour of the work devolved upon the editor.   The task of selecting for every hymn an appropriate text of Scripture, though cheerfully undertaken as a labour of love, entailed a great additional expenditure of time, care, and pains.   The views with which Mr. Conder carried through this important task are sufficiently indicated in the preface to the Hymn-book.

In the following year (1837) Mr. Conder published a second volume of poems, under the title of " The Choir and the Oratory, or Praise and Prayer."   This title was " intended to express the twofold view with which the poems " were " composed, some being designed for the use of the choir or congregation, others for the devotional retirement of the oratory."

"The greater part of the volume consists of pieces written with no immediate view to publication. The lyrical form given, with a few exceptions, to the poetical translations of Psalms, will show that in these compositions my object has been altogether different from that of the authors of most of our metrical versions, which have aimed at accommodating the Psalms to Christian worship. For many years the study of the Book of Psalms has occupied such attention as I could give to it, under the cherished conviction that it might be found practicable to exhibit the poetry of the Hebrew Scriptures in the rich and varied measures of English versification, without compromising either the fidelity of a chaste translation, or the simplicity and majesty of the original. . . . Can anything be more improper than to employ the same metrical *modes* in attempting to adapt to the genius of English poetry an elegiac complaint, an ode of triumph, a choral hallelujah, and an acrostic of axioms? "Paradise Lost" could not have been composed in heroic couplets; and how much of the charm of the "Faery Queen" lies in the magnificent stanza! But by translators metre has been apparently regarded as altogether arbitrary and inexpressive, or as a mere method of adapting words to a melody. Thus we find didactic psalms rendered in lyrical metres, and the sublimest odes given in an unbroken series of iambic couplets, the narrative measure of Gay and Scott. . . . I am aware that by these remarks I may seem to challenge criticism to my own attempts to do better justice to the structure and poetic spirit of these wonderful compositions. I can only say that I have bestowed upon them the utmost thought and skill that I could command; yet I am very far from indulging a sanguine expectation that they will please or interest general readers."

Such of the versions of the Psalms, both in this volume and in the "Star in the East," as partake of the character of hymns, are included in the small volume of "Psalms, Hymns, and Meditations," published subsequently to the author's death; but not those which are simply poetical translations, made on the principles indicated in the preceding extract.

In the year previous to his quitting Watford, Mr. Conder published a work on which he had been engaged, at intervals, during several years—a comprehensive treatise on the religions of the world.* These are classified with reference to the revelations, real or supposed, on which they are based. Regarding Judaism as an undeveloped Christianity, the religions at present prevailing are arranged under the following heads :—

1. The Religion of the Bible.
2. The Religion of the Koran.
3. The Religion of the Zendavesta.
4. The Religion of the Vedas and Puranas.
5. The Religion of the Sacred Books of Buddhism.
6. Illiterate Superstitions.

The closing paragraph of the preface to this work thus expresses the principles on which it is composed :—

"The most difficult, or at least the most delicate, part of my task has been to preserve that impartiality which may reasonably be looked for in an account of religious opinions, without affecting an irreligious neutrality, or compromising my own most sacred convictions of truth. To conceal my opinions would have been fruitless hypo-

* Analytical and Comparative View of all Religions now Extant among Mankind, with their Internal Diversities of Creed and Profession. By Josiah Conder, Author of the "Modern Traveller," etc., etc. 8vo. 1838. Pp. 698.

crisy; and I can only hope that I have not suffered them to betray me into any defect of candour or violation of charity. I have not attempted to treat of the Roman Catholic tenets in the character of a Romanist, or of Mahommedism in that of a Mussulman; nor have I scrupled to speak of sects as sects, or of heresies as heresies. The Searcher of hearts knows, however, that my earnest desire and steady aim have been to vindicate the catholicity of Christ's Church, to harmonize the creed of its true members, rather than to exasperate our mutual dissensions; to show that the religious differences among Christians chiefly arise from causes extrinsic to the common rule and supreme arbiter of faith, and to lead to the practical conclusion, that as Christianity is demonstrably the only true religion, so no one needs despair, with the Bible in his hand, of ascertaining for himself, under its various disguises, the genuine lineaments of true Christianity."

Watford, February 17, 1839.

LXVII. . . . You have indeed started three of the most difficult questions that you could have proposed for solution; and upon each of them I have been led to conclusions differing from those adopted by the majority of the orthodox.

The first of your inquiries relates to the inspiration of the books of the Old Testament, upon which I threw out some remarks in the *Eclectic Review*,* during the Bible Society Controversy, which Haldane and Andrew Thomson denounced as neological and heretical, but which I have not seen reason to deem erroneous. Those who insist upon the absolute and even verbal inspiration of every portion of the canon of the Old Testament, rest

* *Eclectic Review*, Second Series, vols. xxiv. xxv. xxvi.

U

their opinion upon the following grounds:—1. The sanction given by our Lord to the Jewish canon as a whole, without discriminating one portion from another. 2. The declaration of St. Paul, 2 Tim. iii. 16. 3. The impossibility of determining what is inspired, if the whole is not, and the dangerous tendency of scepticism on such points. As to the first ground, we know that the Jews themselves made a distinction between the books, which they divided into three classes, and that they attributed to them a different degree of inspiration; it may, therefore, be as fairly presumed that our Lord tacitly sanctioned this threefold division (see " Analytical View of all Religions," p. 516, note; *Ecl. Rev.*, vol. xxiv. p. 382). As to the second, I agree with Dr. J. P. Smith in thinking that the absence of the auxiliary verb, and still more the scope of the passage, justify the rendering in the Vulgate; and, I render it, " all prophetical Scripture (being) also profitable," etc. Mr. Watts, I believe, stands by the rendering of our translators; and I wrote to him at length my views last year. The affirmation that " every writing is Divinely inspired" must, at all events, be taken in a qualified sense. In answer to the third argument, I proposed four criteria of inspiration, *Ecl. Rev.*, xxiv. 388 :—1. Every book of the O. T. is given by inspiration, which is referred to by our Lord and his Apostles, as inspired. 2. Or, the writer of which lays claim to inspiration. 3. Or, the author of which sustained the character of a prophet. 4. Or when the internal evidence of its inspiration is too manifest to be mistaken. This applies especially to the book of Job, its author being uncertain. These criteria establish the inspiration of the whole of the Old Testament *revelation*, and all the prophetical portions, to which Heb. i. 1, and 2 Pet. i. 21, more immediately refer. The Pentateuch must be included among the prophetical writings ; and so were the books of Joshua, Judges, Samuel, and the Kings, by the Jews, probably because they were carried on by a succession of prophets and seers. That David was a prophet is incontestable, and inspiration of the highest character attaches to such Psalms as Ps. ii., cx., etc. As to Esther, the Chronicles, and the Canticles, I have an invincible difficulty in supposing them to have been dictated by inspiration ; and there appears to me more danger of *lowering* the character of inspiration by plácing them on a level with the prophetic books, than of countenancing scepticism by admitting the distinction between a sacred book or ecclesiastical record, and an inspired or prophetic writing.* But you will see my opinion more at large in the article referred to.

I will take your third inquiry next. The general rule I should lay down is, that all ceremonial sanctity is abrogated, and that, under the new economy, the institutions of religion are rather to be viewed as *the means of moral sanctity*. The Sabbath is a means to an end ; and the rule of conscience relates to, and is determined by the end. There can be no *intrinsic* holiness in any portion of time or place. The Sabbath was holy, only as the temple was holy. *That ceremonial sanctity* has not been, as I conceive, transferred to the first day of the week ; and this is intimated, Rom. xiv. 5, and Col. ii. 16. But the primary law of the Sabbath binds us to a weekly day of rest, as a law of mercy to man and beast, to a day of public worship, without which religion could not be maintained in the world, and by which, in all ages and countries, one religion is discriminated from another ;

* As regards the books of Chronicles, it is believed that this opinion was subsequently changed. The spiritual element is, in point of fact, more prominent in them than in the Kings.—E. R. C.

and to a devout reference to what must be supposed to be the highest original end of the institution, even in Paradise—communion with God and the cultivation of piety. The Sabbath being made for man, is to be kept sacred for *his* sake, not for its own. The man who loves the Sabbath, will not be tempted to dishonour it ; and it is only rightly hallowed by the affections. This is " the law of liberty;" superstition is the law of bondage. Yet superstitious scruples have their use, in the absence of clearer views, as an outwork of principle ; and on this account the Apostle, in Rom. xiv., teaches us to respect them, and to guard against leading others into sin by acting upon our Christian liberty. This especially applies to the observation of the Lord's Day ; and while I wish to have my conscience free from superstition on this point, I should be cautious against either giving offence on the one hand, or encouraging a dangerous laxity on the other.

Your second inquiry relates to the Epistle to the Romans. Hodge you shall have, as I have done with him. Stuart's work on the Romans, I do not think very highly of, though I think he is right, in the main, in his view of chap. vii. Generally, his judgment is to be distrusted, though his scholarship is highly respectable. I will write out my analysis of chap. ix., and hope it will serve to remove your difficulty. " Imputed righteousness" is a phrase unauthorized by Scripture, although 2 Cor. v. 21 is usually used to justify it ; and in Scotland, you would be anathematized for not holding to the phrase. It is not worth while disputing about the expression, only avoid using it. What St. Paul says is imputed or reckoned to the believer as the ground of acceptance, is his faith. We are saved and justified, not by the righteousness, but by the blood of Christ, his propitiatory sacrifice : his obedience, *apart from his sacrifice,* is never represented as either vicarious or piacular; and if anything is to be spoken of as imputed to us, it is his death—the price of our redemption. But theology has been deformed by such verbal blunders, which must not, however, be treated as doctrinal errors. We believe in what is *meant* by the imputed righteousness of Christ, that is, free justification; although I strongly dislike the unscriptural and incorrect technicality.

Watford, March 24, 1839.

LXVIII. You have certainly hit upon some of the most difficult problems. It is quite true, that belief must have, to deserve the name, evidence for its basis; but all truths do not admit of the same kind or degree of evidence, and, as Bishop Butler has admirably illustrated in his "Analogy," it is an element of our probation to be satisfied, in many cases, with that probable evidence which it has pleased God to vouchsafe to us.

With regard to the inspiration of the Books of the Old Testament, the subject is confessedly attended with difficulties, and the German neologists make short work of the matter, by rationalizing away their inspired character; while Haldane and others go to the opposite and (as I conceive) absurd extreme of attributing to them an absolute verbal inspiration, which, of course, could be preserved in no translation. That Moses, in the Book of Genesis, made use of pre-existing materials, is in the highest degree probable, and does not, in my judgment, militate against the prophetical authority of the Book. Some traditional records must have been handed down from Noah, derived originally, we must suppose, from revelation to our first parents; and such materials, as well as the Abrahamic history, must have possessed a sacred character, even before Moses collected them and interwove the fragments into a consecutive history. How far any of his historical-knowledge was derived from immediate revelation is doubtful. There is very little in the Gospels that is related on other authority than that of an eye-witness or ear-witness ; yet we believe that the Evangelists wrote under the especial guidance of the Holy Spirit, who was promised to teach them what they should say, and to bring all things to their remembrance. In like manner, there is the strongest reason to believe that Moses, and the prophetic writers of the sacred histories of the Old Testament, were Divinely instructed as to what they should commit to writing, whether in the shape of record, laws, poetry, or prediction ; so that "*it is written*" became a law of belief. The prophetic office was one of authority, and the authority was Divinely attested. Whatsoever, therefore, the prophets said, or wrote, or did, *officially*, claimed the confidence and obedience due to Divine authority. You ask, if St. Paul had written a history of Rome, or a treatise on botany, or on political economy, would it have been inspired? I do not find fault with your question ; it is not an unfair way of putting it. But I do not hesitate to say in reply, that if St. Paul had, *in his apostolic character*, transmitted to the Churches a history of Rome, or a treatise on political science, there would have been every reason for concluding that he was Divinely commissioned and Divinely qualified to furnish them for the instruction and comfort of the Churches ; and to them would have been applicable the language he applies to the O. T. Scriptures—"Whatsoever things were written aforetime, were written for our learning," etc., Rom. xi. 4. "And they are written for our admonition," etc. 1 Cor. x. 11. The Apostle's reasoning in this chapter, and also in

Heb. vii., respecting Melchisedec, as well as the general spirit of the references to the O. T. Scriptures, clearly indicates that the events recorded, the personages introduced, and the expressions used, had often a typical and predictive bearing and design, of which the writers themselves could not be conscious, and which were the result of supernatural guidance. Now, to suppose any portion of falsehood to have mingled with truth in their narratives or declarations, written under such influence, and supported by the official authority of inspired men, is to "make God a liar." To impute falsehood to a part, is to invalidate the whole. It is true, there may be statements which betray the imperfect knowledge of the writers as to physical facts, but we cannot suppose that they were allowed to state anything at variance with fact. For instance, the first chapter of Genesis may seem at variance with the discoveries of astronomical and geological science, to which we can hardly suppose the inspired knowledge or Egyptian lore of Moses extended. Yet that there is any real and necessary contradiction has never been proved, and is not for a moment to be admitted, or it would shake the very foundations of faith. We must, however, take into consideration the *design* of the inspired writer, in judging of the import of any passage. We are sure that the first chapter of Genesis was not intended to reveal astronomical facts, but to correct the false cosmogony of the heathen sages. It does not treat of the origin of existence, but of the visible heaven and earth. No mention is made of the creation of angels and other orders of beings. How the earth *became* formless and void is not intimated. That light exists independently of the sun, or did exist before the sun was made the sun to our earth, modern science has rendered at least very supposable. Indeed (says M——) how else could the

light of the stars have *reached* the earth by that time?
I think Dr. Redford has some valuable remarks on this
point in his "Congregational Lecture;" and Macculloch's larger work will be worth your careful perusal, as
showing the bearings of modern science on revelation.
It may, perhaps, be safely admitted that Gen. i., ii. 1—3,
has something of a poetical character in the very phraseology and construction; yet, by poetry, we cannot allow
the idea of *fiction* to be conveyed, and it is venturing on
very delicate ground to apply the phrase to the lyrical
form and ornamental mode in which this account of the
creation is given. If a poem, it was doubtless the earliest
of all songs, such as might have been taught by angels to
Adam in Paradise.

You ask, what criteria can we take for the internal
evidence of the inspiration of a book. Internal evidence
can scarcely be reduced to any definite criteria. It must
comprise the complex proof supplied by the *contents*, the
originality of the knowledge or doctrine, the character of
the *writer*, the stamp of holy elevation of sentiment; but
this would be matter for a volume. Take the Book of
Job as an instance, in which the internal evidence of inspiration is all but irresistible. In the Books of Samuel,
Kings, etc., the marks of supernatural guidance may be
less obvious; but we have every reason to receive the
testimony of the Jewish Church to their being not only
sacred books, but composed, under Divine direction, by a
succession of prophets. And the way in which they are
cited by the New Testament writers confirms this view,
while it does not appear to me to prove the inspiration
of *all* the hagiographa.

Your query respecting *faith* opens the whole *Sande-
manian* controversy, respecting which, *vide* "Analytical
View," pp. 434, 577; and *Eclectic Review*, Second Series,

April, 1823, vol. xix., p. 327, etc. Faith is belief. Faith in a *thing* is a simple belief of the fact. Faith in a *person* is confidence and trust. But to believe a report upon the strength of testimony is to believe in the veracity and competency of the witness; to believe a promise is to put faith in the promiser. The Gospel message is both a Divine testimony and a Divine promise; and he does not believe upon the Son of God who does not yield the obedience of faith to the authority of God, and exercise the assurance of faith in the Divine mercy. Unbelief involves the rejection of some part of the Divine testimony, and it indicates that no part is received upon the ground of submission to that testimony, or faith in God. You ask, " What is the connection, of cause or sequence, between belief and the state of the heart?" A disposition to believe or to disbelieve, denoted by the words credulity and incredulity, is, with regard to religious truth, a *moral* disposition, indicative of a state of heart and of character. All experience testifies to this fact. A repugnance to believe unwelcome truth is natural;—to receive holy truth, is the property of an unholy mind. On the other hand, the Gospel is in itself fitted to conquer incredulity, to overcome the indisposition to believe, and to work that change of heart which is regeneration; but, while *adapted* to have this effect as truth, the Scriptures clearly teach us that the concurrent influence of the Holy Spirit is absolutely necessary to secure this result. Much that relates to the truths of the Gospel, the scheme of redemption, the orthodox outline, may doubtless be believed as abstract truth, without producing a sanctifying influence. But the *whole truth* cannot be embraced by the heart (which, in this reference, is the moral understanding), without re-acting on the heart to salvation.

Tell me, honestly, whether I have made the matter clear to your apprehension. If I have, it may save you from being bewildered amid the mazes of a senseless logomachy. And now I think I have written enough for one epistle.

Watford, April 7, '39.

LXIX. To come at once to your questions, which I have great delight in solving:—

1. The Apostle, in 1 Cor. vii. 12, does not disclaim inspiration or apostolic authority, but states that he had no special command from Christ to communicate on the subject. Calvin interprets v. 10—" Hac correctione significat, quod hic tradit, ex lege Dei sumptum esse. Alia enim quæ tradebat, habebat etiam ex revelatione Spiritus : sed hujus authorem allegat Deum, quod lege Dei expressum sit." Again at v. 12, "Quoniam nusquam de hoc re extabat in lege aut prophetis certum ac expressum verbum." I greatly respect Calvin as a judicious annotator, but he does not satisfy me here. It is to me very evident that the distinction the Apostle intends to convey is between a positive command of Christ, binding upon all, and what he offered simply as counsel or advice, which he did not wish to be taken as authoritative. Thus, he recommends marriage in v. 2; but in v. 6, he says, he gives no commandment on this head, simply recommending it κατὰ συγγνώμην in the way of *indulgence,* or *permission; pro eorum infirmitate.* To the married, he speaks authoritatively; and the law of God is explicit on the point. And I think that the words in v. 12, τοῖς δε λοιποῖς ἐγὼ λέγω, are improperly connected with what follows, and refer to his previous advice to the *unmarried;* for what follows is in continuation of the directions to the *married,* founded on

the Divine command. Verse 40 looks the most like a disclaimer of inspired authority. But here, too, St. Paul wishes to be understood as giving only an opinion as to the preferableness of not marrying again—not as forbidding second marriage. Then he adds, that he judges this opinion to be given under the influence of the Spirit of God. Δοκῶ has been rendered " I trow," or, "am persuaded." Tyndal renders it, "And I think verily that I have the Spirit of God." Calvin, on this verse, says : " Non tamen videtur ironia carere quod dicit existimo ;" supposing him to refer to the pretensions of the false apostles. This may be, as there occur several fine examples of irony in this very Epistle to the refined Corinthians. But I rather take it more simply, q. d., " Although I only give my opinion that she will be happier remaining a widow, I think that, in expressing this opinion upon a subject on which I have no command to give, no positive instructions from the Lord, I am still guided by the Spirit of God." You will see that your letter has led me to look at the passage very closely ; and the whole chapter is very important, as furnishing a strong proof that the Apostle was most careful not to mingle his own opinions with the doctrines received by revelation from Christ (Gal. i. 12), or to push his apostolic authority beyond the limits of his commission.

2. As to the typical character of historical events, you will find this subject adverted to in one of the four notes to my " Translation of the Epistle to the Hebrews." The facts may not have been, strictly speaking, typical, and yet they may be made to assume a typical character in the account given of them. That is to say, the account may be so framed (and this without the conscious intention of the inspired writer) as to serve the purpose of a prophetic emblem or type. You will see that I consider

the Apostle's argument in Heb. vii. as requiring us to suppose that it was with a specific design Melchisedec appears as he does in the sacred narrative, neither more nor less being recorded of him than answers the purpose of the typical application. "Thus explained, we obtain a fresh proof of the Divine inspiration of the sacred historian, since he could not foresee the typical application; and the argument of the Apostle is rescued from the appearance of either fanciful accommodation or inconclusive reasoning."

On the Quaker Controversy.

Watford Field House, May 5.

LXX. Esteemed and Dear Sir,—I regret that it was not in my power to fulfil your wish by reviewing the controversy in the May *Eclectic*. I could not have accomplished it in time, nor could the editor have made room for its insertion.

In the meantime I have been occupied with reading and writing upon the subject for a different purpose. I am engaged upon the last chapter of an "Analytical View of Christian Churches and Sects;" and in this I introduce an account of Quakerism. I have before me the "Rules of Discipline," Bates's "Doctrine of Friends," Tuke's "Principles," and "Life of Whitehead," Gurney's Works, Wilkinson, Hancock, Ball, Wardlaw, etc., and all your publications. Barclay and Penn I have looked into several years ago, and have not deemed it necessary to go beyond the extracts cited by Mr. Wilkinson in order to substantiate my statements. I think I now pretty clearly understand the history and mystery of Quakerism. Its true character is drawn by the Apostle, Col. ii. 8. It seems to me much more closely related to the Romish mysticism than I had supposed. It is Christianity shrouded in mystical deism, and struggling with it, like a lamp in a vapoury atmosphere. It combines the Platonism of a learned age with the fanaticism of the seventeenth century, and is a skilful combination of opposite elements well adapted to beguile both the proud and the simple. Is it not so? But that God has had a people among the Society I cannot doubt; and this revival, which is passing Quakerism through an ordeal, is detecting and manifesting who have indeed the Spirit of Christ.

We have consented to admit into the *Patriot* an account of the proceedings of the ensuing yearly meeting, which we expect to have furnished by some of your friends. I fear that the old leaven will mar the feast.

And now, my dear sir, permit me to advert to the subject of infant baptism. I believe I have told you that I am in the practice of attending the Baptist chapel in this town, of joining with them in the Lord's Supper, and of occasionally occupying their pulpit; so that you will not suspect me of being very strongly influenced by party prejudices. But I am more and more firmly convinced that the restricting of baptism to adult confession of faith is an error, and, like all errors, of evil consequence.

Baptism is no part, as it appears to me, of a *profession* of discipleship, but is rather an admission to discipleship. The question, then, is, "Who are the disciples of Christ?" Our Lord Himself said, "Suffer the little children to come unto me." The duty of bringing our children to Christ—their *claim* to be taught—their capacity to be discipled—their susceptibility of Divine teaching, will not be denied: why then should it be scrupled to employ this rite of discipleship according to the spirit of the reasoning of St. Peter, Acts x. 47 ? A convert from another religion can only be received on his own profession and desire to be taught. But the children of believers have a claim to be taught, and a correlative obligation of the most binding nature lies on their parents, of which the performance of the rite is a solemn recognition. " I reminded them" (the Baptists in Scotland, who were reported to be negligent of family religion) "that if family religion was neglected, Pedobaptists would be furnished with the most weighty objection against our sentiments as Baptists." Such are the words of Andrew Fuller, a leading minister among the Antipedobaptists. And do they not amount to an admission that the Baptist views have a possible tendency to lead to this neglect of God's great ordinance of family religion ? Does not the denial of this rite to the infant children of believers sanction the dangerous notion that not their baptism merely, but their choice of a religion, and their becoming partakers of Divine grace, must (or may) be deferred till they attain an adult age ? Is it not implied that the child of a heathen stands in the same relation and condition towards God as the child of one who, with his whole household, fears and worships God ? And, further, does not deferring the rite till an adult age divide a Christian family into the baptized and unbaptized, and thus render it a rite of disunion ? In ancient times, and according to Eastern notions, this would have been no trivial consideration. It appears to me very questionable whether unbaptized children would have been permitted to sit at table with baptized persons ; and what we read of the baptism of households (that is, families) as well as a remarkable passage, 1 Cor. vii. 14, sanctions this idea. I am not contending for what is, in technical phrase, termed the church-membership of children; but I cannot think the institutions of the Gospel were intended to supersede or clash with the domestic economy, by which chiefly, if parents were faithful to their charge, the church would be perpetuated.

You are aware that it is the practice of our churches to require an adult confession or profession of faith on the part of those baptized in infancy, prior to their admission to communion or membership. This answers, in some degree, to the original design of the Popish rite of confirmation: We differ from the Baptists only in this, that they defer the rite of initiation—what I should venture to call the rite of Christian education—till the time of admittance to their church fellowship; and they then first bestow the sign of discipleship, as they would upon a heathen convert of yesterday, upon one who, it may be, has grown up in the fear of the Lord—the son of pious members—an attendant with them on the ministry and public worship—receiving him, though a child and nursling of the church, as from the world. Is this rational? Is it Scriptural? Allow me to entreat your consideration of the subject in this light: When a Gentile in primitive times embraced the faith of Christ, did he not renounce idolatry for his offspring and descendants, and pledge himself to bring up his children in the Christian faith? Look at 1 Cor. x. 2, and consider whether all the young children were not baptized unto Moses, discipled or subjected to him as their leader, in the cloud and in the sea. The Apostle evidently borrows the phrase from the Christian rite of initiation, which he applies to the Mosaic church in the wilderness.

I am not surprised that evangelical friends, when led to perceive the evils arising out of membership by birthright in their own society, should be disposed to view with jealousy any practice that may seem to favour the notion of an hereditary title to those Christian privileges which belong only to those whom God has sanctified. The Popish heresy of baptismal regeneration, so tenaciously retained by the Church of England, has, I imagine, produced the opposite mistake of the Baptists, whose opinions I must admit to be rational and Scriptural on this point, in comparison with those who convert a symbolic rite into a sort of incantation. Still, the undue stress which the Baptists lay upon the rite, in another point of view, has been found to produce a fallacious assurance on the part of many; so strong is the tendency to exalt the ritual above the spiritual. Quakerism, which was in part produced by the Popish abuse of the sacraments, seeks to escape from this tendency by substituting the mystical for the ritual; but this is found to be still more fatally opposed to genuine spirituality. How wise is our Heavenly Master, who, knowing what was in man, has instituted but two symbolic rites—each, properly viewed, so replete with instruction—the one implying the necessity of the washing of regeneration and the renewal of the Holy Ghost in all who would enter the kingdom of Christ, and the other perpetuating through the darkest ages of the church, notwithstanding the idolatrous superstition that had become attached to it, the fundamental doctrine of the propitiatory sacrifice, and thus showing forth the Lord's death till He come.

CHAPTER VIII

AFTER fifteen years spent at Watford, Mr. Conder found it desirable, for reasons sufficiently indicated in the preceding chapter, to remove to London, or at least to its immediate neighbourhood, within omnibus range of Temple Bar. Scarcely any motive attracted him to one suburb more than another, so that the selection of a residence was a perplexing problem. At last, Highgate, lying close on the skirts of the still uninvaded country, and lifted more completely than any other suburb out of the atmosphere of the great city, was preferred. Mr. Conder took a house at Holly Terrace, and removed thither in the summer of 1839. Here he resided for six years, and then removed to Clapham, where he continued until the spring of 1851. His family circle having, meantime, diminished, as the sons went out one by one into the battle of life, until it consisted only of himself, Mrs. Conder, and their daughter, Mr. Conder quitted Clapham, and being unable to decide where to fix his home, took lodgings at Kennington, near one of his sons. His stay was prolonged from time to time, until more than three years had slipped away. Circumstances then indicated St. John's Wood as the most desirable locality. He removed thither, near the close of 1854, just twelve months before he was called to enter on that eternal house, not made with hands, which awaits the tired pilgrim at the end of his life-wanderings.

x

These closing years of Mr. Conder's life were, like
their predecessors, years of unremitting and varied intellectual toil. To write their history, were it possible,
would be to fill pages with details of endless Committee
meetings, Public meetings, Deputations to Ministers,
Parliamentary tactics, Newspaper controversies—things
as empty of interest now, as they were full of interest at
the moment; of which time devours the fruit, and treads
out the remembrance. The record would show, what,
alas! any one may prove for himself who will make the
experiment, how ungrateful a task it is to serve the
Public—whether the religious public, or the political
public; and how little there is to encourage a man thus
to spend his strength and life, except the knowledge that
no true work can be altogether wasted; that results do
not cease, because they are unknown; and that at the
Master's coming, no faithful service will be forgotten or
unrequited.

Mr. Conder's labours as Editor of the *Patriot* continued through this whole period, in conjunction with
other literary labours. His spare time was still assidu-
ously devoted to theological and biblical studies, and
more than one of his published works originated in
investigations undertaken for his own satisfaction and
spiritual profit. If he had turned his pen only to tasks
which would have paid him, he might have been a richer
man; but, true to the principles on which he had always
worked, he thought more of the service which his writings
might render to the Christian Church, or to his country,
than of the profits they would realize. And yet the money
would have been of great value to him. Pecuniary difficulties were for many years a source of trial and anxiety.
He felt keenly not being able to give to religious and
benevolent objects as he would have desired (though, in

fact, he gave largely of his time and brains); and the disappointment of several plans by which he hoped permanently to increase his income, was a sore trial of faith and patience. In one of his letters, he says—"'My soul is even as a weaned child;' to be brought into this state is a great attainment. When I think I have got the lesson by heart, I find I have to learn it all over again. God has to bear with very dull scholars." And again, in reference to the failure of plans which had seemed full of promise—"These passages in the Divine Providence perplex me more in trying to find out the meaning, than any cramp text in St. Paul's Epistles. All my plans and projects, though earnestly prayed over, are baffled; and I am constantly tantalized with things that seem presented to me only to be snatched away." It pleased God, in his fatherly providence, not only to keep the faith of his servant from failing under these harassing anxieties, but, when preparing for him trials of a different kind, graciously to remove them; so that for the last year or two of his life, he was probably more free from cares of this description than at any former period. So wonderful is the *timing* of God's dealings, that nothing is to the observant Christian a stronger confirmation of his faith.

The neighbourhood of London offered very few opportunities for continuing the practice of preaching, in which Mr. Conder had been so frequently engaged while living at Watford. From causes which it is not worth while to discuss here, the feeling against lay-preaching is stronger (among Dissenters) in London than in the country; and Mr. Conder had no wish to be thought to trench on the ministerial office. Now and then an opportunity offered, which he willingly embraced; especially when visiting Sheffield, where he frequently occupied the pulpit of his brother-in-law, the Reverend

Thomas Smith. Such visits were refreshing interruptions to the regular routine of toil in London. But he always carried his work with him, and an entire month of complete recreation was probably a thing which he never enjoyed since he left school. Of one of these Sheffield visits, he writes—"It has done me good, although I had not much rest of mind. I wrote almost all the *leaders* for the *Patriot* during my absence, preached two Sabbath mornings out of three, and two Wednesday evenings gave an address at the United Prayer-meeting, and made a speech, as you would see, at a *soirée*. So I was not idle. I enjoyed preaching again, after so long an interval, where I knew my voice would be heard with pleasure and affection; but that does not seem the line in which Providence intends me to exercise the gift intrusted to me. I am more and more convinced, however, that it is a mistake to confound the *prophet* with the *pastor*."

The year after quitting Watford, Mr. Conder was called to lose his pious and venerable mother, at the advanced age of eighty-six. With the exception of this peaceful and happy departure—an occasion of thanksgiving rather than of submission—his domestic circle continued to enjoy a signal immunity from the visits of death, until within three years of his own removal. Cares and trials he had, as every man has, and as every Christian knows that he *needs;* but though they were at times hard to bear, he delighted to express his sense of God's mercies, as far outbalancing these burdens, and forbidding any thoughts of repining. The day after entering on his fifty-eighth year, he wrote—"I am often ashamed of the tenor of my thoughts, too often exclusively, tyrannically, occupied with petty but pressing anxieties and annoyances, as if I cared for nothing beyond them. I seem to feed upon ashes, with golden fruit hanging all around me. For with such a wife and such children, I feel I am one of the most prosperous and favoured of men. But though this fresh life-year does not open very cheerfully, I have no doubt it will in its course be marked, as every one of its predecessors has been, by the Divine goodness; and perhaps bring, in answer to your prayers, in concurrence with ours, relief from the long-continued trial. A cloudy morning often precedes a bright and lovely evening."

At Midsummer, 1848, Mr. Conder was laid aside by a severe accident to his foot, by which the "tendon Achilles" was nearly severed. Skilful treatment, and tender and vigilant nursing, by the blessing of God, averted any fatal results, and the use of the foot was eventually almost completely restored. But he was confined for months to his house, or a carriage; and it is not unlikely that the compulsory rest thus ordained for him, at a time when he was overtaxed with combined toil and anxiety, was the means of averting some serious illness, and lengthening his life. The feelings awakened by this merciful chastening are expressed in the following brief and simple lines, penned in the ensuing spring:—

I was striving in my prayer;
  Was struggling in my will:
Thou didst touch my frame; I bear
  The mark and memory still.
Thou hast spared and bid me live—
Wilt Thou not the blessing give?

Bless me, O my God, and make
  My life a blessing yet!
Bless me richly for their sake
  To whom my heart's in debt.
Bless me, that with mind and pen
I may serve both saints and men.

March, 1849.

In the year 1845, Mr. Conder published the cream of his biblical studies in the form of a large octavo, under the title of "The Literary History of the New Testament."* Perhaps the title was not very well chosen, but it was not easy to find a better. The nature of the work is thus stated in the preface:—"Although numerous works have appeared, both in this country and in Germany, intended to serve as introductions or helps to the critical study of the New Testament, the author of this volume is not aware that there exists any popular manual, affording a condensed view of the literary history, chronology, internal evidence, and distinctive features of the apostolic writings. To supply this deficiency the present work has been undertaken, in the hope, that while it may assist to guide the investigations of the biblical student, it may also serve to interest general readers more extensively in the topics of inquiry connected with the historical and critical illustration of the New Testament." Very great care and pains were bestowed, in this work, on the analysis of the Apostolic Epistles, which had formed the writer's favourite study for very many years; and these analyses will be found to constitute the most important and valuable portion of the work. Great pains were also bestowed on the consideration of the distinctive characters of the Gospels, and the mode of harmonizing their principal difficulties.

The preparation of the chapter on the Apocalypse, in the volume just mentioned, led Mr. Conder to resume and extend his study of that difficult book, and at the commencement of 1849 he published a commentary on it, under the title of "The Harmony of History with Prophecy."† The "historical counterpart to the predictions is given in the form of citations from Gibbon,

* Seeleys, pp. 608.   † Shaw, fscp. 8vo, pp. 532.

Robertson, Hallam, Sismondi, and other popular writers, in whose language there will often be found a precise adaptation to the Apocalyptic emblems, which is the more striking from being undesigned." In its general line of exposition, Mr. Conder's volume coincides with Mr. Elliott's masterly and erudite work, to which frequent reference is made; but it differs in the explanation of some symbols (as the Ten-horned Beast, the Harvest, and the Vintage), and altogether as to the supposed pre-millennial coming of the Lord.

At the autumnal meeting of the Congregational Union at Southampton, in 1850, Mr. Conder read an essay on Dr. Watts, prepared at the request of the committee, on occasion of the assembly being held at the birth-place of the father of modern psalmody, a century (and two years over) after his death. In compliance with the vote of the assembly, this paper was published in an elegant little volume, under the title of " The Poet of the Sanctuary."*

In the autumn of the following year Mr. Conder published a revised edition of the Psalms and Hymns of Dr. Watts. The work had been in hand at intervals for many years, and cost him a vast amount of labour. His hope was, by casting aside all those compositions which have become obsolete, discarding superfluous verses,, correcting objectionable phrases, and arranging all the hymns in one methodical series, to aid in preventing these noble strains from falling into disuse (through the adoption of hymn-books containing but a small number of Watts's hymns), and to furnish an edition suited, in every way, for congregational use.

Immediately after putting this work to press, Mr. Conder, accompanied by Mrs. Conder, visited the lakes

* Snow, 1851, pp. 142.

of Westmoreland and Cumberland, previously to attending the autumnal meeting of the Congregational Union at Sheffield. One of the letters given in this chapter refers to this journey, which was one of much enjoyment. The following two sonnets were among the memorials of the excursion:—

APPLETHWAITE GILL.

(Suggested by the planting of a seedling oak on a spot where Wordsworth, not long before his death, had been seen apparently in devout meditation.)

Here, on the base of Skiddaw, WORDSWORTH stood,
And in this green recess retired, alone,
Communed with God. Here, too, the soil his own,
Where, through deep gill, green slope, and tangled wood,
Leaps the free stream, he once had thought it good
To build a Poet's Home :—then, not unknown
Had been this spot, fronting the mountain zone
That fondly circles Derwent's silver flood.
Sure, Eden could no lovelier scene present ;
And here unfallen man might be content.
But Poets build in verse, their home the scene
Made vocal with their name, to which they lent
Their living spell. Here, where the Bard has been,
This nursling oak shall be his sylvan monument.
September 24.

SOUTHEY'S MONUMENT.

In Southey's changed abode a stranger dwells.
Yet still his favourite sylvan walk remains,
Where Greta in its stony bed complains,
Oft as with sudden rush from gills and fells
The gentle current to a torrent swells.
Still, monarch of the scene, dark Skiddaw reigns,
And Derwent's fairy isles and circling chains
Of wood and crag exert their nameless spells.
A simple slab marks where his ashes lie,
Fast by the church ; while, from the sculptor's art,

Within the aisle his semblance meets the eye :
The marble sleeper makes the stranger start.
The Sabbath throng pass reverently by,
And some turn back to gaze, ere they depart.

Keswick, September 25.

Several of the letters, or portions of letters, given in
this chapter have been selected as conveying the views
of their writer on important topics—theological, ecclesiastical, or philosophical — on which he had largely
thought, read, and written, during many years; and on
which, therefore, his deliberate and matured opinions are
here expressed.

[Sheffield] Oct. 28 [1839].

LXXI. . . . . . What with writing leaders, acting as
uncle's *curate*, a few visits, and receiving company, etc., my
time has been very fully occupied.   Mamma will have told
you how very unwell your uncle has been : to-day he has
come down stairs for the first time since Friday week.
I preached for him both parts of the day yesterday and
the previous Sunday, from Heb. xii. 7, Matt. xxv. 21,
as well as gave the lecture on the Wednesday.   The people
have expressed themselves very much gratified by the
supply; and nothing would do but I must preach last
night a sermon for the benefit of Rotherham College,
the same being placarded and advertised.   In the morning my subject was 1 Cor. ii. 5, in which I showed that
true faith did not rest upon unreasoning adherence to the
religion in which the individual had been brought up—nor
upon the Papal foundation, the authority of the Church
—nor upon the *light within*, the Quaker notion—nor
upon obedience to State authority—nor upon servile
deference to any favourite leader or teacher—nor upon
metaphysical reasonings—nor upon impressions, the

creed of imagination and fanaticism; but upon the demonstrated truth of the doctrine, the experimental knowledge of its power, and the power of the grace of God realized in the practical fruits of faith. Having thus shown that all religion must rest upon *Divine* teaching, in the evening I showed the necessity and office of *human* teaching, of *academic training;* taking as my text, 1 Tim. iii. 6, and showing that a well-trained youth was much fitter for the office than an *old novice.* The morning sermon, more particularly, appears to have produced a satisfactory impression. On Wednesday, I met about fifty persons in the school-room, to form a R. F. Association for Sheffield, which promises to be tolerably effective, if not very numerous and considerable.

Holly Terrace, March 1, 1840.

LXXII. It is lawful to do well on the Sabbath-day, and I think I shall do well to write a few lines to you. And so, my dear boy, we have both been employed this morning in the same honourable and delightful service of teaching others what we have been taught of God. I have been speaking of the privilege of discipleship, in being admitted to the higher knowledge which is the reward of obedience, reserved for the friends of the Master, John xv. 15. I suppose that my congregation has not been larger than yours, if less rude. Mr. Blessly has been called to Portsmouth in consequence of the death of his father. I "*supplied*" for him also last Sunday morning, and you would have been interested in the subject—ὁ Θεὸς ἐν αὐτῷ μένει, καὶ αὐτὸς ἐν τῷ Θεῷ; a phraseology which I conceive to be Gnostic, and to allude to Gnostic (or Buddhic) pretensions; but the doctrine of St. John to be the opposite of mysticism. And I showed, *first*, what the language implied as to the

nature of religion—namely, that (*confessedly*) (1) the
the knowledge of God is the supreme good; that (2) by
this knowledge we are to seek reunion with God; and
that (3), as to have God abiding in us is the highest
virtue, to dwell in God is the highest bliss: *secondly*,
whereby true religion is distinguished from false religion
—namely, (1) that it has its root in faith, the belief of
the truth, which is mental obedience; (2), that it is a
life of which we must have experimental evidence; (3)
that it produces *moral* conformity to the Deity, assimi-
lation of character, not of essence, as the old mystics
dreamed. Now, I dare say, in your reading you will
come across sentiments and language which will illustrate this view of the passage. Mysticism, the Antinomianism of the intellect, and the most subtile form of
error, has prevailed, under some of its Protean forms, in
all ages and nations, from Pythagoras's Indian masters
to Penn and Barclay.

. . . Our Religious Freedom Society movements
are beginning to furnish me with a great deal of work.
My visit to Leicester was in this wise. It being thought
advisable, on public grounds, to come to a good understanding with the reverend Radicals of that place, and to
put a stop to the petty warfare they were waging against
London committees, the Rev. Messrs. —— and ——,
and the Secretary, were deputed to visit Leicester, to
hold a conference with a deputation from the Leicester
Voluntary Church Association Committee. Accordingly,
we left London by the eight o'clock train on Wednesday
se'nnight, and proceeding from the Blisworth station by
coach, reached Leicester soon after four, where we were
met by two of the deputation. At six we entered upon
the conference; and after some hours' brisk debate,
adjourned till ten the next morning. Our second con-

ference lasted till near two. Then, having come to a tolerably satisfactory conclusion, we dined with the Rev. J. P. Mursell; and left Leicester early next morning for Northampton. There we met a few friends by appointment; and taking the steam again at Blisworth, reached London early in the evening. It happened fortunately that Thursday and Friday were beautiful days, so that I enjoyed the excursion. Our Committee have now at last decided upon energetic movements to defeat Sir R. Inglis's motion on Church Extension. A public meeting in London is fixed for the 19th, which will, we hope, be responded to by public meetings in all the great towns. I wonder what the Angel James says to the resolutions at Walsall. If he does not move *now*, let him expect his chapel to be burned down like Dr. Raffles's. But I have strayed into politics before I was aware. And this is a day upon which I like to wash my feet from the soil of this dirty world. And this reminds me of an excellent article in the last *American Biblical Repository*, which I believe Mr. Watts takes in. It is upon the true import of βαπτιζω, which the writer, in gratifying coincidence with my own views, contends to be strictly synonymous with καθαριζω, without retaining any specific meaning as to the mode. I wish I could trace any etymological connection between *bapto* or *baptizo* and our English *bathe*, which seems to me to answer very exactly in its general character to the Greek term. There are two other articles—"Character of American Literature," and "The Book of Enoch"—worth your reading. If you cannot borrow the number, I will send it you.

Highgate, June 12 [1840].

LXXIII. It is quite too late to answer your last letter to me, it was so very long ago; and I did not mean to let it lie so long unanswered, only dear mamma has monopolized the pleasure of corresponding with you of late. But to-night she is too tired even to write to you. What will you say to the grand start she has made—yesterday attending a committee of Highgate ladies as President(ess) of the Bible Association (such as it is), and to-day accompanying me to "The World's Convention"—alias the Anti-Slavery Conference—where we have had a very interesting though somewhat extraordinary meeting. Some of the wild men of Massachusetts wished to force "The Women's Question" on us, some female delegates having been sent to us whom we did not choose to recognise; and after a very animated discussion of several hours, we decided by an overpowering majority against the *Martineauites*. Among the speakers, before the question was brought on, were the venerable Chairman, Thomas Clarkson, O'Connell, Knibb, etc.; and on the mooted point, sundry American delegates, George Thompson, Burnet, your pastor, Dr. Morison, Dr. Bowring (!), Charles Stovel, and half a hundred more. Mamma had a lady's ticket, of which each committee-man had one, and sat with the small group of distinguished "females" (as the odious phrase goes), cisatlantic and transatlantic. But I said I would leave her to tell you all about it.

You will wonder that I could begin my letter (which is, however, not a letter, but only a *scribble*) without adverting to the horrible attempt upon the Queen's life; but I feel to have written to you upon that subject in yesterday's *Patriot*. There is no doubt the young miscreant has been employed by others; but it will be difficult to find a clue to the conspiracy, and in the meantime all conjecture and speculation are useless. You may imagine the intense interest which the event has excited.

[The picture given in the postscript of the " distinguished females," though not from Mr. Conder's pen, is too graphic to be omitted.]

'I am not at all tired, although dear papa kindly thinks I must be, and I fully intended writing; but as it was already late, it was judged better for his ready pen to be employed, and that I should retire to rest, as—would you believe ?—I am again going early to-morrow morning to hear the speeches at the " Convention," which I expected to find interesting beyond anything that could be imagined. In itself it is and will be so, but " this day's uproar" exceeds description; the shouts of those who *would be* heard, and the persevering calls, for those who *ought* to be heard, while several point-blank contradictions of the Americans by each other proved that they were " divided among themselves"—produced altogether such a vulgar clamour as could never have presented itself to my imagination. And all this in the presence of the " ladies" themselves, several of whom were most untidily arrayed in creased and limp dresses, tumbled and soiled collars, coffee-coloured cambric handkerchiefs, hair anything but neat, and nails which served as hieroglyphics for " unwashen hands." I believe, too, the object of the " fair visitors" is, in part, to waken the ladies of England to a sense of their " rights," and the maintenance of the same. If we are thus to start out of our spheres, who is to take our place ? who, as " keepers at home," are to "guide the house," and train up children? Are the gentlemen kindly to officiate for us ?

' *You* will surely be at home to attend the great meeting. Do you remember your *fears* that slavery would be abolished, and there would be " no more meetings," before you were old enough to be present at them? There will, at all events, be one more.'

Holly Terrace, September 18.

LXXIV. . . . And so I am now between fifty and a hundred! I feel it to be a great mercy and privilege to have been spared—I should say preserved—thus long, so as to see our dear boys rising up one after another into manhood, and fulfilling our best hopes; and an exceeding great mercy to have dear mamma preserved to us all, and you all to us. What ought we to render, as a family, to Him who has so greatly blessed and distinguished us! Let us pray to be made and kept vessels of honour, fit for the Master's use. . . .

I may, perhaps, enclose my translation of the 1st of Ephesians, which I should like you to show to Mr. Watts. It is certainly a little puzzling, and, if the Apostle used no punctuation, must, one would think, have been so even to Greeks, to reduce this wave-like flow of words to rigid and precise construction; and to refer all the κατα's and εἰς's to their proper place and function. Nothing but an attentive examination and nice perception of the *scope* can, I think, enable us to do this; and those critics who go merely by what they deem rules of syntax are often demonstrably wrong. There are cases in which what the Apostle *must* mean is very different from what verbal criticism would pronounce to be the grammatical meaning; in which cases I can never conclude that the Apostle disregarded or violated grammar, but infer that we do not know all the rules that governed the use of the language—as, for instance, in reference to the article, that which seems to us arbitrary being determined by reasons, though we may not be able to detect them. It is one thing to try to force our own preconceived notions upon the meaning of the sacred writer, and another to force his own meaning, as deduced from the whole train of thought upon the language he employs, when the words will not voluntarily disclose what they were intended to express. This would be thought a very odd mode of interpretation, and learned scholars would ridicule my notion; but it is sanctioned by nature and experience. Children learn the use of words by inferring their meaning—they make out meanings before they understand the words. So it is in conversing with foreigners. We learn to catch the general meaning before we can acquire the precise knowledge of the words which convey it. And I think that Scripture must often be studied in this child-like manner, and be most safely interpreted by this child-like process.

Holly Terrace, May 2, 1841.

LXXV. I need not say how constantly you are in my thoughts, especially on the Sabbath-day; and I like to take a few moments of this only leisure portion of my time to converse with you. · There is not much in your last letter, written by snatches, to reply to; but your questions relating to moral philosophy will furnish a text. I *have* thought much upon the subject, and you will find the results in my red MS. book, and in the *Eclectic Review, passim.* Moral philosophy is a vague term: it ought to include (1) theology; (2) ethics; (3) law; (4) political science. Paley uses the terms, moral philosophy, morality, ethics, etc., as convertible; but morality is only a part of moral philosophy, if this be, as Paley says, " the science which teaches men their duty and the

reasons of it." Grove (a Dissenting minister, who contributed some of the Saturday papers in the *Spectator*),
in his work on Ethics (2 vols. 8vo), says : " Ethics, or
morality, is a science directing human actions for the
attainment of happiness. The *objects* of this science, by
which it is differenced from all others, are the *actions* of
mankind as capable of being directed by a common rule,
and made subservient to the acquisition of happiness."
I believe that very little that goes under the name of
moral philosophy, or ethics, is much better than the
jargon of the schoolmen; but it is a fine exercise to hunt
down the fallacies you are sure to start at every step.
You ought to read with great attention Sir James
Mackintosh's " Introductory Essay," and my article upon
it (*E. R.*, Third Series, vol. vi., Oct. 1831). Look, too,
at my review of Dr. Dewar's " Moral Philosophy " (vol.
xxv., p. 505). Paley was a lawyer, not a philosopher;
he is always clear, but often unsound and fallacious.
Adam Smith (" On Moral Sentiments ") I regret I never
have been able to find time to read, but only know at
second hand. I believe it is one of the most valuable
works of its class. Then you must not forget Dr.
Wardlaw's volume, and my dispute with him about conscience. Archbishop King and other writers of his
school, you must encounter by-and-by. But call no man
master in this branch of philosophy. The dispute about
the moral sense is little more than mere logomachy. An
action is right or wrong in reference to a rule, not in
reference to a sense : it is virtuous or the contrary according to the nature or motives of the agent. The basis
of moral obligation must be the relation between the
Creator and the creature ; and the true moral sense is a
sense of accountableness. Why am I obliged to do what
is right ? Because I must give account of my actions.

Y

How am I to know what is right? In the absence of revelation, from the undefaced traces of the law, which is the transcript of the will of the Creator written on the heart, Rom. ii. 14. But this law must relate to a law-giver; and the sense of right and wrong which "witnesses" to the law must be an instinctive or natural consciousness, or rational conviction that certain acts are approvable or acceptable to God, or the contrary. And true virtue is the desire to please God, and be approved by Him. The definitions of virtue proposed by Paley, Archbishop King, President Edwards, Bishop Butler, and others, are all fallacious. See my article on Joyce, *E. R.*, vol. xix., p. 97. With this clew I think you need not be puzzled, but may amuse yourself with threading the labyrinth of moral theorists.

(To the Rev. H. M.)

Highgate, December 30, 1841.

LXXVI. . . . Ought I not to be perfectly happy? No, you will say, but unspeakably grateful; and I feel this. That God has greatly favoured and blessed me, I am constantly sensible. But, in this world, unalloyed peace and joy, even with all the materials around us, are not to be realized; and we must be taught, in some way or other, that happiness depends upon living very near to God, and very dependently upon Him. There are anxieties, too, arising out of our treasures; and for the last week or two, fears for F.'s safety, exposed as he has been to many dangers, and anxiety at not hearing from him (he was expecting to leave France from day to day), occasioned me much mental suffering. So it is, when we have not afflictions, we make them for ourselves by distrust or over-anxiety. And then there is the weariness of spirit which the work, and care, and fag of life induce, when we reach my side of fifty. But for all that, I think I am happier than at five-and-twenty; and if it shall please God to spare my health, and avert overwhelming calamity, I shall be willing to labour on at my post of honourable responsibility, as " ever in my great Taskmaster's eye."

I do not know whether even to so old and sincere a friend as yourself, I should have disclosed so much of my sources of domestic pride and comfort, had not your letter given me so pleasing an account of your own domestic and ministerial happiness. To rejoice with those who rejoice, we must be tolerably happy, or supereminently Christian. To weep with those who weep is a lower attainment.

Holly Terrace, March 6, 1842.

LXXVII. It has pained and vexed me very much that you should have had so much cause to wonder at not hearing from me; but I know you will have attributed it to no forgetfulness. I have wished to write to you, and have in vain sought for an opportunity since your last (to me) of Feb. 5, in which you give an account of your visit to Stafford. You take a right view of the spirit of the Plymouth Christians, which is more ascetic than Pauline; but, like much of the ancient asceticism and mysticism, has been caused, at least in part, by what was defective or criminal in the conduct of professed Christians. The worst is, that spiritual censors, like the hermits, withdraw from those circles in which they ought to set a better example. They act like a physician, who should renounce the company of his patients, and rail against their ailments. No doubt we are all to blame, in respect to the negative faults of much of our conversation. Ministers are especially in danger of seeking for a relief from the monotony of theological studies and pastoral business, in political and other chit-chat. Indolence and false shame also have much to do with the avoidance of spiritual subjects. Yet it would, I am persuaded, often be found, that if introduced, the subject would be welcomed and responded to, that seems excluded by common consent. It is a great art, and a *gift* to be sought and cultivated, to converse profitably and appropriately, and yet not with mere professional feeling and *knack*.

I wish to know whether your college has taken any part or interest in the affair that has excited so much stir among the metropolitan colleges, in reference to the authority exercised by the trustees of Coward. The Baptist students of Stepney are, I understand, zealous for the sacred right of insubordination. I have known of several little insurrections in academies, and believe that very rarely has an insurgent or insubordinate student turned out well in after life. Tutors are not always all that could be wished, and committees and trustees are apt to be very arbitrary, and not over-wise; but still, blessed are the meek, blessed are the peacemakers, rather than those who are pugnacious even in the cause of right. . . .

I am glad to find you have time to read the *Patriot*, and are interested in the articles. Those relating to France are from two "*cœurs méchants*," one from the secret correspondent you know of, but must not hint at, the other a French gentleman wholly unknown to the other authority, but whose political views are in precise accordance with his. The information obtained from these sources is very important, and more authentic than the greater part of what appears in the daily papers.

March 20, 1842.

LXXVIII. I am seizing a few moments of the quiet leisure of this day to answer, as well as I can, your politico-theological question. It is, I think, quite certain that the New Testament contains no political doctrines, and that the injunctions to subjects and to bond-servants, respectively, to submit to magistracy and to their earthly masters afford no sanction either to an imperial despotism like that of Nero, or to slavery, but leave the question which you raise to be determined by reason and the principles which lie at the foundation of law and social order. Political rights, strictly speaking, are created by law, and differ from natural rights which are inalienable and common to all. The rights of a people, as distinct from its rulers, must be derived from the national constitution or some conventional arrangement. But extreme circumstances may justify, that is, make it right, to have recourse to a power which does not belong to the party as a right. Power creates rights for itself, as we speak of the rights of conquest, *i.e.*, rights acquired by conquest; and so, a government *de facto* is looked upon as becoming after a time *de jure*, it being for the interests of society that, even where the original title is not good, lapse of time should preclude its being questioned. The right of a people to change its government may be a legitimate constitutional right; or, where it is not so, as against the sovereign, it is the right of the nation itself in respect of all *foreign* interference. But as to the right of resistance, that must needs be supposed to exist under a constitutional limited monarchy, when the limits of the constitution are violated by the government. Under a despotic government, the people have no rights, and their consent is a mere fiction. It might as well be said, that the negroes in the West Indies consented to their being held in predial bondage. Individual submission and obedience under such a state of things may be, and seems to be prescribed as the duty of a Christian—his private duty, for political duty he is not in a condition to perform, having no political rights. But your question is, whether the mass of a nation might not establish a representative government on the ruins of a despotism. Unquestionably, when they had by conquest obtained the right and power. To acquire this, they must have made war upon the despot, by rebellion or conspiracy. It may be right, but it cannot be *a* right, to do this : war suspends all rights. If your question is, which part ought a Christian to take in a national struggle for freedom, the answer would be, with that which has justice and humanity on its side. The New Testament certainly contains nothing to make it binding upon him to side with the despot against the people under such circumstances; but there are many considerations which would prevent a Christian from promoting an insurrection or civil war, or raising the standard of resistance against even an unjust government. It behoves him, as a Christian, rather to suffer wrongfully ; and, as a patriot, he might well tremble at incurring the responsibility of attempting any violent change. No changes, in fact, are permanent but what are effected by opinion, and are gradually prepared, though, it may be, suddenly consummated. Tell me if this view of the question satisfies your inquiry.

I do not know all the circumstances of the case you refer to as presenting " exceptions ;" but W. H. would in my view confirm the rule, as a man in whom the spirit of piety is, I fear, awfully wanting. Students ought undoubtedly to be treated as men and as gentlemen, and be made to act and, if possible, feel as such ; but the discipline of the army makes gentlemen ; and the most rigid discipline in a college may consist with a due respect to all the liberty which the inmates of an establishment can have a right to claim. I really have not examined the matter sufficiently to give an opinion upon the late squabble, but can readily believe Coward's Trustees to have acted with unwise harshness.

April 3, 1842.

LXXIX. . . . . I have finished my "Exegetical Analysis of the Epistle to the Ephesians," which has enabled me to enter more completely than I had done into the richness and beauty of this portion of the Pauline writings. I am just beginning to work upon the Epistle to the Philippians, which is of a very different character, but full of *heart*. I should like to think that my *horæ biblicæ* would be of some advantage to you hereafter; and perhaps you may do by them as Matthew Henry did with the MSS. of his father Philip—edit them, or work them up into a complete key to the New Testament, which is still a desideratum. I look to you as David did to Solomon, to fulfil what is in my heart to do, but which is not permitted me. You have chosen the most honourable species of service. I do not count my editorial functions and political duties to be less the service of God than preaching the Gospel; and I have been apparently *ordained* to the more secular service. But the pastoral work is the more honourable and excellent, when discharged under the constant inspiration of the Spirit of Christ, with all singleness of heart and love to the souls which Christ has redeemed. Your consecration to this work is a great joy to me; and it is my constant and fervent prayer that the Great Head of the Church may be pleased to spare you to be a pillar of the temple, a standard-bearer of the truth, mighty in the Scriptures, and wise to win souls. Nothing less than great usefulness will, I am sure, satisfy you, for these are no ordinary times, and much will be expected from you. But you will feel that your strength and your wisdom are not in yourself, but must be drawn for day by day.

April 2, 1843.

LXXX. But for the date inscribed at the head of your last letter, I could not have believed that a month had well-nigh elapsed since I received it. The Sabbath seems the only day upon which I can command leisure for a quiet, thoughtful conversation upon such themes; and quickly do the hours glide away—too quickly I often feel. The mention of the day recalls Dr. Stroud's papers. His long-delayed concluding letter is announced for the May Number. I have kept back my reply till I should see all that he had to say; but, as he has been so long in producing his sequel, I regret that I did not print my reply at once. I quite concur in all you say respecting the moral part of the Mosaic code—the necessary perpetuity of all that is strictly ethical, all that is taught as *truth*, which must be distinguished from what is ordained, under penal sanctions, as *law*. The Mosaic economy combined a system of theocratic government with a system of symbolic instruction, of prophetic ministration, and of grace in the spiritual promises; and these two collateral systems, though differing as law and gospel, or as exterior and interior parts of the same dispensation, were blended together. The spiritual part consisted in the teaching of the prophets from Samuel to Malachi, and was quite apart from the Levitical institutes and the penal laws. Ethics and law may prescribe or involve the same great moral principles, but they are still very different modes of exhibiting and enforcing what is true and right. Law is essentially prohibitory, compulsory, penal, "working wrath." Moral teaching addresses itself to conscience and the affections. I do not know whether you will find these distinctions useful; they are trite, but not always kept in view. Now, as to the Decalogue, I view it as partaking of the double character of a fundamental law—a code of which the rest of the Mosaic legislation was but an exposition and development, and of a summary of moral principles, carrying with it an internal spiritual import, of which, even under the old dispensation, the spiritually enlightened could not be ignorant or unconscious. The fifth commandment, indeed, differs from the form and character of a law, as being preceptive, not prohibitory, and having a promise annexed to it—a *bounty* upon obedience, instead of a penal sanction. The tenth, too, is so strictly ethical and *spiritual*, that it could not be penally enforced as law, but was "exceeding broad" as addressed to the conscience. Then, as to the fourth, it is also a moral precept in its very form, "*Remember;*" and in the reason assigned, differing essentially from the Mosaic *law* of the Sabbath, which was a severe penal law, partly founded upon the moral precept, but partly on the peculiar political character of the Theocracy. The word law is used indiscriminately in Scripture in reference to ethical precepts and to penal legislation; but it is impossible to suppose that St. Paul, for instance, when speaking of the law as he does, 1 Tim. i. 7—10, means the same thing as when using the same word, Rom. vii. 7—14. . . .

And now I find I must break off. I intend that this sheet should reach you on the day that Greswell has rendered so honourable above all other days in the Calendar.

"Be this thy very law of thought,
To think, feel, act, like *Him.*"

H. T., April 13 [1845].

LXXXI. You have chosen a very knotty subject. If I understand your theme, it is, whether the government of a church by a single elder, or what *the Brethren* stigmatize as the "one man system," is conformable to the apostolic model, or, in the absence of positive rule, to general expediency. I think we may safely assume that our Lord and his apostles have left us at liberty to follow the wisest plans, all regulations of the kind being but a means for an end; but at the same time that the apostolic plans, so far as they can be ascertained and followed, are likely to prove the wisest under all circumstances. I apprehend that the first churches were synagogues, and that the synagogue government was generally adopted. This is maintained by Vitringa, Lightfoot, Stillingfleet, and others, whose works you may some day perhaps find time to look into. Now every synagogue had, I imagine, its ruler; but this ruler was not the only elder or bishop, still less the only minister or teacher. There was the ὑπηρέτης (Luke iv. 20), perhaps the same as the chazzan, or the angel of the apocalyptic churches; perhaps the presiding clerk, reader, or minister, but not a teacher. We confound the person who presides over the *service* with the person who presides over the *society*—the dean with the bishop. In fact, several distinct offices, it seems to me, are mixed up in our modern pastor; he is reader, preacher or prophet, ruler, visitor of the flock—perhaps sole elder, etc., all in one. Yet, in *small* churches, this may be partly necessary or unavoidable, and partly expedient. The primitive churches were large bodies, and, from custom and external position, required to be brought under a sort of municipal self-government, in relation to secular matters, which would neither be advisable nor practicable now. Your question relates not to teaching by a single pastor (against which the brethren peculiarly rebel), but to governing by a single elder. But why should this be ? The ruler of the synagogue, we are told, was "the moderator of the college of elders." You know my opinion about deacons—that they were assistant ministers, not chapel-wardens, as ours are. What is greatly wanted in our churches is either the separating of all secular matters, money matters, etc., from the office of deacon, or the confining our deacons to such matters. Let those secular officers be *annually* chosen by the people. Then, choose three or four elders to assist the pastor in ruling, visiting, and watching over the flock. I think our "clerk" would be a most useful officer (answering, perhaps, very nearly to the chazzan or *hyperetes*), were he an elder duly qualified to preside over the arrangements of the service, subordinate to the minister, and *ordained* to the office, instead of being a psalm-singing drudge or hireling, often not even a member of the church. We ought to have trained *readers*, (how few ministers can read a chapter decently!) who might greatly relieve the pastor. Why not give lectures to your young men upon reading and elocution ? But, after all, *government* must ultimately rest in a single head, whatever he be called.

The unsatisfactory state of our churches, to which you refer as presenting much to vex the eye and grieve the heart, does not result, I think, from any defects in our system, except such as are accidental, but from the same causes that led to declension and decay in the churches of Ephesus, Sardis, and Laodicea. Formalism and indolence, a prayerless and perfunctory discharge of official duties in the half-educated pastor, faults which begin at, and in, the academy, originating in imperfect conversion or essential inaptitude—these must work spiritual desolation in our churches. Then, when a church has once got into a bad state, some form of Antinomianism is sure to spring up and choke the seed; and a faithful pastor is deemed an enemy, and is doomed to reap sorrows from the sins, perhaps, of his predecessor. But, if a spirit of prayer is but awakened, the showers of Divine influence will not be withheld from the ministry of God's truth in the spirit of the Great Teacher. How often does the Apostle repeat, God is faithful! What we chiefly need, I imagine, is more *family* religion, predisposing for the public ministry, and cherishing any impressions made. Heads of families are not often addressed, prayed for specifically and affectionately, and counselled, as they are by Mr. Forster, who is continually holding up to the view of his flock the family relation and economy, as God's ordinance. No man ought to be a deacon or officer of the church who does not rule well his own house. If the cautions and directions of apostolic Scripture are set at naught, how can we wonder that disorders spring up? I do not know whether you can work upon any of these hints. I should like to hear from you to what circumstances or evils you more especially advert. But still more, I should be glad to talk over these matters. I think of saying more upon the subject of our churches in the *Patriot*, but it requires much wisdom to know what to say upon so delicate a point. I do not believe *censors* do much good. Physicians should be good tempered, or seem so. We must do all the good we can, and leave the result unanxiously with Him whose affair it is to govern all things. This is what I endeavour to do, though I confess that my mind has been filled with anxious and disturbing thoughts about the present position of public affairs, both in the church and in political society, as well as with domestic solicitude as to our future dwelling, and other things. How much easier is it to teach others than to teach one's self! Pray for us, and for *me* specifically, as we always do fervently for you, rejoicing at every remembrance of you.

Clapham, July 13, 1845.

LXXXII. You say in your paper, "If our much boasted system should be judged defective in the matter of the eldership, are we quite sure that it is perfect and apostolical in all other respects?" Now, there is a *Plymouth tone* about this remark which I do not like. I have never been accustomed to hear our system boasted of, but more commonly picked to pieces by Dissenters themselves. Episcopalians, Presbyterians, Wesleyans, —all boast of their respective systems: *we* defend ours, rather than boast of it. It may be not the less true and apostolic for all that. But then we must understand what the system really is, and not take it from the "feeble and mutilated outline," or rather skeleton, to which it may have shrunk in modern practice. I think you should study the idea of Independency in the writings of Robinson, Owen, and those who may be regarded as its modern founders, before you pronounce upon its discrepancy, as a system, from the New Testament model.

As to ordination, if you will look to my "View of all Religions," p. 385, you will see that the difference between the Presbyterian and the Independent divines turned very much upon this point—that the latter ordained to office on a previous election; the former to a function or faculty, that of the ministerial *order*. The notion of an indelible character imparted by ordination is strictly Papal and Episcopal. Nothing short of sacramental grace imparted by episcopal hands can give *that;*

and Presbyterianism, in mimicking Episcopacy, becomes
simply ridiculous.

Then, as to elders who are not ministers or teachers,
but "ruling elders;" these are not peculiar to the Presbyterian polity.   Cotton, of Boston, U. S. (1645), considers ruling-elders, together with the pastors and
teachers, as making up the presbytery of the church, and
defends even, against Bishop Bilson, their right to maintenance by the church: "But let the Lord appoint
ruling-elders, according to the simplicity of the Gospel,
to assist his ministers in the work of government, that
they might attend the more to labour in the Word, if
they shall expect from the church any maintenance for
the work's sake, Oh! that seemeth a strange matter," etc.
("Hanbury's Memorials," ii. 561).   He contends, too,
that "in churchwardens and vestrymen are some footsteps and remnants, and as it were *rudera* of that ancient
and holy ordinance, so much as is escaped out of the
ruins of antichristian apostacy."   "What other thing
soundeth the very name of churchwardens, *guardiani
ecclesiæ?*"   I have no doubt you would find abundant
proof that the founders of Independency did not arrange
their system to their own mind, but framed it as nearly
as they could after the pattern in the *Book*.   You are
combating a shadow in labouring to prove what no one
denies, a plurality of elders, not all of them *prophets* or
teachers, in the primitive church.   But then you must
not, with our translators, render Acts xx. 28, to *feed* the
church of the Lord, but to *tend, rule*.   It is, I believe,
generally referred to feeding with instruction, but without any sufficient reason—perhaps to suit the theory of
preaching bishops.

Further, there can be no doubt that, in our office of
deacon (the Dissenting churchwarden), we have an elder-

ship practically recognised; and some of our deacons are rulers indeed with a vengeance. In some churches there is by far too much government; and sometimes the pastor is nothing, the lord-deacon everything. I should have thought you would not have taken so one-sided a view of the system. A large church requires, of course, a different government or governmental staff from a small one, which might not even furnish materials for a full complement of officers. So, I conceive, the "church that is in thy house," whether it denoted a Christian family, or a company accustomed to assemble in a private house, would be under somewhat different rule from a Christian synagogue. But, ordinarily, a church *was a synagogue*, with its president, elders, and chazzan or messenger, or rather clerk and secretary. The offices or functions of prophet and evangelist were probably distinct from the *staff* of the synagogue. The evangelist was, I think it is clear, a missionary, or travelling preacher. The prophet was the local preacher or teacher, 1 Cor. xiv. 3; and the Apostle wished they were all able to prophesy, rather than to speak with tongues. There might, then, be more prophets or preachers than one in a church; but the gift seems to have been a distinguishing and not very common one. Therefore, special honour was to be given to those elders who laboured in the word and doctrine (1 Tim. v. 17), *i. e.*, who exercised the gift of prophecy. Judas and Silas (Acts xv. 32) being themselves prophets, *i. e.*, preachers, exhorted and confirmed the brethren. I take it that the prophetic office, which was not Levitical, and was older than the synagogue polity, was always in the Jewish church, and was continued down through the Christian—an office ordinarily connected with scholastic training (as there were schools of the prophets), and with appropriate gifts. To reconcile James iii. 1, with

1 Cor. xiv. 5, 39, it is only necessary to suppose that the assumption of the *professional* character of a rabbi or teacher, from ambition or conceit, was an evil to be deprecated; and the church was too soon infested with such pretenders, against whom the people are cautioned, 1 Cor. xiv. 37; *ib.* xii. 3; 1 John iv. 2, 3. Still, to be able to speak to men "to edification, and exhortation, and comfort," was an attainment to which *all* were encouraged to aspire. Consequently, though an elder might or might not be a prophet, a prophet was not, as such, an elder—he was, like your father, if I may say so, *a lay preacher;* and to speak boldly, I consider myself as exercising, alike by my pen and by word of mouth, the proper gift and function of a New Testament prophet.

It would be found much easier, however, to bring back our churches to a nearer conformity to the primitive model, than to restore the meaning of words, and to get them to acknowledge that *you* are a bishop and *I* a prophet—that a lay elder is a presbyter, or that a deacon is a minister. Nor is it worth while to dispute about words. Happily, there is nothing in our system to forbid our conforming as closely as we can to the apostolic model; and though I believe with you, that a considerable latitude of adaptation to circumstances is allowed us, yet the nearer we keep to the primitive rule in principle, the better our system will work. We must take care, however, not to mistake, with the Plymouth Brethren, the Corinthian church for a model, instead of its being a beacon.

LXXXIII. . . . Where do you get your notion of *ordained teachers?* Were the prophets ordained? I know of no ordination but either to an office or to a specific mission. Teaching is not an office, nor a function restricted to office. Office is a charge implying rule and responsibility, as that of rulers of a synagogue. Elders were not ordained as elders, but ordained rulers: I mean, were not made elders, but rulers, by appointment or ordination.* There are many Jewish synagogues in London, each having its rulers and officers; yet, if I am not mistaken, all the London synagogues (except those of the *new school*), acknowledge one chief rabbi, and are, in a sense, one synagogue. The word synagogue is used with the same latitude and diversity as church—applying either to an assembly or to a society. Thus, the Jews of Liberta, Cyrene, and Alexandria, according to Greswell, formed one synagogue. There must have been more churches than one in Rome when Paul arrived in that city. I cannot, however, attach *much* importance to these questions, and am open to further light. I have not yet had time to look into Davidson, or to read Wardlaw. Shall I send them to you? I feel sure of this: that ordaining men to write hymns, to edit religious works, to be authors, is quite as rational and scriptural as ordaining them to preach the gospel. Hence, licensing the press and licensing preachers have generally gone together when Church authority was in the ascendant. I consider myself, alike in writing and in preaching, to be discharging the prophetical function as defined, 1 Cor. xiv. 3.

I have just been dipping into Davidson's Lectures, and light upon this, at page 152, "as long as there were prophesying and teaching, besides other spiritual gifts, in the primitive churches, the elders would probably devote themselves to the work of general superintendence and

---

* Wardlaw, I see, denies this; but why were they called bishops, if elder implied what elders were ordained to?

Z

rule, much more than to that of instructors." This quite accords with my views.

March 29, 1846.

LXXXIV. . . . Now, touching the offending couplet of my last hymn, I hope that you will like this better—

> "And love and duteous deeds shall be
> Our life's incessant liturgy."

I would have defended my division of "shall be" by *Virgilian* precedent, and, if I mistake not, by examples from our elder poets, but I give up; and the above is pronounced an improvement. I am pleased that you like the other hymn best, although I readily subscribe to all you say on behalf of good Dr. Watts. That hymn of his is certainly one of the most beautiful in the language, and deservedly popular, although, I fear, its popularity is partly owing (as is often the case with popular compositions) to its lower pitch of sentiment. What I mean is, that while pious believers can attribute a higher meaning to the expressions than they naturally suggest, common minds can derive pleasure from the mere poetry. It is thus that the "Pilgrim's Progress" pleases all readers; although what a different book it is to the delighted child, the mere man of taste, the pious rustic, and the instructed experimental Christian! "There is a land," etc., would read very differently to a mere lover of poetry, and to a dying saint; yet it would be admired by both. Mine would be insipid and unintelligible to a mere *professor*. But it is worth while sometimes to write for one's self, and for the few who will sympathise with the feeling.

I have been reading to-night in the family circle, instead of a sermon, my review of Joyce on "Love to God,"

in an old volume of the *Eclectic*. Have you ever read it?
Some of my best and most useful writing is scattered
through those forty-six volumes, and I often think I
should like to select some of the best for republication;
only it would not sell! I refer especially to such as this
article, and those on Coppleston on "Predestination,"
Dwight's "Theology," Principal Hill's "Lectures,"
Lawrence and Pring on "Physiology," Dewar's "Moral
Philosophy," Brougham's "Natural Theology," Erskine.
etc., on "Faith," etc., etc. I have almost materials
enough for an "Outline of Theology." But I feel as if
I had nearly done enough. Only one does not like what
one has done to be lost.

I meant to have adverted to the subject of your discourse, but must defer it. Lift up your voice against
those German gnostics and neologists. The Epistle to
the Hebrews distinctly recognises the threefold character
of our Lord in the triple type, Moses, Aaron, and Melchisedec, the greater than David.

Sheffield, Oct. 22, 1847.

LXXXV. You will have gathered from my leader
upon the subject, that the York meetings were of a highly
interesting and satisfactory character. A very solemn
impression was produced by the recent death of Mr. Ely;
but in all respects it was one of the best sustained series
of meetings I ever attended. Wells exceeded himself in
the unaffected eloquence and good sense of his speeches;
and his rebuke of one of Mr. J——'s croaking lamenta-
tions was one of the most effective and admirable I ever
heard—its perfect good humour and respectful tone preventing its being in the slightest degree offensive. These
truly fraternal meetings must be productive of the happiest effect. On the Wednesday some hundred or more

of us, with leave of our learned and reverend chairman, flocked to the afternoon service at the Minster. It was the anthem day, Dr. Camidge presiding at the organ. The voluntary was Beethoven's Hallelujah Chorus from the "Mount of Olives"—I need not say how admirably given on the beautiful organ. The anthem was but a verse, but very sweetly sung. I attended also the morning service on Friday, when the Te Deum was sung. It is a glorious old edifice; but I thought the service would have been more in keeping had it been in Latin. The lesson from the Apocrypha was all very well; but that from the New Testament sounded to my ear quite out of place—not at all in agreement with the *genius loci.* By the way, the attendance of so many black coats and white cravats produced an evident sensation; and the precentor, immediately after giving out the anthem, turned to a gentleman, and whispered, "Is Dr. Campbell among them?"!! We all behaved very decorously. . . . We walked on the walls, but I had not time to see the chapter-house, as we left York by the three o'clock train.

To-day we have all had a delicious walk to the Riveling Valley, the scenery being lighted up by bright gleams, interchanged with light flying showers and busy clouds; and Mont. and Miss Gale have been drinking tea. I find you saw but very little of the poet. The *Patriot* and the "Apocalypse" have furnished my pen with ample employment since I have been here. I have just finished the exposition of chap. xvi., and have passed the line which separates the past from the undisclosed future. Think of it—Time's clock is near upon striking γέγονεν, *actum est.* I preached on the Sunday evening after my arrival here, from John iv. 42, but took no part last Lord's day. I expect to take the morning service on the next, and to plead the cause of British missions.

Sept. 29, 1847.

LXXXVI. . . . I spent part of the morning in working out, to my own satisfaction, the problem of the Vintage in Rev. xiv., having previously satisfied myself that the Harvest denotes the religious wars that followed the Reformation, from 1560 to 1713; the Vintage, you will perhaps be startled to find, extending from 1740 to 1815. But, when you come to, compare the history with the prediction, you will see that this is no uncertain conjecture. We are shamefully, I was going to say atheistically, ignorant of recent history—of the dealings of God with his church, and the great anti-church, in these latter days. The manner in which Elliott leaps over the three centuries between the Reformation and the French Revolution is surprising. They must be indicated in the prophecy; and yet it is only under the figures of the Harvest and the Vintage that they can be referred to.

As to the deadly wound of the Beast, my explanation is different from that of any preceding expositor, but I have no hesitation in saying it must be the right one, as the Beast is the revived Western Empire, not the Papal monster. The wounded head must have been *the existing governing head*—that of the Carlovingian Empire, which was apparently extinct in the hiatus of seventy-four years which occurs between Charles the Fat, the last of the Carlovingian race, and Otho the Great, who claimed to be the successor of *Charlemagne and the Cæsars.* (Robertson's "Charles V.;" "View of Europe," sect. iii.; Gibbon, chap. xlix.) Had the prediction not noticed this temporary extinction of the empire, it would have been wanting in an essential feature of correspondence to the facts.

I have no fears of the Papacy in a political point of view, but we seem on the eve of the Seventh Vial, if not under it. Our obvious duty and safety are to keep clear of being mixed up with Rome in her sins. But the end is not yet. The 1260 days will not have run out before A.D. 2029 or 2041; by which time we shall all be, I trust, in the better country.

Clapham, July 20, 1848.

LXXXVII. My dear Friend,—Your kind letter of inquiry ought to have obtained a prompt reply, but at the time it reached me I was not allowed or able to use my pen; and a reply was a task to which, under the anxieties and duties of the time, my dear wife was unequal. I have had a most merciful escape. The wound was so serious, that had inflammation ensued, there would have been immediate danger of a fatal issue. The tendon was nearly severed: it has apparently reunited, and promises me the entire use of my foot, so that I have to bless God for escape also from permanent lameness. The wound is now completely healed, and my medical attendants have expressed their surprise and satisfaction at the very favourable progress of the wound from the first. I have suffered, of course, from pain and weariness, from the bandages, and from the effects of confinement, but far less than I could have expected. It has been a season greatly to be remembered for the gracious kindness of God, who has not only averted immediate and multiform danger, but sustained my dear wife and myself in a patient and confident trust in his goodness. I owe much to great medical skill; and not less to constant, tender, unwearied nursing. I am now resuming the use of my pen. . . .

Meantime, I have been much impressed with the removals that have taken place, while I have been raised up again—as I trust for future service. I was particu-

larly struck with the (to me) sudden death of Mr.
Gunn; then Dr. Payne; others of my acquaintance in
private life; and now Dr. Hamilton! He who has the-
keys of the Grave and of Death, openeth, and no man
shutteth. He is sovereign, and giveth no account of his
matters. But He is unerring in wisdom, and doeth all
things well.

I do not know whether you have been passing through
town; but, till within a few days, I have seen nobody,
being still confined to my room, and obliged to be kept
quiet. *Now*, I should be very happy to see you. Failing
this, let me hear how you all are.

What times we are living in! As regards the Church,
what need of prayer to the Divine Head to "give apostles
and prophets," pastors after his own heart, and efficient
standard-bearers, to fill up the thinned ranks, and carry
on the war against the mighty! Do you study the
Apocalypse? I have an Exposition complete and ready
for press, if I can but find a publisher. You can recognise, I take it for granted, the pouring out of the seventh
vial upon the air, and know what time it is by the
prophetic chronometer. I find many of our ministers
practically reject the Apocalypse as unintelligible. This
is a sad error; as if there were no medium between
monomania and lethargy or indifference. Many of our
Professors have adopted neological views respecting it.
My work will vindicate, if it appears, its Divine character,
and distinct, legible, unequivocal import and fulfilment,
up to the present most remarkable European crisis. But
"the end is not yet."

January 13, 1849.

LXXXVIII. . . . As to myself, my general health,
as increased bulk and weight, and my aspect indicate,

has been improved by my five months' *rest*. I cannot walk very far without fatigue; but as the leg is *all right*, I hope that it will gain strength; and I am told that I must not be disappointed if a year should elapse before I walk again as well as ever. I trust that the discipline has not been wholly without fruit; and that the Lord has spared me for service and usefulness.

My work on the Apocalypse, though prepared in 1847, has undergone thorough revision during my confinement, and I hope that it may be accepted as a first-fruit offering. The feeling you express respecting the study of the Apocalypse, I find very extensively prevalent among our pastors—too often degenerating into an irreverent incredulity as to the possibility of making anything of the Book. This is surely a most undesirable state of opinion among the spiritual guides of the people. It is a *weak* place in the body—a something to conceal. To rescue the study and use of the Apostolic prophecies from this general neglect and misapprehension, has been a principal motive to undertaking the work. I have no disposition to blame you; but the want of interest in the study of the allegorical which you express, must equally preclude your satisfaction in studying the prophecies of Ezekiel, Daniel, and especially Zechariah. I hope that you will find that I have succeeded in translating the symbolical into the historical; and in both accounting for the diversity of interpretation, and removing the stumbling-blocks in the way of a pious student of the Book. I am myself perfectly satisfied as to the certain correspondence between the predictions and the events which I have endeavoured to illustrate; and as to the future, I do not attempt to do more than explain the import of the figurative language. I am sure you will be interested in the work as throwing light

upon the mystery of God's providence; and I shall be
very glad to find that its perusal imparts to you any
measure of that satisfaction which I have derived from
composing it.

Keswick, September 25, 1851.

LXXXIX. . . . We have turned to the best
account the delightful weather we have had up to this
morning. Tuesday was a splendid day, with a golden
sunset, and the most exquisite aerial tints on the mountains that guard Derwent's lovely water. Wednesday,
the gold was turned to silver beauty, presaging the
approaching change. We visited a romantic spot in the
neighbourhood, where Wordsworth owned a little slip of
the soil, at the foot of Skiddaw. We have not taken any
long excursion since our visit to Buttermere (of which I
think I gave you an account), in company with the two
clergymen and their wives. They left Keswick on the
Thursday; and I then availed myself of the first leisure
to find out the "Independent minister," whom, I think
I told you, I have been much pleased with; and this has
led to our making personal acquaintance with Miss
Rolleston, of whom I have often heard Hone speak with
enthusiasm; an accomplished and extraordinary person,
skilled in Hebrew, reads Syriac and Sanscrit, writes no
despicable verse, draws, is enthusiastically attached to
this mountain region with its local traditions, and, what
is best of all, is a pious and excellent person, active, and
influential, and not ashamed of the reproach of Dissent,
though, by birth and connections, a churchwoman of the
"Clapham sect." There has come here, to visit her,
another remarkable personage, the sister of the Arch-
deacon of New Zealand, herself of the Plymouth fraternity,
but a very pleasing, strong-minded woman, who, having

lived in New Zealand and visited America, seems to think nothing of making a trip next year to Jerusalem, being much interested in the work of conversion among the Jews. These two ladies have been our companions in our little excursions the past three days, and I had them as auditors last evening, in giving an address at the neat little chapel erected here at the cost of one of the seceders from Quakerism at Kendal, who has become a Plymouth brother; in compliance with the request of Mr. Dallow, the minister, a simple-hearted, excellent man, who is on the most brotherly terms with Mr. Davidson. These "brethren" are, in fact, open-communion Baptists, with a slight tinge of peculiarity, and with Millenarian notions, but nothing fanatical or sectarian, so far as I have seen. I forget whether I told you that I was to preach at the "Independent chapel" on Sunday. It is a small and rude place, and I have no doubt that if such a church as your Sturminster model could be erected here, it would soon be filled. It is quite discreditable to us as a body to have no better place of worship here. I had the place full, and a, very attentive auditory in the evening. I spoke from Heb. i. 2.

. . . You will have recognised as mine the articles on Father Newman and his Mystifications and the *British Quarterly's* croakings. So far as I can learn, the state of our congregations in Cumberland affords cause for much satisfaction. I am sure that a hopeful view of things is the most healthy, and I should think the most becoming in the Master's sight.

CHAPTER IX.

GOING HOME.

MERCIFUL and wise in their severity are those sharp strokes of sorrow, which loosen the heart-roots from their fond hold on this earthly soil, and so prepare the Christian for being transplanted into the winterless Eden above. The life whose progress we have been tracing was approaching, though unconsciously, very near the threshold of immortality. But in the narrow space which yet intervened there were some rough steps to be trodden, and some bitter lessons of patience, submission, and faith to be learned;—some sweet ones, too, of the power of God's love, and promises, and Holy Spirit, to comfort his children in affliction, and to make his strength perfect in their weakness.

The arrows of death, which for more than twenty years had been falling all around the family circle, without touching it, except in the instance of Mr. Conder's venerable mother, now began to fall thickly within it. At the commencement of 1853, Mr. Conder was called to follow to the grave the remains of his highly esteemed and valued brother-in-law, the Rev. Thomas Smith; in the summer, of Mrs. Conder's stepfather. At the close of the same year, his eldest grandson, a child of whose loveliness and promise the writer will not trust himself here to speak, was called away to a world for which he seemed more fit than for that in which he left us behind. After little more than a year, Mr. Conder's youngest granddaughter followed her brother, in the spring of the same year which closes this biography.

A heavier affliction than these, or probably than any other in Mr. Conder's life, was the illness of his beloved wife, in the autumn of the same year in which his family circle was thus visited with the unaccustomed presence of death. For some time, what we, in our ignorance, are wont to call "the worst," seemed inevitable; by the blessing of God upon skilful and indefatigably kind medical treatment, and devoted and tender nursing, fatal results were averted; but health was not restored, and thus, though the edge of the trial was abated, its weight was not removed. "Thus," wrote Mr. Conder, to a friend, towards the close of 1854, "thus are our trials and consolations blended, and we shall see hereafter how graciously, and tenderly, and wisely we have been dealed with."

At Christmas, 1854, Mr. Conder removed to St. John's Wood, little supposing that the following Christmas would bring the appointed time for his quitting "this earthly house of our tabernacle," and entering on the "house not made with hands, eternal in the heavens." This closing year, but for the trials already indicated, would probably have been one of the happiest of his life. Cares that in former years had pressed heavily had been removed. He still felt himself equal to his work, except when suffering from occasional indisposition, and fully capable of enjoying prolonged life, if it were God's will; while at the same time he felt (as he himself said) that he had reached an age at which each added year of life was to be regarded "as a *boon;*" and the removal of one after another of his coevals uttered to his ear a solemn note of admonition, not unheeded. His interest in public affairs, and anxiety to serve the Christian Church, and in especial his own denomination, were as intense as ever. The new residence, chosen for the sake of being near one of his sons, was more commodious and cheerful than either of his previous London abodes. The locality was pleasant and healthful, on the crest of the outermost wave of the deluge of bricks and mortar which incessantly rolls onward over the green fields. He found himself surrounded with a circle of friends, old and new, amongst whom he felt more at home than had been the case for many previous years. The Sabbaths were days of much quiet enjoyment; and he highly prized the ministry of the Rev. Watson Smith, at that time minister of New College Chapel. Neither his habits of criticism nor his pulpit labours had spoiled him for being a candid and attentive hearer and a devout worshipper. Indeed, the praises and prayers of the house of God were to him still more important, as means of feeding and invigorating spiritual life, than the preaching. When residing at Kennington, he would occasionally attend the Weighhouse, not so much for the sake of the masculine and impressive address from the pulpit, which he well knew how to appreciate, as for the sake of the refreshment and profit afforded by the worship. He believed public worship capable of being made both delightful and profitable, to a degree which our churches have as yet hardly imagined, much less attempted. Yet he greatly enjoyed earnest, thoughtful, and scriptural preaching, and often expressed his satisfaction in this respect while residing at St. John's Wood.

It seemed as though a busy and anxious life might have in store a tranquil and serene, yet not inactive, evening. But the sun was already on the mountains.

With much to chasten and sadden his heart, but with much more to cheer and solace it, and to inspire gratitude and faith, the pilgrim was being gently led to his journey's end.

In addition to domestic sorrows, his mind was often severely tried and harassed by public affairs, religious and political. Few hearts cherish a more intense concern for the welfare of their country, and of the Church of Christ, than was habitual with him. Though he accounted "the hopeful view of things the most healthful," yet there was much in the state both of his own denomination, and of the church at large, which inspired him with acute anxiety. He regarded the movement of which Professor Jowett's writings are the exponent with indignation, and almost distress; and his sense of the dishonesty of men who can sign the Articles and eat the bread of the Church of England, and employ themselves in teaching, on the one hand, Popery, or, on the other, Infidelity, was sometimes expressed with a force and bitterness that seemed surprising in one of so mild and Christian a temper. Amidst all, he ever held fast the animating and soothing conviction that "the Lord reigneth," and therefore, however appearances may be against it, the cause of truth must be the winning cause.

The alteration of the stamp duties on newspapers led to the publication of the *Patriot* three times a week. This step, taken against Mr. Conder's judgment and advice (and which has since been found a mistaken one), entailed on him much additional labour, which speedily told upon his constitution. At sixty-five it is late to change one's habits. Considering the intense wear and tear of his brain, his health all through life had been remarkably good. He had always been subject to occasional sudden attacks of indigestion, which had latterly become more frequent and serious.' In this respect, however, his removal to St. John's Wood seemed to produce a beneficial change. But toil and care had told upon a constitution naturally vigorous. Though yet wanting some years of the three-score and ten, active business life had begun so early with him, and his intellectual powers had been, so prematurely taxed and developed, that he had in reality lived a long life. His strength had for some time imperceptibly declined, and he looked older than his years.

The chief literary labour which engaged his spare hours during these months was one singularly fitted to prepare his mind for the passage into eternity. If he had known that it would be his last work, he could not' have chosen a more suitable one. This was the collection, and revision, not of his poems as a whole, but of those which he regarded as belonging to the class of "Hymns," excluding many of his versions of the Psalms of Scripture, but including those which are adapted for singing. He was interrupted in this work by his last illness. He had already carried half the volume through the press, and the last sheet printed from his revision concludes, remarkably enough, with the collect inserted at the close of this chapter.

The materials were left by him in such a state of preparation, that nothing was needed but to superintend their passage through the press; and the volume was published very shortly after his decease. The reader, who wishes to appreciate his religious character, must be referred to those pages for a portraiture more complete and authentic than can be attempted in these. As his versions of the Psalms were the fruits of his calmest hours and favourite studies, so his hymns—some composed after

preaching or hearing sermons on striking texts, some in
sleepless hours at night, and some in seasons of severe
trial and spiritual conflict—are the records of his deepest
personal experience as a Christian. They belong to all
periods of his life; but, as might be expected, those composed near its close are simpler in expression, and deeper
in tone. The following brief hymn seems to express the
prevailing temper of his mind, in contemplating the approaching termination of his pilgrimage :—

> What joy, when life seems almost spent,
>   And our departure near at hand,
> To feel serenely confident
>   That we in Christ accepted stand!
>
> That life's great combat is achieved,
>   That we our course assigned have run;
> Have kept the faith we have received,
>   And that our Master's work is done.
>
> But, oh! for service poor as mine,
>   Too high a prize the victor's crown.
> The honours which thy hands assign,
>   Lord! at thy feet I'll cast them down.

In the beginning of November, 1855, shortly after
completing his sixty-sixth year, Mr. Conder was seized
with what speedily proved to be an attack of jaundice.
From this first attack he appeared to rally. His last
letter, dated December 1st, speaks of his recovery as
making progress, though very slow and tedious. But in
the course of about ten days, a change for the worse took
place, and he was reduced so low, that it became evident
that recovery was all but hopeless. For another fortnight the balance fluctuated between faint hopes and
growing fears. All that medical skill could do was done,
and the disease itself was subdued; but the fearful pros-
tration of strength baffled all efforts to reinforce the ex-

hausted energies of life. Extreme weakness unfitted him, for the most part, for conversation, and even for enjoying, except a few times, being prayed with or read to. On one occasion, however, he roused himself, and spoke at considerable length, expressing very clearly his state of mind, and his wishes as to what should be done in the event of his decease. If it were God's will, he would have wished, he said, to live, not from "any clinging to life," but for the sake of his wife and daughter; and he felt it a duty to use the best means of recovery, while resigning himself into God's hands. When strong enough to bear it, he found comfort in hearing some of his own hymns read to him, especially those most directly referring to the Saviour. His hymns, he said, while they reproved him, comforted him. Some few evenings before his death, he desired to have read the hymn commencing,

> They whom the Father giveth
> By covenant to the Son,
> Must live, because He liveth,
> And Christ and they are one.*

And also the following, which he said he had composed for a death-bed hymn, and which chanced to be in the very last sheet that had come from the printer's, and lay waiting for the pen that was never to be busy again. As it was very difficult for him, from extreme weakness, to fix his attention, he had it read three times, and then said that he had it by heart. "Now you can sleep upon that," said one of his children. "Oh, yes," was the earnest answer, "and *die* upon it."

> Upholden by the hand
> On which my faith has hold; ,
> Kept by God's mighty power I stand
> Secure within the fold.

* "Hymns of Praise, Prayer, and Devout Meditation," p. 155

A A

Weak, fickle, apt to slide,
  His faithfulness I've proved;
Because I in the Lord confide,
  I never shall be moved.

Beset with fears and cares,
  In Him my heart is strong:
All things, in life and death, are theirs,
  Who to the Lord belong.*

The last portion of Scripture that was read to him
was part of the 14th chapter of St. John's Gospel. When
his son rose from prayer, he raised his hands, smote them
together twice or thrice, and said, with emphasis and
great feeling, "Blessed be God, I believe. I understand
it, and I believe it. Blessed be God!" His son said
something of the foundation laid in those words for our
faith being a rock; to which he fervently responded,
"Yes; a rock!" After this he spoke but little. The
last morning (December the 27th) he could only bear a
very brief prayer, to which he gave a fervent "Amen."
He sank into a quiet sleep; and soon after eight o'clock
in the evening, so gently that the boundary between sleep
and death was scarcely visible, his spirit dropped the
mantle of flesh, and entered into rest in the presence of
his Lord.

The end had come sooner than he or others expected;
but it could not be said to have come prematurely. Measured by labour and by experience, though not by mere
lapse of years, his life had been a long one. The wish
cherished in earlier years, "that he might finish his
course," was not denied. No great end of life was unac-
complished, no great task undischarged, no unreached
goal yet in view. He might still have worked on, cheer-

"Hymns of Praise, Prayer, and Devout Meditation," p. 166.

~ and happily; and still have learned more completely
me lessons, whether of thankfulness and joy, or
'n and patience, which past years had taught.
saw that it was time to call him to nobler
sweeter, happier sources of wisdom.
s to those from whom he was sepa-
t there was nothing to regret,
to God.
ney Park Cemetery, on
nd esteemed friend,
feeble state of
the funeral
ost judi-
been
h

onder
d prove
im, they
qualified
rect and en-
years of the
as the author
ed for him the
biblical critic, and
omplishment—and
editor of one of
t unassisted, JOSIAH
place among Noncon-
mper which distinguished
n by those who wish ever
ken in love, and who know
keth not the righteousness of
r departed brother's mind for-
coarseness and vulgarity, while
elevation imparted to his ordinary
n of pure and beautiful English.
erved his God and his generation.
e devoted his powers to the cause of
usness. We will not think meanly of

In the foregoing pages it has been the editor's effort and design to let the life which he has undertaken to record tell, as far as possible, its own tale, without comment from him. He cannot, perhaps, more fitly fill this closing page than with a few sentences from Dr. Morison's funeral address—the honest tribute of a hearty, but discerning friend. The lines which follow were read in the course of that address, and were (as already mentioned) the last which their author corrected for the press.

"It is not an exaggeration to affirm that Josiah C was no ordinary man. If Nonconformists should themselves unmindful of their obligations to will be undeserving of another champion equall to assert and defend their claims. As their co lightened annalist—as the conductor for man only *Review* they could then call their own of not a few productions which have ear reputation of a scholar, a theologian, a a man of general knowledge and acc as the wise, and prudent, and energe their best newspapers, though n CONDER will deserve a name and formists while the world stands.

"Nor will the taste and te his literary course be forgott that the truth should be spo that 'the wrath of man wo God.' The culture of o bade every approach to his poetic fervour and compositions the char

"Well has he s Most actively has truth and righteo

fully and happily ; and still have learned more completely those same lessons, whether of thankfulness and joy, or of submission and patience, which past years had taught. But his Master saw that it was time to call him to nobler work, and. deeper, sweeter, happier sources of wisdom. Heavy as the sorrow was to those from whom he was separated, on .his own account there was nothing to regret, but full reason to give thanks to God.

His remains were laid in Abney Park Cemetery, on the 3rd of January, 1856. His old and esteemed friend, the Rev. Dr. Morison, though in a very feeble state of health, most kindly undertook to conduct the funeral service; an office which he discharged in the most judicious, feeling, and appropriate manner. It had not been the intention of the family to ask any minister to preach a funeral sermon, but the late excellent and amiable president of New College, the Rev. Dr. Harris, expressed, in the kindest manner, his wish to render what he considered a tribute due to the memory of the deceased. Such a suggestion could not but be gratefully responded to. The sermon was preached at New College Chapel on Sunday, January 13th, from the words, "There remaineth, therefore, a rest to the people of God."* Little did either the preacher or his hearers anticipate that within a twelvemonth he would have entered into that rest, and his own funeral sermon be preached from the same pulpit, and that to himself his own striking words would so soon be applicable :—"He knows the secret now. He hath passed through the portal, and entered into rest. He is made free of the universe, with heaven for an inheritance."

* The sermon was published under the title of "The Divine Rest;" together with the address delivered by Dr. Morison at the funeral. (Snow, pp. 32.)

In the foregoing pages it has been the editor's effort and design to let the life which he has undertaken to record tell, as far as possible, its own tale, without comment from him. He cannot, perhaps, more fitly fill this closing page than with a few sentences from Dr. Morison's funeral address—the honest tribute of a hearty, but discerning friend. The lines which follow were read in the course of that address, and were (as already mentioned) the last which their author corrected for the press.

"It is not an exaggeration to affirm that Josiah Conder was no ordinary man. If Nonconformists should prove themselves unmindful of their obligations to him, they will be undeserving of another champion equally qualified to assert and defend their claims. As their correct and enlightened annalist—as the conductor for many years of the only *Review* they could then call their own—as the author of not a few productions which have earned for him the reputation of a scholar, a theologian, a biblical critic, and a man of general knowledge and accomplishment—and as the wise, and prudent, and energetic editor of one of their best newspapers, though not unassisted, JOSIAH CONDER will deserve a name and a place among Nonconformists while the world stands.

"Nor will the taste and temper which distinguished his literary course be forgotten by those who wish ever that the truth should be spoken in love, and who know that 'the wrath of man worketh not the righteousness of God.' The culture of our departed brother's mind forbade every approach to coarseness and vulgarity, while his poetic fervour and elevation imparted to his ordinary compositions the charm of pure and beautiful English.

"Well has he served his God and his generation. Most actively has he devoted his powers to the cause of truth and righteousness. We will not think meanly of forty years of devoted toil, because it did not please God to add a few more to them. We are thankful for every remembrance of him, as of one who had much of the mind of Christ in him; who not only trod the paths of literature with a dignified and intelligent step, but also walked humbly with his God; adorned every relation of human life, as a son, a husband, a father, and a friend; and whose last hours were sweetly irradiated by the bright shining of the Sun of Righteousness."

O God, to whom the happy dead
Still live, united to their Head,
 Their Lord and ours the same;
For all thy saints, to memory dear,
Departed in thy faith and fear,
 We bless thy holy name.

By the same grace upheld, may we
So follow those who follow Thee,
 As with them to partake
The free reward of heavenly bliss.
Merciful Father! grant us this,
 For our Redeemer's sake.

THE END.

London: Printed for John Snow, 35, Paternoster Row.

WORKS

PUBLISHED BY

JOHN SNOW, PATERNOSTER ROW.

MR. CONDER'S LAST WORK.

Just Published, in 18mo, cloth, price 3s. 6d.; gilt edges, 4s.,

HYMNS OF PRAISE, PRAYER, AND DEVOUT MEDITATIONS. By JOSIAH CONDER.

"Truly beautiful in poetic diction, and invaluable as specimens of ardent and enlightened devotion."—*British Mothers' Journal.*

"We suspect that Conder's Hymns, like Watts's Hymns, will do most to make its author known to devout minds in the next generation. His lightest work will live the longest."—*British Quarterly. Review.*

This day is published, in 8vo, price 1s.,

THE DIVINE REST. A Discourse occasioned by the Death of Josiah Conder, Esq., delivered at New College Chapel. By the Rev. JOHN HARRIS, D.D., Principal of New College. Together with the Funeral Address at Abney Park Cemetery. By the Rev. J. MORISON, D.D., LL.D.

Shortly will be published, in post 8vo,

SCENES AND ADVENTURES OF AN AGENT OF THE BRITISH AND FOREIGN BIBLE SOCIETY, in the north-east of Europe, Russia, etc., during the Early Part of the Present Century. By the late Rev. JOHN PATERSON, D.D., edited, with a Preliminary Notice of the Author, by the Rev. W. L. ALEXANDER, D.D., of Edinburgh.

Third Edition, in One Vol. 12mo, cloth lettered, 5s. 6d.,

THE CHRISTIAN'S DAILY TREASURY : containing a Religious Exercise for Every Day in the Year. By the Rev. EBENEZER TEMPLE.

DR. LIVINGSTON.—AUTHORISED EDITIONS.

This day is published, in demy 8vo, price 3d.,

SKETCHES OF THE REV. DR. LIVINGSTON'S MISSIONARY JOURNEYS AND DISCOVERIES IN CENTRAL SOUTH AFRICA. With a Map and Portrait.

This day is published, with Map and Portrait, price 1d.,

TRAVELS AND DISCOVERIES OF THE REV. DR. LIVINGSTON. Written expressly for the young.

This day is published, in 18mo, cloth, gilt edges, price 2s.,

THE VIRGIN WIDOW; or, The Triumphs of Gospel Truth over Hindoo Ascetic Superstition. By a CHRISTIAN MISSIONARY.

THE WAY TO LIFE. The Great Question Answered. By the Rev. J. WILLIAMS. Price 6d.

This day is published, in fscp. 8vo, cloth lettered, 2s.,

THE UNITY OF THE FAITH; or, Jesus as the Manifestation of God in All Ages. "Prove all things."

CHEAP EDITION.

This day is published, the Second Edition, revised, in post 8vo, with Frontispiece, cloth elegant, price 6s.,

VOICES OF MANY WATERS; or, Travels in the Lands of the Tiber, the Jordan, and the Nile. With Notices of Asia Minor, Constantinople, Athens, etc., etc. By the Rev. THOMAS W. AVELING.

WEDDING PRESENT.

Twenty-third Thousand. Cloth, 1s. 6d.; white silk, 2s. 6d.,

COUNSELS TO A NEWLY-WEDDED PAIR; or, Friendly Suggestions to Husbands and Wives; a Companion for the Honeymoon, and a Remembrancer for Life. By the Rev. JOHN MORISON, D.D.

This day is published, in 18mo, cloth, gilt edges, price 1s.,

THE BROTHER BORN FOR ADVERSITY; or, The Similarity of the Saviour's Sorrows and Sufferings to those of his Followers.

"Forcible, experimental, and rich in Christian experience."— *Record.*

This day is published, in fscp. 8vo, cloth, price 1s.,

PRACTICAL HINTS ON THE MANAGEMENT OF THE SICK-ROOM. By R. HALL BAKEWELL, M.D.

"The excellent hints and directions contained in this little book supply a want which has long been felt, and will prove valuable to the friends and nurses of patients."—*Christian World.*

Fifth Thousand. In 8vo, with Map, and cloth lettered, price 12s.,

CHINA: its State and Prospects, with Especial Reference to the Diffusion of the Gospel. Containing Allusions to the Antiquity, Extent, Population, Civilisation, Literature, Religion, and Manners of the Chinese. By the Rev. W. H. MEDHURST, D.D., Forty Years a Missionary to the Chinese.

Third Edition, in fscp. 8vo, cloth lettered, price 1s. 6d.,

SEVENTY SCRIPTURE CHANTS. Selected and Arranged for Congregational and Social Worship by the Rev. NEWMAN HALL, LL.B.

This day is published, price 2d., by the Author of " Come to Jesus,"

CONGREGATIONALISM FOR CHRIST. By the Rev. NEWMAN HALL, LL.B.

Price 6d., cloth gilt 1s.,

REST IN CHRIST FOR THE WEARY. By a CLERGYMAN.

"A priceless gem. Many an aching heart will be healed by the counsel and sympathy contained in this excellent manual."—*British Mothers' Journal.*

This day is published, price 3d.,

FAMILY GODLINESS. By the Rev. J. GREGORY.

Second Edition, in small 8vo, cloth elegant, 5s.,

PAUL THE APOSTLE; or, Sketches from his Life. By the Rev. HENRY J. GAMBLE.

Fscp. 8vo, cloth, 4s.,

SCRIPTURE BAPTISM: being a Series of Familiar Letters to a Friend, in Reply to " Christian Baptism," recently published by the Hon. and Rev. Baptist Noel, M.A. By the Rev. HENRY J. GAMBLE.

This day is published, in 8vo, cloth lettered, with Portrait, price 10s. 6d.,

THE EARNEST MINISTER. A Record of the Life, and Selections from Posthumous and other Writings, of the Rev. Benjamin Parsons. Edited by the Rev. E. P. HOOD.

Second Edition, much enlarged. Now ready, in 18mo, cloth lettered, price 1s. 6d.,

THE EASTERN LILY GATHERED. A Memoir of Bala Shoondore Tagore. With Observations on the Position and Prospects of Hindoo Female Society. By the Rev. E. STORROW, of Calcutta.

Post 8vo, cloth, 9s.,

RECOLLECTIONS OF A TOUR. A Summer Ramble in Belgium, Germany, and Switzerland; including Sketches of the Minor States of Germany, the Fatherland of the Reformation, Modern Reform in Continental Churches, and the Condition of the Dispersed Jews. By the Rev. J. W. MASSIE, D.D., LL.D., M.R.I.A.

"It will henceforth be a choice companion to those who shall travel the same regions, and form a most interesting and valuable substitute for such travel to those who can spare neither the time nor the money."—*Christian Witness.*

Post 8vo, cloth, 8s. 6d.,

THE EVANGELICAL ALLIANCE; its Origin and Development. Containing Personal Notices of its Distinguished Friends in Europe and America. By the Rev. J. W. MASSIE, D.D., LL.D., M.R.I.A.

Post 8vo, sewed, 2s.; cloth, 3s.,

LIBERTY OF CONSCIENCE ILLUSTRATED, and the Social Relations sustained by Christians as Members of the Commonwealth considered. By the Rev. J. W. MASSIE, D.D., LL.D., M.R.I.A.

Cloth gilt, elegant, 1s.,

THE CONTRAST: War and Christianity. By the Rev. J. W. MASSIE, D.D., LL.D., M.R.I.A.

Fourth Edition. Just published, in 8vo, cloth lettered, 8s. 6d.,

ELEMENTS OF MENTAL AND MORAL SCIENCE. By the Rev. GEO. PAYNE, LL.D.

Third Edition, revised and greatly enlarged, post 8vo, cloth elegant, price 9s.,

THE LAMPS OF THE TEMPLE. Crayon Sketches of the Men in the Modern Pulpit, including Melvill, Gilfillan, Binney, Pulsford, Spurgeon, etc.

"There is a power and splendour about these sketches that would make the reputation of half a dozen writers. They are 'studies' of the highest order, claiming and deserving the attention of every thoughtful mind."—*Jewish Herald.*

In fscp. 8vo, cloth lettered, price 4s.,

THE RELIGION OF MANKIND: Christianity adapted to Man in all the Aspects of his Being. By the Rev. JAMES SPENCE, D.D., of Poultry Chapel, Author of "The Tractarian Heresy," etc.

Third Thousand, post 8vo, cloth, with many Engravings, 8s. 6d.,

JAMAICA: its Past and Present State. By the Rev. JAMES M. PHILLIPO, Twenty Years a Missionary in that Island.

"A volume of enchanting interest, which equals those of Williams and Moffatt, presenting a most instructive and entertaining view of the state of society in Jamaica, and written in a spirit which inspires implicit confidence in the narrator."—*Patriot.*

Four vols., fscp. 8vo, sewed, 1s. 6d. each; cloth lettered, 2s.,

THE HISTORY OF THE REVIVAL AND PROGRESS OF INDEPENDENCY IN ENGLAND, since the Period of the Reformation. With an Introduction, containing an Account of the Development of the Principles of Independency in the Age of Christ and his Apostles, and of the Gradual Departure of the Church into Anti-Christian Error until the Time of the Reformation. By JOSEPH FLETCHER.

In fscp. 8vo, the Second and Cheap Edition, with important Additions, price 4s. 6d.,

SPIRITUAL HEROES; or, Sketches of the Puritans, their Character and Times. By the Rev. J. STOUGHTON.

In post 8vo, cloth elegant, price 8s., morocco, 12s.,

EVENINGS WITH THE PROPHETS; a Series of Memoirs and Meditations. By the Rev. Dr. BROWN.

"Dr. Brown's 'Evenings with the Prophets' has a charm and a value peculiar to itself. Its subject is one of the most sublime that can be entertained, and the method of handling it is consistent with its own picturesque beauty and excellence. It abounds with sweetest music, it overflows with 'still waters,' it sparkles with heaven-descended thoughts, and it is presided over by the very spirit of a sanctified genius."—*Glasgow Christian Journal.*

In one handsome volume 8vo, cloth lettered, 12s.,

SERMONS BY THE REV. DANIEL KATTERNS. "Models of that vigorous, manly, and mind-breathing eloquence which attests the earnestness of the speaker, and stirs the deepest thoughts and feelings of the hearer or reader."—*Evangelical Magazine.*

Forty-fourth Thousand, beautifully Illustrated, price 2s. 6d., or post 8vo, cloth, 8s.,

A NARRATIVE OF MISSIONARY ENTERPRISES IN THE SOUTH SEA ISLANDS. With Remarks upon the Natural History of the Islands, Origin, Language, Traditions, and Usages of the Inhabitants. By the Rev. JOHN WILLIAMS.

"He knew not whether he would not willingly put away at least half the folios which he possessed, rather than part with one volume which had recently been published by the Missionary Williams."— *Archbishop of Canterbury at the Bible Meeting.*

Cheap Edition. Sixth Thousand. Now ready, with beautiful full-length Portrait, etc., price 3s.; or in 8vo, price 12s.,

THE LIFE OF THE REV. JOHN WILLIAMS, Missionary. Compiled from his Journals, Correspondence, and other Authentic Resources. By the Rev. E. PROUT, Home Secretary to the London Missionary Society.

In one volume, handsomely bound, cloth lettered, with Portrait, price 6s.; or in morocco elegant, 10s. 6d.,

THE CHRISTIAN MERCHANT: a Practical Way to make "the Best of Both Worlds," exhibited in the Life and Writings of Joseph Williams, of Kidderminster. By BENJAMIN HANBURY. Third Edition.

"We can conceive of nothing more profitable or delightful to Christians in business than to be able to spend an hour in the perusal of this work."—*Jewish Herald.*

Eighteenth Thousand, beautifully Illustrated. Cheap Edition, 3s.; or, the Library Edition, cloth, 12s.,

MISSIONARY LABOURS AND SCENES IN SOUTHERN AFRICA. By the Rev. ROBERT MOFFAT, Twenty-three years an Agent of the London Missionary Society in that Continent, and Father-in-law of Dr. Livingston.

Dedicated to Her Grace the Duchess of Sutherland.
In post 8vo, with portrait, 6s. 6d.,

AUTOBIOGRAPHY OF A FUGITIVE NEGRO: his Anti-Slavery Labours in the United States, Canada, and England. By SAMUEL RINGGOLD WARD.

"A noble book by a noble man—physically, intellectually, and morally; and we are sure it will meet with a noble reception by the liberty-loving sons of Great Britain. The story of his life will speedily be read by tens of thousands. It is a volume of deep and romantic interest."—*Christian Weekly News.*

In 18mo, cloth elegant, 2s. 6d.,

SCENES OF THE BIBLE; a Series of Scripture Sketches. By the Rev. WILLIAM CLARKSON, Missionary from India.

This day is published, in small 8vo, cloth lettered, price 5s.,

LIFE SPIRITUAL: its Nature and Progress. By the Rev. GEORGE SMITH, Trinity Chapel, Poplar.

By the Author of "Come to Jesus."
Just published, a New Edition (Nineteenth Thousand), crown 8vo, with Portrait, 4s.,

THE CHRISTIAN PHILOSOPHER TRIUMPHING OVER DEATH. By the Rev. NEWMAN HALL, LL.B.

Second Edition. This day is published, in fscp. 8vo, price 3s.,
cloth lettered,

HOW TO SUCCEED IN LIFE. A Guide to the
Young. By the Rev. J. B. LISTER, of the Congregational
School, Lewisham.
"There is not a page nor a paragraph which presents not something really of importance."—*Christian Witness.*

Second Edition. This day is published, in one vol., post 8vo,
cloth lettered, price 9s.,

FEMALE SCRIPTURE BIOGRAPHY; preceded by an
Essay on "What Christianity has Done for Woman." By
the Rev. F. A. Cox, D.D., LL.D.

This day is published, in fscp. 8vo, cloth lettered, 1s.,

THE PRISON OPENED AND THE CAPTIVE
LOOSED; or, the Life of a Thief as seen in the Death of a
Penitent. By the REV. JOSIAH VINEY.

This day is published, in fscp. 8vo, cloth, price 3s.,

NAAMAN; or, Life's Shadows and Sunshine. By the
Rev. T. W. AVELING.
"The volume is alternately interspersed by brilliant conceptions, beautiful figures, weighty sentiments, and strokes of pathos. It cannot fail to obtain extensive favour with the Church of Christ."—*Christian Witness.*

Fifteenth Thousand, 8vo, sewed, 2s.,

ANTI-BACCHUS: An Essay on the Crimes, Diseases,
and other Evils connected with the Use of Intoxicating Drinks.
By the Rev. B. PARSONS.
"We conjure our readers to give this volume an attentive, candid perusal, from a decided conviction that, in proportion as its circulation is promoted, and its contents are impartially read, will be stayed one of the most dreadful evils that ever afflicted the human race."—*Methodist New Connection Magazine.*

FOR THE USE OF ANXIOUS INQUIRERS AFTER
SALVATION.

Fortieth Thousand, with Portrait, 1s.; cloth lettered, 1s. 6d.,

THE CONVERSION AND DEATH-BED EXPERI-
ENCE OF MRS. LITTLE: to which is added, A GUIDE
TO PEACE WITH GOD.
"I believe it is one of those hallowed productions which the Lord Jesus will make use of for years, if not for ages to come, in winning souls to himself."—*Rev. R. Morison.*

JOHN SNOW, 35, PATERNOSTER ROW.

01340778

01340778

92C.75
C
CONDER

INSERT

BOOK CARD
PLEASE DO NOT REMOVE.
A TWO DOLLAR FINE WILL
BE CHARGED FOR THE LOSS
OR MUTILATION OF THIS CARD.

www.ingramcontent.com/pod-product-compliance
Lightning Source LLC
Chambersburg PA
CBHW070952240525
27223CB00015B/805